# WORLD PERSPECTIVES

A European Assessment

# WORLD PERSPECTIVES
A European Assessment

## Revised and Updated
English Edition

### JACQUES F. LESOURNE

*Professor of Economics and Industrial Statistics*
*Conservatoire National des Arts et Métiers, Paris*

Translated from the French by
Sharon L. Romeo, University of Birmingham, U.K.

**Gordon and Breach Science Publishers**
New York · London · Paris · Montreux · Tokyo

© 1986 Gordon and Breach Science Publishers S.A. Post Office Box 161, 1820 Montreux 2, Switzerland. All rights reserved.

**Gordon and Breach Science Publishers**

P.O. Box 786
Cooper Station
New York, New York 10276
United States of America

P.O. Box 197
London WC2E 9PX
England

58, rue Lhomond
75005 Paris
France

14-9, Okubo 3-chome
Shinjuku-ku, Tokyo 160
Japan

Originally published in French as *Les Mille Sentiers de l'Avenir*,
© Editions Seghers, Paris, 1981.

**Library of Congress Cataloging-in-Publication Data**

Lesourne, Jacques, 1928 –
 World perspectives
 Translation of: Les mille sentiers de l'avenir.
 Bibliography: p.
 Includes index.
 1. Twentieth century – – Forecasts.  2. Civilization,
Modern – – 1950 –   I. Title.
CB161.L4913   1986      303.4'909049      86-18366
ISBN 2-88124-179-4

## To Renaud

"I can make you no other gifts
than this sombre light
Men of tomorrow, breathe on the
coals
It is for you to say what I see."

ARAGON
*Les Poètes*

# CONTENTS

# FACING THE FUTURE

"Peoples, Tomorrow is not a monster lying in wait for us."

Victor Hugo
*Les Quatre Vents de l'esprit*

# Questions

By the end of this century, my son, who is just being introduced to the rudiments of grammar, will be twenty-seven. By the year 2025 he will be fifty-two. All of a sudden, this future which has seemed so remote to our uncertain reflections, becomes a very near tomorrow; it becomes the focus of my questions, and those of millions of men and women in the developed world from Vienna to Los Angeles, from Boston to Nagasaki.

As I confront these questions I want to discard both optimism and pessimism, both dreams of a fairy tale future and fears of ultimate catastrophe.

I want to discard the childish belief in rosy-tinted futures, where there will be no more class struggle, the equal development of all nations, harmony between all human societies, and higher ethical standards brought about by scientific knowledge.

I want to discard the childish fear of millenial years, of an inevitable nuclear holocaust or world-wide pollution, and a total rejection of any technological development which questions the way we relate to our bodies, our intelligence, the species, or the cosmos.

In my opinion the mature approach is to use the word 'future' in the plural, for it is no more than the range of possible futures. Futures which announce the clashes and convergences of countless actors: governments, the media, political parties, big business, the people, scientists, prophets, writers and artists... Of course, I have a feeling that there will be strong trends, created by behaviour patterns that will only change direction slowly; of course, I expect many smooth continuities, but I can also identify possible ruptures which may give rise to cumulative divergences in the various areas of development. Coming events should be the preoccupation of prospective analysis, a prospective analysis which goes beyond forecasting, though it sees itself only as thoughtful preparation for action.

Usually superficial extrapolation makes forecasting come to grief. Prospective analysis attempts to free it from this constraint by describing possible futures based on the plans which are being worked out by the actors within the global system. This ambition is as necessary as it is immense. Necessary, because it takes into account simultaneously both universality and the actors, and this makes it possible to understand how potential futures are generated. Immense, because it forces one to complete the relations of science with conjectural connections. And no team undertaking prospective analysis can escape the subjectivity imposed on it by its own nature, its origins and the institution which takes it under its wing.

Here prospective analysis joins hands with history in its mad desire to give back to people living today the potential futures whose seeds lie in the present. But it wears itself out needlessly when it tries to be a history of the future. This is because we can only perceive fragments of the human environment that our children will inherit. We may get a rough idea of its dimensions, but we do not know its cathedrals, much less its songs of love or death.

Whether it is trying to help some decision-maker to see something, or whether it addresses itself to some social group or other urging it to change its behaviour in order to change its future, it is very difficult to separate prospective analysis from the will to act. That is what I (like so many before me) am seeking to do in this book. Why? Because, of the innumerable inquiring minds, I have been fortunate enough to have been able to dedicate more than three years of my life to this investigation, surrounded by a mine of information covering nearly all the countries of the world. And because I am convinced that over the next quarter century the so-called developed countries will have to face a five-fold challenge.

Firstly, there is the challenge of the rise of the Third World, this collection of peoples who have not been able, or have not wished to adapt to the shock of the Industrial Revolution which began two centuries ago in Georgian England. Overwhelmed by Western civilisation and changed by it, they are in the process of forging a-new identity, and they aspire to playing a role in world affairs more commensurate with their central position in tomorrow's world.

There is the challenge of peaceful coexistence with the Soviet Union, that conservative heir of the October Revolution whose military power grows as the messianic force of its ideology loses vitality.

There is the challenge of competition between developed countries. This competition has intensified following the emergence of Japan, the reconstruction of Western Europe, and the changes in American power.

Then there is the internal challenge of the superposition of traditional social demands and new social demands born of an evolution of values. Both sets of demands are equally difficult to satisfy, and tend to test economic and political institutions.

Finally there is the challenge of relations with the ecosphere, between an ever increasing number of human consumers and a finite world. In the opinion of some who extrapolate the exponentials of the last quarter century too hastily, this is the only real challenge.

None of these challenges is truly new. If one follows the slow road leading from the Industrial Revolution to colonisation, the various socialist experiments, two world wars, and post-war economic expansion, it becomes evident that these challenges all have their roots in history. This does not make their conjunction less awesome, for they arise in a geographically limited world that is experiencing tremendous changes, and where there is a numeric explosion of those who, while realising themselves, become at once the salt of the earth and hotbeds of trouble for the human groups to which they belong.

Let us not fall into the ridiculous trap of forgetting the challenges which confronted our fathers and the cataclysms which have wiped out whole civilisations. But in order to confront our own challenges we must face them candidly, for our response will, up to a point, determine the fears and hopes of those who follow us.

# Ariadne's thread

But how should we organise the mountain of facts, figures, predictions and available analyses into a whole that makes the futures intelligible?

By constructing a world model with ten to fifteen regions, ten to forty sectors, a dozen natural resources, and a few revenue groups? A praiseworthy and useful endeavour. But lumping countries together in regions erases the sociopolitical realities that national societies constitute; cutting the world up into sectors leaves out the transnational company actors; stressing description in terms of quantitative economy pushes cultural, military and political factors etc. into the background.

What about juxtaposing partial prospective analyses? By taking an interest in South Korea, Iran, Mexico; by scrutinising the strategies of actors in the car, iron and steel, and textile industries; by studying the spread of ideologies; by examining military power relations. The specialist may get something out of it, but it dissolves the conjunction of challenges which is at the heart of our futures.

So then, what should we do? Both things. For it is during the development of this complex game of building blocks that the conceptual framework emerges, through processes that associate indiscriminately scientific sequences and conjectural constructions.

Thus it is at a deeper level than that of formalised models that interpretations of our futures can be formulated. Hence, the itinerary is personal without being arbitrary.

Therefore, the arrangement of the subjects in this book is dictated by the result of my own reflections and can only be clarified by reviewing my own progress.

In the beginning, about a decade ago, a feeling of revolt. Revolt against the naïvety of the political debate, against the inadequacy of the common interpretations of social facts, against the ignorance of the immense and varied scientific knowledge apparent in the usual reading of the evolution of societies. A revolt resulting in an attempted analysis that expressed itself in systemics.

The choice of this language did not reflect a desire to force an external interpretative framework on the facts clarified by the various sciences, but rather resulted from the conviction that all of the sciences are, in their own way, in the process of constructing a systemic approach suited to them by presenting in the form of systems the part of reality that they have taken as their object. What then is a system? A set of elements linked by a set of relations. And where does the interest in a theory of these objects come from? From the slow rise that permits the passage from simple systems that only change inputs into outputs, to systems with aims that follow defined objectives more or less efficiently, on to learning systems that improve their own procedures, then to self-organising systems which, through their research activity, create and invent new structures or set themselves new aims, and then finally on to societies with systems created by the interaction of several self-organising systems.

As for the synthesis,[1] it was derived from studying the contribution of the sciences to the knowledge of the individual, organisations, economic systems, national political systems, and the system of international relations. It showed that while complex systems were able to develop, whether from their own initiative or in response to their environment, they could, during their development, create control deficiencies that rendered them incapable of overcoming certain challenges. Through a loss of power, through the inadequate pursuit of information, through the incoherence of their objectives, through a loss of memory, imagi- nation and judgement, and through the inability to learn new behaviour patterns. It could therefore be summed up in one hypothesis – that of the existence of a triple control deficiency: on the individual level, on the level of political systems, and on the level of the international system.

Individual deficiency is the product of the relationship between affectivity and the intellectual faculties.

Endowed with a nervous system that is the product of a transformation of simpler nervous systems, the human species retains an archaic affectivity whose fundamental motivations are fraught with dangers, an affectivity that orients the use of intelligence, and which, because of its aggressive, gregarious and altruistic aspects, is ever in danger of hurling one community against another, even in the name of noble sentiments. From the quest for power to the need for self-assertion, from curiosity to narcissism, these motivations are no more than short-term objectives for the blossoming and self-preservation of the individual; the intellectual processes have little influence on them and cannot guarantee either coherence or the widening of their horizons.

For its part, the simultaneous development of the neo-cortex and society opens up infinite perspectives of knowledge and power, but intellectual capacities are limited and man is incapable of predicting all the consequences of his actions. All the more so since motives interfere with the processes of the neo-cortex by slanting perception, curbing the imagination, orienting intelligence, and rejecting disagreeable conclusions, while at the same time letting the intellectual processes have absolute freedom when their interplay can satisfy the need for curiosity.

In other words, the dragon of intelligence, controlled by affectivity, is only free when serving it, and though it can explore the world, its ability to anticipate things is not enough to allow it in return to channel affective agression. Individual rationality finds itself doubly limited. Thus the functioning of the individual is at once the source of collective rationality and the principle obstacle to its emergence.

As for the second control deficiency, it concerns the great political systems and takes the form of both an inability to master these systems and a defect in the processes of formulating their objectives.

On one hand, confronted with the size of the systems to be controlled, the great number of demands being made on them, leaders, lacking adequate means, initiate profound changes whose direction and extent escape them, or they are content to contribute to short-term regulation by acting on variables that would tend to move away from their usual desired range.

On the other hand, the diffuse objectives of the political system are the result of a compromise between leaders seeking the level of support necessary for their survival (as leaders) and these same leaders' pursuit of their own aspirations, especially of an ideal type of society. The operating conditions of this double mechanism then make it possible for rational behaviour based on limited perspectives within partial sub-systems to lead (in a long-term, world-wide future) to real catastrophes.

From Athens which threw itself into the Peloponnesian War to the declining Roman Empire, from the Czarist Empire to France between 1930 and 1940, history is a burial ground of political systems that fell victim to the second control deficiency, for nothing guarantees that national political systems are capable of producing answers which would allow them to face in the long term the external and internal pressures that they are subjected to.

And finally, the third control deficiency is the result of three characteristics of the international system. It is a non-hierarchical system without world-wide regulation. It is a system in which the quest for security is a constant necessity, for no national government dares to imperil the existence of the territorial state. It is a system that offers no protection against war.

The interaction of these three control inadequacies, on the individual, national and international levels, makes it possible to understand that mankind has not mastered history, and if up to the present it has managed, as a species, to rise above the challenges that have confronted it, it is because the conditions of the biological and social environment have only varied within very narrow limits so that short-term adaptations have sufficed.

The question may then be asked, "Does this interpretation of the past and present offer a clew for an understanding of the future?"

It was only after pushing this personal synthesis into the background that the answer made sense. For several years I had to give first place to a detailed and varied analysis of the facts, to the use of models, and to the integration of partial data in a set of global scenarios.[2] And it was only after having completed this journey that it suddenly became obvious that *the possible histories of the future could be interpreted by beginning with the conjunction of control inadequacies on the national and international levels, with individual control inadequacy constantly interfering, but always through the other two.*

The attempt to make a synthesis of the past thus showed itself to be a framework for reading the future.

Governments, or rather, the political systems of nation-states meet at the junction of these two deficiencies. About one hundred and fifty in number, equal in rights but very unequal in fact, they share all the land and a great part of the seas. Their existence (or at least that of most of them) is assured for the foreseeable future.

For every one of these nations, the actions of the others are a source of uncertainty, and throughout their cooperations and conflicts, they find it difficult to manage the two main phenomena that will characterise the functioning of the international system in these final years of the century: the emergence of a multipolar world that is no longer dominated by the omnipotence of the United States: intensification of the interdependence of states. Cultural, military, political, and economic interdependence. An interdependence that is being woven by the flows of people, energy, raw materials, grain, industrial products, and information. An interdependence in which the spheres of influence of the big banks, transnational companies, scientific associations, religious institutions, and military presences, overflow everywhere all the rigid nation-state frontiers as they appear on the world map.

Increasingly occupied with this attempt to master international problems, the governments of the developed countries, especially in Western Europe, are at the same time confronted with a growing internal contestation. The gradual, heterogeneous adoption of new values adds new social demands to traditional ones. While the market is not always very suited to satisfying these new demands, central bureaucracy is torn between the duty to soften shocks from the outside, the obligation to respond to internal pressures which presuppose the reinforcement of the Welfare State, and the need for decentralisation in order to deal with minor problems. Hence difficulties for the market and the Welfare State, two institutions on which the prosperity of the last quarter century has been built. Thus control deficiency on the national level may be analysed through these interactions between values, structural flexibility, and economic growth.

*Daniel Bell has rephrased this observation in a succint sentence: "Governments have become too small to solve the big problems, and too big to solve the small ones."*

But this interpretation of the next few decades comes up against one great objection. Is not humanity's coming up against the physical limits of the planet the major characteristic of the possible futures? Won't the world population (which is growing exponentially) collapse suddenly following the vertiginous rise of infant mortality? Because of a lack of energy. Because of the disappearance of raw materials. Because of the exhaustion of arable land. Because of the extension over the planet of the black blanket of pollution. Does not the shadow of the catastrophe predicted by D.H. and D.L. Meadows[3] force us urgently towards zero growth, forgetting in the confusion the political, economic and social aspects and the three control inadequacies, and concentrating our attention on the physical limits of growth?

This question must be tackled frankly and examined carefully. But discussing it, far from brushing control deficiencies aside, rather returns them to the foreground, because the problems of our relations with the ecosphere can only be understood through an interpretation of the functioning of human societies.

It is up to the reader to accept or reject this overall view, to find it stimulating or trite. The route is fascinating enough, and the landscape sufficiently varied for each person to extract his own conception of modernity. As for ourselves, once the prerequisite of physical limits has been dealt with, it will suffice us to follow the clew. It will immediately lead to the analysis of the control deficiency of the international system, through the description of the emergence of a multipolar world and the examination of the rise of interdependence. In the next stage, it will expose the control inadequacies of the national systems in developed countries through the study of the contestations and ossification within industrial societies. Then and only then will reflection be able to take in the possible futures with all their continuities and ruptures. That will be the hour of scenarios for the specialists, and pictures of the futures for the layman.

But, as we know, these pictures cannot be the anticipated reconstruction of future histories. They only make sense in relation to actors. You the reader. I the writer. And the group of societies to which we belong (even though it cannot be the sole reference): that of Western societies and among them of European nations. Hence the final question. How can these societies respond(both for themselves, and as members of the family of human societies) to these questions put to them so insistently by the possible futures?

# PHYSICAL LIMITS?

"Facility is deleterious to civilisation."

Arnold Toynbee
*An Interpretation of History.*

# Of ponds and waterlilies

Does the increased consumption of non-renewable resources caused by the multiplication of people and the rise in their living standards jeopardise our future existence or that of our descendents to such an extent that it is now urgent that we turn around population growth and set a ceiling for it?

As an answer to this question, some people propose the image of a round pond with water lilies which double their surface area each week. The water lilies take a long time to cover the first half of the pond. In just one more week, they spread over the second half and come up against the edges of the pond. A lovely but inaccurate metaphor, for this mechanical vision of the growth of an exponential eliminates all the regulations of complex systems.

Thus, in the medium term, demographic evolution is a datum that may be calculated from fertility and mortality rates by age groups. However, in the long term, history testifies to the influence of social changes on population, and there is no evidence that such flexibility no longer comes into play, although the details of precisely how it works are not very well known.

Similarly, what happens when a resource becomes more rare? Its price goes up. It becomes economically worthwhile to intensify exploration for it, and to reorient technological progress in order to lower extraction costs, to begin to use more difficult sources, to obtain it by recycling and recovery, to stop using it in areas where it may easily be replaced, to economise on its use in other areas (thanks particularly to investment in equipment), and to decrease slightly the production of goods which require it... Step by step the whole social and economic system adapts itself and the final result cannot be compared with the initial shock. Besides, the greater the initial shock, the more stringent will be the regulations set up to reduce its effects.

There is one corollary. However rare a resource may be, it always has a value – though not necessarily that of the market – which is its cost to the community, and it is unreasonable to consent to spending more money in order to economise on its use. Scarcity does not invalidate economic calculations. Rather, it calls for them. This is wonderful food for thought for those who are always suggesting that we save copper, or chrome, or energy, without bearing in mind the extra trouble to people, or the the fact that it might mean increased consumption of other equally rare resources.

However, this discussion on the strength of regulatory mechanisms and the part played by prices, demands three essential complements.

All adaptation requires time. Short-sightedness about the future may make some actors ignore the future development of a resource until they are absolutely forced to react. Would such a situation then constitute a problem of long term physical scarcity? No, that would be a misapplication of the term. They are forced to confront a problem of transition.

Scarcity does not only have time limits. It is also geographically localised. If one more child is born in Texas, it will probably be welll off; if it is born in Bangladesh, it will probably be poor. The grain reserves of the Midwest do not automatically feed the inhabitants of Ethiopia. The mining resources of one country are not freely available to all others. Thus there are often local scarcities which depend both on regional situations and on the overall system. Should one classify them as long-term physical shortages? Obviously not, for, were it not for geopolitical obstacles, they would vanish. However, there remain certain cases where the regulatory mechanisms are inadequate. There are situations in which man's behaviour can create irreversible discontinuities in the functioning of our environment and make it teeter towards other balances. This may be a trivial phenomenon on a local level. A town expands or a motorway is cut through an area and several square miles of arable land disappear. Such a problem is much more serious on a regional level. Which of us does not know of tracts of land that have been turned into deserts by certain agricultural methods, or seas where all life has been gradually killed by pollution? It follows then, that it is absolutely vital to establish agricultures which may be kept going indefinitely without causing breakdowns that bring them to an end. But it is on a global scale that the issue assumes its full significance. What will happen if man accidentally causes changes in climate distribution? What if he allows non-degradable toxic chemicals to build up? Here we are raising the whole issue of the calculation of risk in modern society. We can be sure of one thing, and that is the absurdity of exaggerated answers. Reject nuclear power plants without taking into account extra deaths in coal mines. Absurd! Create an artificial dichotomy between 'natural' and 'chemical' foods. Absurd! But it would be equally absurd to reject long-term risks on the grounds of remoteness or uncertainty. We have to develop sound procedures for calculating risks. They must not be based either on the illusory assumption that all risks will be eliminated (the dam must never break, the tanker must never leak), or, naturally, on a refusal to take them into account. But at the same time, such procedures will be useless if they are not incorporated into the political system. Gone are the days when, shielded by their knowledge, technicians could take upon themselves alone the responsibility for the technological risks taken by society.

Thus, whether we are dealing with scarcity, delayed reaction, local shortages, or risks with irreversible consequences, we should refer, not to lilies and ponds, to projectiles and armour, or to cars and precipices, but to self-organising social systems under pressure from active agents working within criss-crossing regulations. Whence this paradox: there is no question that better clarifies the part played by control deficiencies (on both the national and international levels) than the one relating to the physical limits of growth which nonetheless seems only to involve the balance in volume of our resources and the uses that they are put to.

I have announced my destination. Now we must pass each stage and consider the facts:

First of all, let us examine the demographic phenomena, for human population and the volume of goods that each person will consume determine the size of future demands.

Next, let us consider data on the principal natural resources: energy, food, mineral raw materials, and the physical environment.

# People and population

Are we on the eve of a demographic disaster? Are we on the brink of having the planet's resources destroyed by a proliferous, ravenous human race that is incapable of controlling its birth rate? Will the geometric increase of the world's population continue happily at the rate of two per cent per year, doubling in thirty-five years, heading for fifteen and then thirty billion?

Probably not. The most significant thing to happen in the last few years has been the beginning of a timid and uneven decline in fertility in Third World countries like Tunisia, Mexico, Jamaica, Sri Lanka, South Korea, Costa Rica, and several islands - Mauritius, Barbados, and Fiji, for instance. Between that and the uncertainties surrounding the Chinese population, it is possible that world population may reach 6 billion by the year 2000, around 9 billion in the year 2025, finally reaching a plateau of about 12 billion, which is three times 1975 figures.

But it is social, economic and psychological changes in the Third World that will have the greatest influence on the rate and extent of this tremendous transition: development plans geared to satisfying basic needs, a more equal distribution of wealth brought about by a rise in agricultural productivity, the spread of education, changes in women's status, and the continuation of family planning programs. There is no doubt that these are the factors that will have the most impact.

The world will not collapse under the weight of its population, but the move to 12 billion is no trivial matter. An increase of around 8 billion people has far-reaching implications:

• Let us first do a rough calculation. It will mean a greater demand for natural resources in the future. If these are shared more equitably, an average world income of four or five times present levels will mean an economically developed world.

With its population increased by a factor of three, world production will have to reach 12 to 15 times present levels. Bearing in mind future technological progress and probable changes in production structures, it would be pessimistic to keep the same coefficient for natural resources. A coefficient of 6 to 7 would seem to be roughly right. Let us file that information for the moment.

• Secondly, in the course of the next century, demographic growth will bring about a radical change in the world map of population distribution. By the year 2000, North America, Western Europe and Japan will represent only 15% of the world's population (850 million). The population of the Third World will be more than five times this figure. Of these, 1360 will be in Southern Asia, and 1150 in China. Eight developing countries alone (China, India, Indonesia, Brazil, Bangladesh, Pakistan, Nigeria and Mexico) will account for more than one half of the world's population. As for the 12 billion projected for the year 2075, more than 5 billion may be in Southern Asia, more than 2.5 billion in Africa, and only 10% in North America, Europe, and the Soviet Union. In the Twenty-first Century, the average man will be an Asiatic, or a Muslim. He will be a man who will see himself as an heir of Mohammed, Ghenghis Khan, Lao-tze, or Akbar. He will look at European history the way we look at the history of the warring kingdoms of China. He will read Descartes and Kant just as we skim though Confucius. Behind all the platitudes and excesses of diplomatic rhetoric, do we perceive the quiet force of these numberless hordes? Do we realise that they are waiting for the day when each man will have an equal say in world decisions? The image which portrays the developed world as a privileged island surrounded by a growing sea of poor, is a rather simplistic one. A good many decades will roll by before the Bangladeshi peasant whose harvests are periodically destroyed by fowls sees himself as the equal of the Harvard graduate. But for all that, the demographic balance of the world is in the process of changing, and it is our (i.e. the developed world's) strategies that will determine its effect on the political balance.

• Thirdly, these demographic changes will generate many problems, as much in developing, as in developed countries.

In the Third World, despite the fact that situations may vary from country to country, rapid population growth demands a high level of investment simply to maintain the current level of facilities per capita. It swells the active population and depresses wages. It speeds up migrations to the great urban centres. It makes the struggle against malnutrition and poverty more difficult. It leads to an age-based structure which forces each worker to maintain a higher number of inactive people. As for urban problems, a few figures are enough to give us an idea of their scope. By the end of this century, all the great urban centres will be in developing countries: the population of Mexico City may reach 28 million, Sao Paolo 24 million, Calcutta 19 million, and Lagos 9 million. In these urban centres half of the population will be under twenty. Public services will be overstretched or non-existent. They will be the permanent homes of millions of unemployed. They will constitute a constant threat to governments which will be more vulnerable to these volatile plebeians, ready to back any political coup, than to the undernourished rural masses.

What a striking contrast with the developed countries! In North America, Japan and Europe (up to the Ural) each generation hardly replaces itself. The schools are going empty, and soon the universities will follow suit. At the same time, the growing number of elderly people is beginning to weigh on health systems. Some predict an overall decline in total world population. Others, including myself, foresee long periods of fluctuation in fertility, with the overall trend being towards a stationary population, resulting in pressures on socio-economic structures. It must be said that demographers are not a very helpful. They are good statisticians and serious economists, but they are not in the least interested in the psychological determinants of birth rates. We are familiar with the radical changes in attitude of the younger generation of women, and men's uncertainty concerning their role in the family. But what part do these factors play in such different cities as Tokyo, Munich and Los Angeles? For the fact is that the down-turn in fertility rates has been almost simultaneous.

● And these regional differences will have a further effect: they will be the cause of huge migrations. All we needed was some 'boat people,' a few hundred thousand Vietnamese (one ten-thousandth of the world's population) for the world to be moved. The developed countries felt obliged to open their borders and let them in, if only in trickles. Everything would seem to point to this as being only a shadow of things to come. Not only are we far from seeing the end of ethnic and political score-settling within or between Third World countries (whether in Latin America, Africa, Western, Southern, or Southeast Asia), but the difference in wealth between North and South are a strong motivation for emigration. And the immigrants of the future, far from trying to assimilate Western civilisation, will organise themselves into minority groups in order to develop their culture and maintain their identity, for they will no longer be fascinated by the values of the North. What will be the vulnerable areas? The long border between Mexico and the United States. It has already been crossed by about ten million illegal immigrants which the United States government no longer has the political power to eject. Then there is the Mediterranean with its immense human reserve: Turkey, Egypt and the Magreb. Finally, we have the Soviet Union's long frontier with Iran, Afghanistan and Turkey. And on top of that, within the Soviet Union itself, there are the frontiers of the Islamic republics.

• Finally, the geographic diversity of the demographic landscape raises one last question. How will these adolescent Third World countries peopled with adolescents get on with the mature societies of the West burdened with old people and centuries of uninterrupted creation? On one hand we have a violent, passionate, stormy people possessed by the charisma of their leaders; on the other hand we have a society of sceptics, technicians, preoccupied with security and caution. Need we recall the raving crowds at Nasser's funeral and the Negus half-smothered by prime ministers acting as bodyguards? Need we recall the hundreds of thousands of Moroccans who marched on the Sahara in response to their king's call? And the multitude that welcomed Valéry Giscard d'Estaing at the Kinshasa stadium? And the fleeting glimpses of Khomeini's tribunals? Contrast this with the rather formal serenity of the Bundestag, the quietness of an English election campaign, or a plane-load of American grandmothers disembarking at Miami. If one agrees with Alfred Sauvy that the dynamism of a country and its attitude to the future is determined by its age distribution, then the developed countries can do the world no better service than to boost their birth rate. This would not constitute an illusiory attempt to keep up their part of world population, but would be done in order that the moderate increase of their population might help to shatter rigidity, stimulate creative action, and awaken a faith in the future that will bring about real exchanges with the rest of the world.

# Energy: three crises and two transitions

Here is an excellent example of the fact that physical limits really boil down to national and international control inadequacies. Despite some significant areas of uncertainty, the data relating to this problem are relatively simple, if one starts off with two statements.

Firstly, long-term world energy production will in no way be limited by the volume of resources. What are the facts? Here they are in a few words. We shall agree on a convenient unit of measurement which is the (metric) Tonne Oil Equivalent, or, in specialists' jargon, TOE.

We have three points of reference: in 1980, world consumption was a little over 6 billion TOE; by the year 2000 it will probably have reached 10 to 12 billion; a very optimistic estimate places total consumption over the next 200 years at 10,000 billion TOE.

On the other hand, at less than sixty to seventy dollars a barrel, resources of oil, natural gas and coal are each estimated to be some hundreds of billion TOE. Other resources (heavy crude, asphaltic sand, oil shales) are estimated at 1000 billion at least. Reserves of cheap uranium and thorium for nuclear energy are limited, and without breeder reactors they would only provide 100 billion TOE, but as energy prices rise, resources increase; the rate of recovery for oil improves; deep sea deposits become accessible, and the volume of reserves of coal and unusual sources of fossil energy increase. For example, in 1978 the World Energy Conference estimated world coal reserves to be 6750 billion TOE.

With the new forms of energy, dimensions change: the appearance of breeder reactors means that fission will bring a yield of 10 to 100 billion

TOE from uranium and thorium reserves. And once it is mastered both economically and technically, fusion should produce between 25 and 250 million billion TOE. Apart from solar energy, the renewable sources of energy (forests, farms producing energy from plant sources, hydroelectricity, glaciers, winds, geothermics, oceans, and tides) could create 4 to 5 billion TOE per year at reasonable prices.. Finally, direct sunshine constitutes a considerable potential, even if only a tiny proportion of the 100,000 billion TOE which the earth receives each year is recoverable.

We may therefore conclude that we can manage for an indefinite period to maintain our annual energy consumption at six to seven times present levels. This can be achieved if we adopt energy systems based mainly on nuclear energy (breeders or fusion reactors), and a variety of secondary sources. Once these systems are established, energy costs should stop rising.

What then is the problem? This is where the second statement comes in: the structure of the balances of primary energy supplies will inevitably evolve slowly. History shows that it has taken between fifty to a hundred years for a new source of energy (coal or oil) to take over half of the world market. The development of nuclear energy is now going through the same process.

Oil production is likely to reach its highest levels around the end of this century. At this time it will still represent 35 to 40% of world energy consumption, compared with 49% in 1974. Under such conditions, and because of the fixed nature of energy stocks, we shall not be able to avoid two successive transitions:

● During the first, which will not have been completed at the end of this century, the sources of energy which are presently still at the research stage will not play a very decisive role and if we are to have an impact on the energy situation between 1990 and the year 2000, only three options will be open to us – reductions in growth apart. They are: the adoption of energy-saving policies, the development of nuclear energy, and greater coal production.

Since the classic nuclear power plant is no more than a new way of burning fuel, this first transition does not confront the basic issue which is the consumption of resources which are running out.

● On the other hand, the second transition will be characterised by enterprising efforts to use renewable or partly renewable sources of energy: basically, breeder reactors, nuclear fusion and solar power... We need to set up these new sources of energy without delay.

Once one has faced an issue, it is always easier to perceive the difficulties. Let us continue our analysis by considering first of all the question of consumption. The world average is 1.4 TOE per person per year. But in fact there are huge disparities between one region and another.

In the United States it is 8.1 TOE; in the Third World it is 0.23. The higher the national income, the greater the consumption of energy, but the relation between the two depends very much on the price of energy and the structure of the national income. In developed countries, when the national income goes up by 10% energy consumption only goes up by 5 to 8%, and these rates will fall even further in the future. Due to industrialisation, a 10% rise in the national income in developing countries often produces an increase of up to 15% in energy consumption. Thus, the countries whose growth is most threatened by the energy transition are not the developed ones, but the non-oil-producing countries of the Third World. And what about the influence of prices? Here we must distinguish between the long and short term. Sharp price increases such as the ones experienced in 1974 and 1979 set off an inflationist recession, a perceivable drop in the growth of national incomes, and a slightly sharper fall in the consumption of energy. On the other hand it seems likely that a steady, long-term price rise without periods of shortage will bring about an appreciable reduction in the consumption of energy and a slight fall in national income. The economy would have time to adapt. Thus, according to certain models, the United States could, following present trends, reduce its annual energy consumption over about twenty years by around 40% with only a very small percentage drop in national income. And already, between 1973 and 1981, the amount of energy consumed per unit of output has fallen by 16% in the OECD as a whole. In other words, there is no doubt that energy saving has great possibilites, but its cost increases significantly as its volume expands or delays are reduced.

Energy production for its part is inclined to come up against many constraints. It involves overturning huge areas of land and dealing with significant volumes of materials and water in order to facilitate the massive extraction of combustible solids; the immobilisation of vast surfaces in order to install solar receivers; risks peculiar to nuclear energy such as the contamination of power station employees, the pollution of wide areas due to a serious accident or sabotage, the improper elimination of radioactive waste over long periods of time; a possible change in the climate due to emissions of carbon dioxyde produced by burning fossil fuels... In addition, the majority of future sources (deep sea oil deposits, coal extracted by new techniques or liquified, nuclear energy, shale oil, and large-scale solar power), as well as huge savings in energy consumption will mean the mobilisation of very large amounts of capital. Whereas in 1975 the world devoted 2% of its income to investments in energy, by the year 2000 it may have to increase this to 4% (6% for developing countries) and the highest percentage will only be reached twenty five years later. None of these problems are insurmountable.

But some of my readers will be thinking, "Your vision of things is *passée*. Isn't the energy problem behind us? Even Saudi Arabia is experiencing trade deficits." Wrong! We should not confuse long-term prospects with a short-term development which is accounted for by economic recession, the crisis of heavy industry and oil. Certainly developments of the past few years have postponed difficulties for ten years, and to-day oil experts believe that the price of crude oil will continue on a downward trend for a few years. But dependance on the Middle East should increase once more after 1995, and an annual rise of between 3 to 5% of the real price of oil is likely in the last ten years of the century. Thus, one cannot exclude the possibility of a third oil crisis.

However, faced with this situation, what do the governments of developed countries do? Their response does not measure up to the challenge, and there is no better example of the inability of national political systems to devise coherent objectives, or to take the long term into account. And this incapacity is precisely characteristic of control deficiencies on a national level. In France, in 1974 a prime minister just escaped being remembered by posterity as rejoicing in the protection afforded us by our friendly relations with the Arab world. And though the persistence of *Electricité de France* has made a nuclear programme possible, all we needed was an election for the continuation of this programme to be questioned one fine day, as if it were some trivial matter. As we have no oil, we pride ourselves on having ideas, even if these ideas remain on the shelf. Policies relating to energy saving in transport, domestic consumption and industry continue to be feeble. And as for becoming involved in foreign coal mines, for years, it has been done either rarely or not at all. It would be easy to list countries one by one. The schema is always the same. Public opinion neither wants to save energy, nor to have anything to do with nuclear power. It doesn't want damage done to the environment either. And besides, the year 2000 is far away. So governments speak reassuring words, play for time, or give the impression that they are doing something.

"Why bother with government policies?" some will ask. "Isn't it enough to allow market forces to run their course? Haven't the 1975 and 1980 price rises proven to be the most powerful incentive for energy

saving?" That is indeed true, but there is no denying that had
adjustment to the first oil crisis been more rapid, the second crisis might
have been less extensive. And when one considers the world-wide human
suffering caused by the economic and social consequences of of this
second crisis, one must conclude that state intervention complementing
the workings of the market may be justifiable.

But if it were not for the deficiencies of the international control system
caused by the unequal distribution of resources between countries, the
energy transition would be quite different. In the case of oil. the countries
which currently make up OPEC possess almost 70% of all known
reserves. As for the countries of the OECD, they have 10%. Of this
figure, Japan has practically none, and Europe less than 2%. The Soviet
Union, the United States and China alone possess 90% of the world's
coal reserves. The Federal Republic of Germany, The United Kingdom,
Australia and Canada share 7%.

So overall, the United States is in a favourable position. Japan has
nothing, while Western Europe doesn't have many possibilities, and the
Soviet Union is very well off. In the Third World, the situation varies
widely from country to country. This is all the more so since much
geological prospecting is yet to be done.

That is why the world may yet face three energy crises that must be
identified.

• Firstly, *a substitution crisis* caused by the gradual running out of cheap
oil and its replacement by other forms of energy (by itself it need not be
dangerous as long as oil-consuming countries accept that they must
adapt).

• Secondly, *a capacity crisis*. This could be the effect of a dual cause.
There are OPEC countries that do not invest in prospecting or extraction because they believe that it is not in their interest to increase
production even if they can afford it, even if prices guarantee that it
would be profitable. And there are large oil companies which do not
necessarily look for oil in the places where they are most likely to find it,
but rather in places where, taking into account political risks, the
expectations of profit are highest. North America, for example!

• Thirdly, *a political crisis* with supplies abruptly cut off in the wake of
political tension, wars or revolutions. Two examples are already part of
history. They are the Yom Kippur War and the the change of regime in
Teheran. Confrontation between producing countries and the outside
world, and a revolution. It is far from unlikely that such events will not
recur. In addition, it is only through better control of the oil market by
the economic agents, combined with a reduction in demand brought

about by the earlier price rise, that the consequences of the war betwen Iraq and Iran have been limited.

Revolutions! No developing country that is a big oil producer is free from the risk of revolution, for, the flow of petro-dollars by facilitating waste and corruption, widening the gap between rich and poor, and encouraging more liberal mores, weakens the social fabric.

It was frenzied economic growth, capital-intensive to the point of absurdity coupled with extravagant military spending, which paved the way for a new Mahdi, a prophet of Islamic puritanism to topple the Shah with the help of groups which subscribed to liberal and Marxist European ideas.

Threatened as they are by the urban masses, orthodox Muslims, and the Palestinian diaspora, no government in the Arab Near East can be sure of its future. The United States has trusted the stability of the world to the wisdom of a few Saudi families. A new Churchill could well repeat the old Churchill's observation that: never has the fate of so many depended on the behaviour of so few. Who can guarantee that Ibn Saud dynasty will last forever? It must manage the greatest fortune in the world, and at the same time govern a kingdom which is barely emerging from nomadism and the Middle Ages.

And what about Mexico? Do we really believe that oil will make it more stable? It is a country where the gap between rich and poor is widening rapidly, where the rate of population growth is one of the highest in the world, where just a few years ago there were student and peasant revolts, where the capital city will probably become the largest urban centre in the world. It's culture is steeped in violence and death. Already, a drop in the real price of energy, a repercussion of the second oil crisis, has eaten up its foreign reserves, and plunged the country into a much publicised financial crisis.

As for the political problems between Western consumers and oil producers, they will be cropping up all through this book: conflicts over North African and Mexican immigrants, the Palestinian issue, the consequences of changes within Egypt, Turkey, Iran, Saudi Arabia, to name a few.

Possible paths for the future?

A transition achieved with the help of steadily increasing oil prices. This would fix world consumption in the year 2000 at between 11 and 12 billion TOE. The OECD countries which consumed 1.4 billion TOE in 1975 will be consuming 5 to 6. Third World countries, including China, will move from a consumption of 0.8 to 2.8–3.2. The remainder will be taken up by the Soviet Union and Eastern Europe. Of all the commercial energy produced in the world, oil will account for 35 to 40%, natural gas 14 to 16%, coal between 22 and 16%, nuclear energy 13 to 18%, and other sources, 7 to 8%.

An alternative hypothesis proposes: a chaotic transition without physical shortage, but with a succession of sharp price rises in the real price of oil, followed by falls. Some developed economies subjected to a series of erratic recessions with inflationary tendencies. A development in which, the more the United States reserves its own fossil fuels exclusively for its own use, and delay making economies in energy consumption, the more serious the situation of some Third World countries, Western Europe, and Japan will become. All this brings with it the risk of political destabilisation in these countries.

The third and final possibility: a transition characterised by major crises, and at least partial oil supply cuts. The resulting scenario? American paratroopers take over Saudi and Iranian oil wells. Meanwhile, other oil-producing countries cut down deliveries in retaliation, and the Soviet Union, taking advantage of the situation, continues to increase its political influence in the region, always avoiding a nuclear confrontation. Then, day after day, long patrols along the pipelines, terrorist activity in the oil fields, hijackings, small bombs planted in railway stations or on the beaches of Western countries. Some countries using their very advanced technology to develop national sources and new forms of energy. The whole world admiring the efficiency of a revitalised American machinery capable, at least temporarily, of overcoming the national control inadequacies. But freeing ourselves from oil will take time, a lot of time... and the situation is deteriorating. Beyond, prospective analysis ends, and the novel of anticipation begins.

Presently the trend of oil prices is downwards, but let us not assume, as we did around 1970, that the future must be the same as the present.

# War on hunger

Twelve billion people? Can we feed them indefinitely using a system of agriculture that does not pose a threat in the long term to the ecological balance? Can it be done with the help of advanced technology, despite urban development and erosion, both of which destroy arable land?

The question is even more crucial when we bear in mind the fact that several hundred million of the present four billion suffer from malnutrition. Which of us has not at some time or other felt our heart contract when we see Third World children, living skeletons with swollen stomachs, and over-large eyes set in heads that look too heavy for their slender necks? Are these UNICEF pictures the harbingers of a famine that will spread over the whole world?

It all revolves round the direct or indirect demand for grain in the year 2000 and beyond.

Grain production in 1977 was about 1200 million tonnes. According to certain relatively trustworthy estimates of population and revenue, by the end of the century, demands will have risen to 2300 tonnes. To meet this need, there would have to be an increase in grain production (compared with 1977 figures) of: 95% for OECD countries, 230% for the Soviet Union and Eastern Bloc countries, 210% for China, and 300% for the rest of the Third World. Is that possible? Yes it is. Such a level of world demand for grain would not come up against the physical limits of production, though some countries might find it difficult or even impossible to produce their supplementary needs, given present infrastructures or national resources. These countries include Japan, many European countries, Bangladesh, Nepal, most of the countries in the

Sudano-Sahelian zone, and the great oil-exporting countries. As for the others, the necessary rate of increased production is not, all things considered, imcompatible with their past performance or their biological potential. Besides, most of the countries which cannot effect a rapid increase in food production could, if necessary, ensure their populations physiologically adequate rations from national resources, by combining nutritional planning and fair and equal distribution of what is available.

How do I justify this relative optimism? Because it is possible to cultivate large areas of unused land, even if they are not equally distributed between countries. Because it is possible, between now and the end of the century to increase irrigated areas by 50%, especially in countries of Southern Asia, and tropical Africa that are short of food. Because it is possible to increase yields by 50 to 100%, even if this proves difficult in certain developing countries, not so much because of physical limits, but rather due to constraints arising from other resources or institutions. But what about energy? And the raw materials needed to produce manure? And pollution caused by pesticides? None of these things should prove to be a major constraint. Take the case of pesticides, for example. The use of biopesticides, biological pest control, and integrated control should allow us to remain within the limits of the absorption capacity of ecosystems.

The outlook is less favourable for the Twenty-first Century. If you will excuse the roughness of the sketch, it may be summed up in four statements:

1. The increased demands for food come almost exclusively from the Third World.

2. If the inhabitants of these countries adopt the present diet of its middle classes, available ressources should provide adequate nutrition for the whole population.

3. On the other hand, if higher income levels in the Third World create a per capita demand for animal protein comaparable in quantity and quality with present demands in OECD countries, it could prove very difficult to achieve the necessary level of grain production within the framework of the normal potential of traditional agriculture; in fact, in cases where unfavourable climatic changes or inadequate soil conservation policies may come into play, it would be impossible.

4. In this case, two main options would be open to humanity: either to push traditional agriculture to its absolute limits, cultivating at enormous expense (around 15,000 to 30,000 dollars per hectare), every bit of land that climate and soil make potentially suitable for agriculture, using

the different factors of production up to the point where the physical laws governing photosynthesis and the accumulation of carbohydrates in grains impose a biological ceiling on additional increases in production, and by this method obtaining a world grain production that would be about 30 times present levels; or else, on top of all agricultural exploitation, and at prices significantly higher than at present, turning to the industrial development of biotechnology to obtain a whole range of non-traditional food products.

But one note of caution. It is vital that governments, both in the North and South keep a watchful eye on productive land, and not allow this precious heritage of all humanity to be destroyed by deforestation, erosion, increased salinity or alkalinity of soil, or uncontrolled urban expansion.

Altogether, we have a balance that could be relatively favourable, if it were simply a question of managing the world's food resources efficiently. Unfortunately this is not the case. Unfortutely, the children in the UNICEF pictures are not a nightmare. They are real. And once more, we must bring up the issue of national and international control deficiencies.

For there are two complementary images of Third World agriculture. One stresses a considerable expansion of agricultural and food production in developing countries in the fifties and sixties. In 25 years (1950 to 1975), both agricultural and food production went up by 130%. The other insists on little investment in this sector which received one fifth to one tenth of gross investment in most developing countries, despite the fact that the agricultural sector employed the majority of the population. In all the many and varied national situations this issue shows up the functional deficiency of political systems. In the last ten to twenty years, Third World governments have often seen industry as the only means of modernising their economies, and accelerating growth. And consciously or unconsciously, they have often adopted investment policies or prices which do not favour agriculture, forgetting that usually, in the first stages of industrialisation, their countries needed a dynamic agricultural sector capable of providing food for rapidly growing urban markets, basic products for manufacturing industry, and savings for the development of the social and industrial infrastructure.

What are the economic consequences of these strategies? A slow and erratic increase in agricultural productivity, a very modest accumulation of capital in the agricultural sector, inadequate flows towards other sectors of the economy, an increasing dependence on imported food and raw materials for industry. These imports in turn use up a large chunk of limited foreign exhange resources, and thus reduce imports of intermediate products (such as manure) and of equipment which are necessary for the development of infrastructures, as well as for agricultural or industrial production. The slow rise of incomes in agriculture has retarded the emergence of consumer goods industries and agricultural industries upstream or downstream of the primary sector, thus undermining governments' industrial strategies.

As for the human consequences, they are well known: rising malnutrition, apparent and real underemployment in rural areas; in the case of urban centres, minimal improvements, and sometimes worsening of health and education standards. This situation has slowed down the fall in fertility, encouraged migration to the towns, and increased pressures on resources to such an extent, that in certain sensitive areas (such as the Sahel or Bangladesh) the destruction of plant life has caused ecological disasters. In certain countries, the food intake of low income groups has deteriorated in recent years.

A host of local problems indeed, but they all have common causes. Hemmed in, depending on the region, by tribal or feudal structures, and often dominated by great landed proprietors, the rural masses cannot articulate their demands and exert pressure on governments. And as for governments, the support of peasants (passivity will do) is less important to them than that of the urban proletariat. It was not the peasants of Azarbaijan or Kuzistan who forced the Shah into exile, but the petty bourgeoisie of the bazaars, and the common people of Teheran, Isfahan, and Shiraz. And it would seem that the assassination of Sadat was the work of a few officers and the Muslim Brotherhood of Cairo,

But apart from their place in local society, national agricultures are part of the system of production and trade in world agriculture. And here Western countries play a key role. On one hand, their huge markets have encouraged the Third World to develop a tropical agriculture geared to large-scale exportation. In many developing countries this reinforces a two-tiered agricultural sector. It creates a structure where one finds side by side large modern farms with rising productivity, and tiny subsistence farms which provide basic food needs, but with very little improvement in per capita production. On the other hand, Third World markets play a major part in the agricultural policies of Australia, the EEC, Canada and the USA. If farming incomes are to be kept close to those of industry without increased government intervention, the exporters of grain (and to a lesser extent, the dairy producers of the EEC) need Third World markets. Without them, they would have to increase subsidies or accept a restructuring of agriculture, and in some areas this would cause unemployment. Food aid, subsidised sales, and commercial export help to avoid all this.

In the democracies of Westen Europe and North America, farmers constitute a very powerful minority. This sometimes pushes these countries to adopt certain measures which have a direct effect on the Third World. In some countries they hinder export, while in others (those with a food deficit) they retard vital reforms. Control deficiency in the international system reinforces the effects of shortcomings in national political systems.

So it is not so much the biological limits of agricultural production, or lack of progress in farming techniques, but the social and political organisation of the world, both on the national and international levels, that will determine how many people will die of hunger tomorrow. The battle is far from won.

# No general shortage of minerals

I shall make my remarks brief because the subject is not as important as the ones which we have just dealt with. And if for the laymen it seems similar to the issue of energy, the likeness is misleading. In the short term it is difficult to substitute equipment or labour for energy. This is not the case with minerals. Naturally, each one has its range of uses, but it is very rare to find one that may not be replaced by another for some things. Another alternative is recovery and recycling. It is this adaptability which makes the production and consumption of minerals so flexible, and which so far has defied the makers of models. This is true whether they look only at one metal and easily depict a non-isolatable subsystem, or at metals as a whole and get lost in the undergrowth of uses and substitutions.

One thing is certain, the comparison of reserves[4] with projected consumption does not lead to the conclusion that there will be an absolute, universal physical scarcity, even if it is conceivable that difficulties peculiar to certain minerals may crop up. Thus, for a high rate of world economic growth, the relation between reserves and the probable accumulated demands of the next quarter century may be, 6.2 for aluminium, 10.3 for chrome, 4.6 for manganese, and 8.2 for vanadium, to name a few. Admittedly, the situation for copper, lead, zinc, molybdenum, tantalum, tungsten, and above all silver, bismuth, mercury and asbestos is not so promising. But when one bears in mind possible substitutions and resources which are not accounted for in calculations of reserves, there is room for considerable improvement. Furthermore, even if asbestos, bismuth, and other relatively rare minerals like barium, fluorite, germanium, graphite, gypsum, indium, and mica were to disappear completely – which is unlikely – it would be technically posible to do without them, even though this might mean difficulties in certain applications.

But if we were to end the discussion at this point, we would be side-stepping certain important problems.

Firstly, the fact that the centres of consumption and production are separated constitutes a risk. This is not, as one long-lived legend would have it, because OECD countries are on one side and Third World countries on the other, but because a small number of countries holds most of the world's reserves of the twenty most important minerals: almost 40% for the group comprising the USA, Canada, Australia, and South Africa; 19% for Brazil, Chili and Indonesia. On the other side of the coin, Western Europe, Japan, most Eastern bloc countries, and more than two-thirds of the developing countries have very limited reserves. On the level of individual minerals the concentration is even more marked. You may judge for yourself: 96% of the World's chrome is in South Africa and Zimbabwe; 90% of the manganese, in South Africa, the Soviet Union and Australia; 74% of the molybdene, in the USA, Chili and Canada... More than three quarters of fifteen out of twenty minerals are to be found in only five countries.

Should we therefore fear the formation of mini oil cartels? Generally speaking, no. Why? Because of the possibilities of substitution. Because of the more varied political distribution of producer countries. But we cannot exclude the possibility of temporary crises; the world of metals has its Saudi Arabia, and this means that there is no guarantee of future stability. South Africa holds three quarters of world chrome reserves, four fifths of platinum reserves, almost half of manganese, and one fifth of vanadium...

Another characteristic of raw materials markets is oligopoly. Five major companies ensure 96% of platinum production, 72% of that of molybdenum, 62% of that of nickel. The pattern is the same for almost all metals. It goes without saying that these big multinational companies do not themselves have any intention of adopting discriminatory policies; however, since most of them are essentially American, they could receive directives from their government which would have this effect. The case of nickel is vividly remembered by everyone in the profession. Furthermore, in the future, following nationalisation or state participation in new operations, governments, especially those of Third World countries will have an increasing influence on many markets. This will inevitably bring with it a greater risk of political discrimination.

Finally, there remains the possibility if world economic growth takes off again in the 1990s of an inadequate creation of production capacities, and, to top it all, a considerable price rise in the medium term. Already, the fall in investment over the past few years has been spectacular, and two of the factors which contribute to this phenomenon may persist in the future. In Third World countries there is political risk, ranging from changes in tax regulations to nationalisation without indemnity. In developed countries there is uncertainty about supplementary costs and delays engendered by the proliferation of legislation designed to protect the environment.

Let us remember the lesson of these metals with their poetic or barbaric names, from tantalum to columbium. It seldom expresses itself in terms of physical shortage, or in mining language. It has to do with political science, and speaks about what happens to communities which find themselves more and more interdependent, while wishing at the same time to be less and less so.

# Threats to our physical environment

Physical environment. The term has its limitations, but when put in opposition to social environment, it allows us to eliminate provisionally, and somewhat arbitrarily, the harm that people do to each other. Over the past few years, few subjects have been the subject of such entrenched positions. For some, it is the trivial hobby of old marchionesses or bearded academics. For others, it is a field on which the game of man's future and that of all creation is played. It is, admittedly, a complex issue.

Complex because of the wide range of subjects that it covers: from the disappearance of this or that coleopteron to heavy metal poisoning.

Complex because of the variety of geographical scales. From the pollution of the Potomac to world climatic changes.

Complex because of differences in reversibility between such things as the inexorable desertification of the Sahel, and emissions of nitrogen oxide over Tokyo which a few years of precautionary measures have eliminated.

Complex because of the disparities of the risks that mankind imposes on the ecosphere.

It is therefore hardly surprising that the subject should be fraught with confusion, that it should mix conscious and unconscious anxiety about the future, the fear of being Prometheus unchained, the desire for a bucolic return to Mother Earth, the rediscovery of beauty, and the will to accept responsibility for the consequences of our actions beyond the limits of economic calculation alone.

Let us forget for the moment reversible local effects, blackened facades or rivers with dead fish. If 1.5% of national income, and 5% of world capital were devoted to protecting the environment, it is likely that pollution could be reduced to very low levels. Let us concentrate on the crucial issues: climate, water, and toxic products, not to mention that other essential question – soil conservation.

The effects of man's action on the climate, and the effect of climate on man. There is hardly another subject that merits our consideration more; so all the more so because of its complexity, for despite all the measurement campaigns, the progress made in theoretical analysis, and powerful computers, our ignorance is encyclopedic. Research. We must do research involving meteorologists, oceanographers, agronomists, economists, and sociologists, so as to take full advantage of the period of grace in which we are not yet obliged when making decisions to take into account the impact of our activities on the climate.

What are the causes for alarm?

Firstly, the regular increase in the concentration of carbon dioxide in the atmosphere produced by the burning of oil, coal and gas. This could raise the average world temperature. Oh, perhaps by no more than a degree! But the distribution of this increase could be enough to change climate distribution, relocate deserts, reduce the world's agricultural production, and change the boundaries of the great agricultural areas. There will be winners and losers. Let us imagine for a moment a conference convened by Javier Perez de Cuellar aimed at limiting carbon dioxide emissions, or in other words, rationing the consumption of combustible fuels. You can imagine the row that would cause. Fortunately we have one or two decades left to study the phenomenon and seek solutions.

Another controversial subject. The effect of man-made effluents on the ozone layer, especially nitrogen pentoxide and the chloro- fluoro-carbons. But it would seem to be generally agreed now that a reduction of less than twenty percent of the ozone layer would not affect the temperature. However there are those who fear the increase in ultraviolet radiation.

No doubt the effect of heat given off by large zones of economic activity will be felt more on a local level. However, in the very long term, it is conceivable that we shall have to study very carefully the localisation of these emissions globally in order to bring effects on the climate to acceptable levels.

Finally, urbanisation, intensive irrigation, and the disappearance of forests, also have an impact on climate. But I do not believe that we shall be troubled with anything other than local problems in this century.

In which direction is climate changing? Every summer and every winter the good folk complain about it. Periodically an honourable (or reputedly honourable) institution publishes a report which comes sometimes to one conclusion, sometimes to another, and at other times to none, which is more serious. The fact is that it is highly unlikely that knowledge will have progressed far enough to provide answers to the question in the next ten years. On the other hand, it would seem that fluctuations in climate have become more significant in recent years. If this were to be amplified, we should expect much wider changes in world food production and the spread of famine in some areas.

After climate comes water. Will the coming decades see water supply problems on a global scale? It would seem not. Nonetheless, extending drinking water supplies for the rural areas of developing countries will be a major task. Do you know what percentage of rural populations in African countries such as Burundi, Gabon, Madagascar, Sierra Leone, Kenya, The Gambia, Togo, Zaire, Ethiopia, and Guinea have access to drinking water? Less than 5%. And even supposing that the objectives of the second decade of development were accomplished and maintained up to the year 2000, the number of people in these countries without access to drinking water would grow from 92 million in 1970 to 433 million at the end of the century. But this is not caused by physical limits any more than all the host of environmental issues that involve problems of water. This is true whether one is dealing with the pollution of certain zones with hydrocarbons, or the impact of irrigation projects in terms of erosion, salinity, and water-transported diseases.

As for toxic chemicals, the importance of their effect on the environment is disputed. The fears? That the damage done to man and other animal species by the level of chemical pollution in the environment may produce 'errors' in their genetic programming. Initially, these errors may have minor consequences, but transmitted and accumulated over generations, they could become tragic. Is not the present increase in allergies, anomalies of the immune system, and spontaneous abortions a tell-tale sign of this kind of threat? The risk is aggravated by accumulation along food chains. Thus the concentration of DDT in Lake Michigan is 0.0085 ppm; in invertebrate primary consumers it is 0.41 ppm; in secondary consumer fish it is about 5 ppm; and in gulls who are tertiary consumers, up to 3177 ppm. From sediment to the gull, we have an increase by a factor of 374,000! Among the dangers? About twenty heavy metals such as mercury, lead, arsenic, cadmium, the PCB's (polychlorobiphenyls), pesticides that are mutagens and carcinogens, traces of which are found in water... However, innovations in the chemical industry should change the picture considerably by the end of the century.

If I were to summarise my convictions on the jungle of problems related to the physical environment, I would state them thus:

In the foreseeable future, these questions are very unlikely to be an obstacle to world economic growth, even though they may generate serious local difficulties.

They may well prove to be delicate problems in a world of competing sovereign states where the activities of each one inflicts ecological damage on the others, or on the community (the third control deficiency...). The issue of climate is a case in point.

They call for coherent action in the face of uncertainty. Action which takes into account both the long-term risks and the cost of resources devoted to protecting the environment. Action not characterised by a heedless lack of foresight or the faint-heartedness of conservative societies which forget that death and destruction are the other side of the coin of creation and life.

# Return to the real frontiers

Are we nearly up against the wall of the world's physical limits? The survey which has just been presented leads us to a conclusion which, although not reassuring, is infinitely less black and white than the alarmist and simplistic pronouncements that we have been hearing over the last ten years. My own conclusion is as follows:

1. Even though humanity should be increasingly concerned about the impact of economic activity on all aspects of the environment, overall world economic growth should continue over the next half century without coming up against long-term physical limits. But it will be necessary, especially on a national scale, to exercise control over certain aspects of this growth.

2. On the other hand, man is going to experience a tremendous period of transition in his dealings with the ecosphere. It will be tremendous in length: from half a century to a century. It will be tremendous in extent: a tripling of the population from 4 to 12 billion, profound changes then mutations in agriculture, the massive substitution of sources of primary energy in the wake of a decline in the production of classic oil. During this period, we shall constantly have to adapt the flow of resources to the needs resulting from demographic growth, and economic development. These will be sources of difficulties as well as serious national and international conflicts.

3. We shall have to ask ourselves a number of questions during this period of transition, and most especially over the next twenty-five years. They cannot be separated from the socio-political challenges which will

confront national societies for whether one is dealing with bringing down birth rates, migrations, the development of agricultural production, food aid, access to energy, mining resources, the growth of nuclear energy, non-proliferation, or fixing the price of oil or basic raw materials, we are faced with an 'exploding' world where the globalisation of resources and needs at the planet level has a limited meaning.

Thus, the preliminary survey of the physical limits offers no leads for a reading of our futures.. It throws mankind back upon itself. Upon "Man know thyself," upon the reality of control deficiencies.

On the international scale, the reality of governments engaged simultaneously in games of competition and cooperation. Games of competition over energy and raw materials that will not lead to an ideal situation regarding efficiency or distribution. Games of cooperation concerning the management of man's common heritage – the climate, the oceans – but games in which the one who ignores the rules will derive considerable short-term advantages.

On the national scale, the reality of political systems which only exercise short-term control, and which may be indifferent to the situation of the coming decades, adopting either a swashbuckling or timorous attitude to uncertainty.

Our dealings with the ecosphere? We must incorporate them into a political and economic vision of the world. We must listen to the great historians when they speak of the rise and fall of empires.

# TOWARDS A MULTIPOLAR WORLD

"The heterogeneity of civilisations, henceforth merged in the same system, will perhaps, in the long run, develop more serious consequences than the opposition of two regimes or two doctrines which the majority of the people of the world claim to adhere to."

Raymond ARON
*War and Peace among Nations*

# A new turning point in history

The Renaissance was the last great turning point in human history. When will the next one be? We are living through it right now.

From the sixteenth century the small European promontory began to establish a dominant system of values which extolled individual achievement through mastering the world with the help of knowledge, strength, or wealth. That marked the beginning of the explosion of Western civilisation, and, from that time, all human societies have been swept along into its vortex. Amerindian civilisations were destroyed. Central and South America were colonised. The nomads of Central Asia were pushed further and further eastwards. The peripheries of Africa, India, the East Indies, and the Philippines were dotted with trading posts, in a wave which petered out on the shores of Japan. Black Africans were transplanted to the New World. Then, once the domination in Europe of South over North, of Spain over England came to and end, North America was brought into the central fold of the West. At the same time, the Industrial Revolution was developing in Georgian England, a shock which would submerge all the other continents and give birth to the Third World. And the Third World is simply the group of human societies which have not adapted to this change. Outside Europe and North America, the Japan of the Meiji era was to be the only one, or almost the only one to take up the challenge, becoming the first example of a mixed culture, an outpost of the West.

The triumph of science, the development of its economy, the rise of its military power, internal conflicts, and changes in the relative power of its great nations, all combined to make the Nineteenth Century the century of Europe. First industrial nation in history, and defender of free trade, Great Britain was to give way to Imperial Germany in the first quarter of the century. A reminder that growth is not acquired, and that maturity and decline can follow the royal road of expansion. Two important facts. As early as 1870, the average size of blast furnaces in the Ruhr was by far greater than that of their British counterparts. And the organic chemistry industry was developed by the Germans rather than the English. But already, Tocqueville was announcing in his famous book[5], that from the heart of the Steppes and from the heart of the Prairies, the two superpowers (the United States and Russia) were advancing on the frontiers of Europe. And the two world wars which shattered German power were to bring about the emergence of the bipolar world of 1945. Meanwhile, the great light in the east of 1917 would complete the break-up of the West. A division which some were to experience twice, in 1920–1925 and 1945–1950, as the beginning of a world-wide socialist revolution which, when all was said and done, only gave birth to a bureaucratic Empire.

Up to 1939, convinced that its domination over the South would last for a long time yet, the West only looked at the East and itself. At the time of the invasion of Poland in that year, were not four-fifths of the dry land and three-quarters of the world's population controlled by the West of those days? And were not 25% of both the former and the latter part of the British Empire? But, by 1965, twenty-five years later, the process of decolonisation was almost complete. This phenomenon was not anticipated by the pre-war generation.

Thus, the new turning point in human history has a double foundation.

● Firstly, Western civilisation which, throughout the last century made tremendous efforts to absorb its internal proletariat (a task which has been almost completed), now finds itself faced with the vast external proletariat of the Third World. According to Toynbee, this is a problem which other great civilisations have had to face. Most of them have fallen into ruin. But in this era of the shrinking world, things are different. Feelings of guilt and charity towards this proletariat and calls for strict management, are hopelessly indadequate. We must refer not just to ethics alone, or to a calculation of costs and advantages, but rather to history. It is full of examples of societies whose inability to adapt has set them on a one-way road to decline. It also shows us societies whose creative power has helped them to survive and expand despite great upheavals in their environment. Bearing this in mind, a positive response by advanced industrial societies to new national and international circumstances, and in particular, to increased interdependence with the Third World, is a response that could ensure the long-term political and economic security of these societies. And this applies as much to foreign relations as to their own domestic affairs. If one is to believe the memoires of the great heads of state, it is the main preoccupation that colours their feeling of responsibility towards future generations.

• Secondly, the great shift of the centre of gravity of the West continues. It began in the Mediterranean, reached the Low Countries at the beginning of the Seventeenth Century, became English for around two hundred years, for a moment was German, settled in United States between the two World Wars, and moved westwards from the Atlantic coast towards California. The Pacific is becoming a pole of history. But will the United States maintain the leadership role which it has held exclusively from 1945 to 1975? We can't be sure. Will it have a successor? There are scarcely any candidates. The Soviet Union? Its power may reach its zenith before the end of the century. Japan? It will not have a strong enough position in world economy. China? It is only just waking up. So once more, we are beginning to see the outlines – but this time on a global scale – of a multipolar political and economic system.

These two great components of the movement of history have been evident in the last quarter century. But what have been the essential changes that have taken place during this period? The coming of communism to China, followed by that country's break with the Soviet Union. The arrival of Third World independence. The rise of Japan and the creation of the Common Market. The end of Stalinism, and the development of East-West cooperation. The birth of the Non-Aligned Movement in Bandung. The creation of the Group of 77. All of these developments have not excluded a certain stability, thanks to the balance of power between the two superpowers.

Hence an unprecedented economic boom, and world production which between 1948 and 1973 showed an average growth of 5% per annum. From 1959 to 1975, per capita income increased annually by 3.2% for developed countries, and 3.1% for developing countries. In the space of a mere quarter century, international trade has increased by a factor of 6.

This extraordinary growth explains the functioning conditions of the international system, and national systems during this period:

• For about a quarter of a century, the international system had a regulator that was as much economic as it was political. Despite its great

military and ideological rivalry with the Soviet Union, the United
States emerged from the Second World War in a position of undisputed
dominant economic power. It could dictate the rules of the game
sanctioned by the de facto agreement of its European Allies. Thus it
was that a set of rules was established which facilitated an efficient
reallocation of the factors of production on a global scale, a phenomenon which some have called an International Economic Order. Its
principal components are well known: free trade, the internationalisation of the movements of capital, an international division of labour
that favoured increased productivity, a monetary system that ensured
stable exchange rates, all of this supported by a few inter-governmental
organisations with precise functions – the IMF, GATT, OECD, and
the World Bank.

• As for national systems, they benefited from a oneness of objectives,
and a structural flexibility inherited from the political, economic and
social upheavals of the war in Europe and Japan, and Third World
decolonisation.

For the vanquished (Germany and Japan), and for the semi-
vanquished (France and Italy), the consensus on growth did not only
express the desire to eliminate poverty or own televisions. It conveyed
above all the will to rediscover their soul, to re-establish, beyond the
immediate past, the continuity of the distant past. By giving themselves
a future, proof of collective ability. That was why this consensus thrived
so well in countries like France in the midst of other political cleavages.

For the elite of the Third World, the consensus on development
conveyed less a will to eliminate hunger than a desire to acquire the
symbols of power, to erase colonisation, to become, or become once
again, a nation.

Structural flexibility was the fruit of the Second World War, or of the
independence struggles. These smashed the social oligarchy, questioned
certain classes, mixed people, and switched elites. This structural
flexibility at once made possible the rebirth of the initiative of the social
and economic actors, and the mobilisation of resources to serve the aims
of the community.

The result?

In the North, a spectacular levelling of the differences in per capita
income between the United States on one hand, and Western Europe
and Japan on the other. The re-emergence of Japan and Germany at the
fore of the industrial powers. The intensive industrialisation of France
and Italy for the first time in their history. The result was the relative

decline of the GNP of the United States. In 1955 it represented two-thirds of the GNP of the great Western countries; twenty-five years later it constituted less than half.

In the South however, there has been a varied pattern of growth due to cultural, economic, social, and political peculiarities of the different societies. The rate of growth per capita for the Third World as a whole in the period 1950 to 1975 was around 3%. China achieved 3.4%. South Korea, Iran, Taiwan, and Iraq attained more than 5% per annum, while India reached about 1.5%, Bolivia, Chili and Ghana, 0.7%, and Bangladesh, Burundi. Ruanda, and Madagascar experienced negative growth. Even among non-oil-producing countries, per capita incomes range from 1 to 37. From 160 dollars in Bangladesh to more than 6000 dollars in Singapore. The development of the South is also beset with many problems, for, a modern sector coexists side by side with an archaic sector, rapid urbanisation with, often, the stagnation of agricultural incomes, and the gap widens between the rich and poor. Besides, millions of people live in absolute poverty: about 400 million in Eastern Asia and Black Africa, about 40 million in the Middle East and Latin America.

Altogether, the South has experienced a double development generated by similar problems, and increasing heterogeneity. A development created by the conjunction of national responses with influences from the North (the dominant centre of the world's economy) that are at once negative and positive.

But underneath this stability, the bi-polar world of the post-war period contains the seeds of change: the great poles of the North are becoming more competitive than complementary. Their strengths and weaknesses are changing. The relative decrease of American economic influence, important movements of the exchange rates, the embryos of distinct monetary zones, as well as increased competition for developing markets, all these things show that although the economies of the developed countries are, to a large degree interdependent, they have become less complementary than they used to be.

The Third World has been becoming conscious of its own existence. Over the past ten years the oil-producing coutries have acquired the political ability to organise themselves into a cartel. Countries that are in the process of industrialisation have begun to open up the markets of the developed countries. Poor countries have made claims in the name of their poverty. All have demanded a New International Economic Order. The slogan is more or less void of economic content, but loaded with political significance.

As for the face of the Eastern bloc countries, it is more inscrutable than ever. And while the Soviet Union develops its trade with the West, it amasses rockets and warships.

The movement towards a mulipolar world is being prepared. Towards an international system that will be increasingly more difficult to control, and whose poles will be the Third World, the United States, the Soviet Union, Japan, and the European Economic Community.

# Tomorrow, the Third Worlds

How does one imagine the developing world of tomorrow when the present suggests two different interpretations?

There is the reading that stresses parallels: where the shanty towns of Kinshasa meet the suburbs of Santiago, where one finds the disquieting twinkle of the decorations of Chilean generals and African commanders, where the same lost looks of Fulani shepherds and Bengali peasants converge.

And there is the reading that underlines contrasts: between the modern sky-scrapers of Singapore and the tents of Afghan tribes, between the avant-garde architecture of Brasilia and the hovels of Kabilia, between Hong Kong jeans and Indian saris.

We need to go back to the beginning of things; the clash between societies which are making rapid strides and traditional societies; the rise of the dominant centre that prevented the growth of the Third World from being a later image of that of the West. At this stage the respect of strict historical chronology or cultural differences is of little consequence, for the analysis will be able to account for the variety of responses. Then it will be easy to pick up a map of the world and try to think of the future region by region, or country by country.

A high mortality rate and poor sanitary conditions, a stationary population with nearly everyone employed in a very unproductive agricultural sector, a peasantry hemmed in by a more or less feudal structure, a bourgeoisie almost exclusively involved in commerce, an economy where subsistence farming predominates, little-differentiated political structures, a culture rich in myths and festivals, a profound

ethic of interpersonal and community relations, values which do not
favour innovation, a life steeped in religiosity. This was traditional
society before the wave of the Industrial Revolution. This is true even
though there is a wide gap between the Manchu empire and the
ephemeral African kingdoms, between the Mexico of Juarez and the
far-flung provinces of the Turkish empire. Even though, unlike Asia and
Africa, South American societies are the result of a European first graft.

Then comes the shock of the West with the arrival of the soldier, the
missionary and the merchant.

Perhaps the soldier brings colonial peace, but he also arouses a rage
born of impotence, both scorn, and infinite tenderness for traditions
which have not been able to protect. Thus, in the Third World unconscious, memories of gunboats mix with the image of the cruel foreign
Father. A Father who is both loved and hated, whom they have had to
kill in the adolescence of wars of liberation, and this Mother whom he
has raped. A mother who is the object of both disillusionment and love.

Whether he brandishes the cross or not, the missionary is evidence of a
civilisation that has no self doubt. Neither in the area of ethics, nor in the
area of knowledge. Trained as a minister, teacher, doctor, archeologist,
or ethnologist, he can transcribe languages, restore ancient monuments
and reconstruct history; but at the same time he teaches English or
French, gives vaccinations against yellow fever, transmits ethics in
action, recites Marx or Jesus, and belittles the sorcerer or medicine man.
Supreme architect of the consolidation of the psychological cleavage
created by the soldier's sword. Initiator of two imbalances: a drop in
infant mortality, and a Westernised elite.

As for the merchant, he wants to sell, buy and produce. To sell the
whole range of Western industrial products with the distribution network which he has created, and which the local bourgeoisie has become
attached to. Even if the artisan with his beautiful but crudely worked
products disappears. He wants to buy agricultural products and raw
materials for the North. He creates large plantations, and the rift in
agriculture is opened. He opens mines, and natural resources begin to go
up in value. He uses political power to build railways, roads and ports,
and infrastructures that allow the interchange of people and goods to
take shape. Income rises instead of stagnating, especially for those who
participate in the new economy. But through foreign trade, the country
becomes dependent, tied to the decision-making centres of the developed
world. It is a situation which cannot be explained by the liberal
economist for whom the international economic system is neutral in
terms of power, and who only cares about the efficiency of the market

and the pull of the developed economies. Neither can it be explained by the Marxist economist who only thinks in terms of exploitation. For, as things stand, the developed economy has influences on the traditional economy that are inseparably positive and negative.

That is the good fortune and tragedy of the Third World. If a technology is necessary, one need not rediscover it; it can simply be bought. But it will save labour unduly, because it has been developed by countries with high levels of productivity. The Third World can exchange natural resources for equipment, because there are world markets for these natural resources, but the fluctuation of these markets will, in turn, have a profound effect on the value of exports, and on possible imports. If it wants to back investments it can find loans and aid, but only for big projects which can stand up to the bureaucratic procedures of the North. If it wants to educate managers, it will find universities, but the universities will send them back with their heads stuffed with Marxist doctrine or wanting to hold on to Western ways. If it wants means of communication, it can install television, but due to lack of programmes it will have to feature *The mysteries of the West.*

The blessing and curse of relations with the North will therefore interfere with the internal struggles of changing societies. The social and ethnic groups and regions which have forged links with world economy will attract possible investments to their activities; traditional agriculture will stagnate; the towns will spread like a cancer; those who have nothing will hang around those who ensure Western style incomes... Then every colour and shade of revolutionary will appear, invoking every kind of socialism. Peasant mass movements, urban uprisings, *coups d'état* by power-hungry adventurers, or by doctrinarians anxious to write their theories in the flesh of the people. Struggles which the great powers will stir up in the world-wide game that they must throw themselves into. These similarities will give birth to differences. Divergent answers will spring from similar challenges, for there is no one answer, and there is no right answer. Past history, social and family structures, cultural traditions, population size, the sum total of natural resources, strategic positions, the charisma of this or that leader; all these will be key factors.

The first group of these responses sets off the classic approach: development measured by the rise in per capita income and sought through the accumulation of capital, integration into the world market and industrialisation. Relying on the private sector, and orienting industrialisation towards export. But the successes of South Korea and Singapore must be set against the development of Chile or Egypt. Allowing the private sector and state enterprises to coexist, and endeavouring to construct an integrated industrial machinery, as in the case of Brazil; but no one can forget the widening of the gap between rich and poor, and the desolation of the North East. Putting most of the economy in the hands of the State through national companies, as in the case of Algeria. But the rise of basic industries does not compensate for the worsening of the agricultural situation.

Is the way forward through reformist answers which attach importance both to distribution and growth: through policies which reorient investment, policies which transfer revenue, or through land reform? They have often been attempted, but seldom followed through, for these strategies which only question social structures to a very limited extent, come up against power relations: Frei's Chile, Peron's Argentina, and more successfully, but sacrificing growth, we have the Sri Lankan experiment...

Should we therefore listen to those who propose other objectives? Those who set growth aside and concentrate on meeting the basic needs of the poorer section of the population as quickly as possible, on autonomy in order to reduce dependence on the outside world, and on rural development? India has at times moved in this direction, which, until recently, was the one followed by Tanzania, but, in this path also, expectations come up against the harsh realities of action.

Is the road of revolution the answer? China, that vast country, feeds its population, but between 1950 and 1980 it did not manage to devise stable policies, and has not spared itself the expensive errors of the Great Leap ahead and the convulsions of the Cultural Revolution. Pol Pot's Cambodia has sunk into self destruction. Vietnam may have been efficient in war, but it has not stood the test of peace.

All the roads leading out of underdevelopment are rough, and some lead nowhere. Thus, as in excessively tough races, the gap between Third World competitors will continue to widen in the next quarter century, and this to some extent unprecedented in human history. Never have billions of men changed so rapidly in so little time. Never have they left so many miserable wretches behind them.

Where will this great adventure story be around the year 2000? If you were a few years older, my son, we would turn the globe together in order to get to know the Third World of your adult years. We would look at Southern Asia, arranged round the triangle of India. In the year 2000 it will have a population of 1300 million (a little over 20% of the earth's population) with an average annual per capita income of between 400 and 600 dollars.

I would point out Bangladesh and its grim future. It is a country where four out of five people live in a state of utter poverty, where political power does not ensure the mobilisation of internal resources for certain vital objectives, where investments operate without guidelines, three quarters of them being financed by foreign money. Here the problem of development is political in the profoundest sense of the word, and since there is no solution in sight in the sphere of internal social structures, the present situation will persist for a long time, with swings between famines and better years, and, perhaps, increasing political instability.

I would put my finger on India – a continent that will have a population of one billion men at this time. Since 1955 India has pushed for the develpment of heavy industry; fifteen years ago it turned to food crops and small-scale industry. In order to develop its agriculture, India needs to improve the productivity of its small farmers. India's industrial expansion – once remarkable for its engineering equipment sector – is now coming up against the problem of low domestic demand, since export is not enough to keep an economy of this size going. India's social and political structures inhibit the mobilisation of its human and financial resources, but the country is beginning to move, and could increase the annual (per capita) income of its inhabitants by 2 to 2.5% in the next fifteen years, which would be a remarkable achievement. I would describe the many faces of India at the end of the century. A pot-pourri of regions, casts and languages. India with 300 million people in a state of dire poverty, sleeping side by side in their shirts in the streets of Calcutta, or buried in the countryside during the monsoon. India with its world-renowned scientists and researchers. The India that has exploded an atomic bomb. The India of spirituality.

Then my finger would slip over to Pakistan. Our first contact with Islam. 135 million inhabitants in the year 2000. It will possibly acquire nuclear arms. In the Sixties it gave priority to a diversified export oriented industry. 1960 to 1970 were years of rapid growth – 7% per year. But today, profound imbalances dull its long-term prospects: an under-developed agricultural sector despite the fact that the country has considerable agricultural potential, a very capitalistic industrialisation that does not create enough jobs, a domestic demand that is stagnant because the needs of the majority of the population are neglected. Added to that is an ethnic and political fragility that is all the more dangerous because the country is close to Afghanistan and Iran.

In this vast area of Southern Asia, which for internal reasons is experiencing the problem of the most acute poverty, apart from Pakistan, the impact of foreign relations will have only a secondary effect. Aid and the transfer of foreign resources will be needed to get the process of development off the ground, especially in the case of the poorest countries, but they will never constitute an adequate condition.

Thus you will understand that Southern Asia will be a very specific challenge to your generation as it has been to mine. The challenge of making transfers of humanly necessary resources in a context where internal hindrances to development predominate.

Then I would turn the globe to the left and Eastern and Southwest Asia will appear.[6] From the Yalu which flows along the border of Manchuria to the southern coast of Java, by the end of the century, the islands and the continent will have a population of 640 million. What a contrast with Southern Asia! Between 1965 and 1973 industrial production in this region grew by an average of 12.3%, and 30% of this production was exported, against 10% for developing countries with market economies as a whole. But, what heterogeneity! We would draw closer to the map so as to see better the four small countries that announce the industrial awakening of the Third World. In 1975 just these countries alone still ensured almost half of the exports of manufactured goods from developing countries: Hong Kong 17%, Taiwan 13%, South Korea 12.5%, Singapore 6.5%! Some call them New Japans; others say they foreshadow China. Their per capita income at the end of the century? Perhaps 12,000 dollars in Singapore, 8000 dollars in Hong Kong, from 5000 to 7000 in South Korea, and 4000 in Taiwan. South Korea has become one of the big names in shipbuilding. Singapore serves as a service centre for the whole of Southeast Asia. The cause of this progress? A skilled labour force, a less unequal distribution of wealth than in the rest of the Third World, a considerable influx of foreign money, and government policies that actively promote export. But there is one obvious weakness – their dependence on world economy. A fifth companion state is not far off: by the end of the century Malaysia could attain a per capita income of 3600 dollars. And the Philippines, and Thailand? A more cautious estimate of 1200 dollars perhaps, but industrialisation has already begun.

Leaving success behind, I turn to incoherence, and follow with my finger the circle of Indonesia with its 200 million inhabitants, successors of the present 135 million of whom around two thirds live in a state of utter poverty. An area with considerable economic potential: rubber, timber, rice, and oil, but up to the present only hasty strategies. Soekarno's regime has paid little attention to economic problems, then, after the bloodbath of the 1965–1966 repression, it threw its doors open to foreign investment, but the Indonesian authorities did not outline priorities. Consequently, per capita income did indeed go up by 4.5% per year between 1965 and 1973, but the very capitalistic form of investment that has been adopted creates few jobs and limits the expansion of the internal market. As for oil, no one would dream of denying the tremendous waste that has characterised oil exploitation in Indonesia. Because of the chaotic structure of the investments that it has brought about, because of the shockingly bad management with which it began, and because today, it is highly unlikely, bearing in mind the resources of the country, that the last years of abundant oil will be used for long-term development. All things considered, perhaps an annual per capita income of 600 dollars at the end of the century, for developments of these past few years inspire more hope.

Finally we would come to the four socialist countries of the region, each of them very different from the other. The unknown factor is Vietnam, that outpost of Moscow on the Southern borders of China. It is a reminder that this region is a sensitive strategic zone wherer the great powers vie with each other: China, extended through its diaspora, lays claim to the islands off the coast of Vietnam; Japan sells 20% of its exports to the region – its so-called sphere of co-prosperity of the past – and makes significant investments there; the United States is present both militarily and politically.

Then, I would spin the globe and we would find ourselves on the other side of the Pacific, facing this America which, from the Rio Grande to Patagonia is both Indian and Iberian, and you would ask, "But why is this part of the Third World? Are not the culture, languages, and religion broadly European? Did these countries not win theicr independence more than one and a half centuries ago? Is not their per capita income already much higher than anywhere else in the South apart from the oil-producing countries?" Then I would point out the characteristics of the region that link it with the Third World: incomplete demographic transition (except in Argentina) and a population that is increasing by 2.7% per year; an extremely unequal social structure that blocks agrarian reform, slows down the development of agriculture, widens the income gap, and makes industrial growth dependant on increased consumption on the part of the rich, or on export; a political structure in which internal authoritarianism is combined with a risk of chaotic instability, and with political dependance on the United States whose shadow still extends over the continent; in their relationships with world economy raw materials still represent the bulk of exports (82% in 1973 including food products), the substitution of imports is shielded by a

colossal protectionism that has given rise to non competitive firms, and
the promotion of export rests in the hands of multinational companies
that ensure essential industrial dynamism. Thus, the growth of per
capita income from 1950 to 1975 was slower than in the Third World as a
whole: 2.6% per annum, as opposed to 3.0%. In a nutshell: *a continent that
has bungled its first economic take off.* This is an economist's detached
diagnosis, and it is borne out by travel accounts and the images of film
makers: from abandoned children in Bogota to striking Bolivian miners,
from Mexican Jacqueries to Argentina's missing. And yet by the year
2000, with a per capita income of 4000 to 5200 dollars, the 560 million
inhabitants of the region could enjoy a standard of living comparable
with that of present day Italy. But the debt crisis will have lost the
continent ten years. As in the case of Franco's Spain, through revolutions
and counter-revolutions, economic growth will shatter the social structures of the past. Here we find three of the largest countries of the Third
World. Between them they accounted for 42 % of its industrial production in 1973. Mexico, Brazil, Argentina. They will make their mark in
history.

Mexico? A great country of the future and a powder keg: 3.5%
demographic growth per year; half of the population of the United States
by the end of the century; Mexico and its thirty million inhabitants at
this time; such an unequal social structure that in 1970 the poorest 40%
shared only 10% of the country's income; a domestic market that is
confined to the privileged upper income groups, an excessive protectionism which creates inefficiency, expansion controlled by multinationals, and investment that creates very little employment; oil, a lot of
oil, that source of wealth and social disintegration. The Northern
peasant revolts and student demonstrations in Mexico's main square
were not so long ago... Today the tragedy of the drop in revenue brought
about by the foreign debt crisis. Against the backdrop of a violent past
and this culture symbolised by the sugar skulls with their empty sockets
that one sees in shop windows. One of the world's hot spots, and more
important, a country with a long frontier with the developed world.

Brazil? 210 million inhabitants in the year 2000 and perhaps an
annual per capita income of 5000 dollars. Economic growth has been
particularly vigourous: a rise in per capita income of 3.7% per annum for
the period as a whole, and close to 7% from 1970 to 1975! This has not
prevented social inequality from getting worse, but the country has
considerable resourses, and a massive influx of foreign financing. Hence
long-term development prospects remain favourable despite huge regional and social disparities, depite delicate balances between State-owned

concerns, transnational companies and private Brazilian firms, and despite the explosive domestic problems currently posed by the foreign debt crisis. But Brazil, one of tomorrow's greats, has no doubts about its future or its cultural identity.

But I could not leave Latin America without pointing out the places where zones of poverty will persist to the end of the century: some Caribbean islands, Honduras or El Salvador, Bolivia, Paraguay, and in the very heart of proud Brazil.

Once more I shall turn the globe, and crossing the Atlantic I shall find myself in the heart of the Black Continent. Common-sense declares it a sparsely populated area. It forgets fertility rates and agricultural potential. By the year 2000, 550 million inhabitants will spread over it from the edges of the Sahara to the Cape of Good Hope. The scale of per capita income (excluding South Africa)? No doubt between 600 and 700 dollars. A black Africa that is homogeneous because of its culture, the long epic of tribes and kingdoms, European colonisation and recent independence. An unstable black Africa whose borders are often no more than the legacy of old colonial agreements that have Balkanized the continent. A black Africa whose political structures are anarchical, whose leaders spend most of their time abroad and neglect the government of their countries. A poor black Africa despite its mineral resources, for its subsistence agriculture is in an unhealthy state; food production per person has decreased steadily since the Sixties; and industrial possibilities are very limited – no doubt less than 1% of world industrial production in the year 2000. A vulnerable black Africa, very unsure of its cultural identity, often saddled with teams of mediocre leaders, and an education system that produces unemployed people, and dangerously unoccupied urban masses. A black Africa that is becoming a stake between Europe and the East, with Africans too divided to settle their conflicts themselves. The danger? A considerable worsening of poverty. Hence the inescapable need for Africans to attain political maturity, and for Europeans to behave responsibly.

Penultimate stop. I would encircle the long strip of land that stretches from the south of the Mediterranean to the Near East and Iran. The land of Islam and oil with the shore of Israel in its flank. In the year 2000, this cross-roads of continents at the back door of Europe and the USSR will be inhabited by 330 million Berbers, Arabs, Iranians, Kurds, Turks... brought together into a great religious and cultural community by an Islam that is in the midst of a revival, but undoubtedly as divided as it is now by unstable rivalries. Yes, it is in this area, eaten away by the Palestinian cancer, in this area, where practically every regime lives constantly under the threat of a revolution, that 87% of OPEC's oil reserves are to be found. At the same time, it will, for a number of decades, wield considerable political and economic power. What will become of it in the year 2000?

Before making any judgement, we should remember that oil is very unequally distributed: Saudi Arabia, Kuwait, The United Arab Emirates, Qatar, Lybia, all sparsely populated countries, have 23,000 barrels per inhabitant – more than sixty years of reserves at present rates of extraction. For the more densely populated countries such as Iran, Iraq, and Algeria, it is only thirty years, 1800 barrels per inhabitant. Of the countries that have no oil or very little, the more advanced such as Morocco, Tunisia, Syria, and at one time, Lebanon, have a per capita income that is two or three times that of the poorer ones, such as Egypt, Sudan, and the two Yemens. Other data? The risk of explosive situations in certain countries following the arrival of the post-oil era if development strategies or the management of financial assets are not adapted; the shortcomings of an agriculture which makes the region dependant on the United States for food; very inadequate mismanagement of business concerns and the civil service; upheavals of social structures and moral foundations brought about by the influx of oil wealth. Before concluding, I should like to consider a few examples. For instance, the gloomy future of Egypt with its 60 million inhabitants in the year 2000, an Egypt where the per capita income has only increased by 1.4% in the past twenty-five years, and which receives about 50 dollars per person in aid each year. An Egypt that is generally short of food, and which, for the moment, has no coherent economic policy... Then we turn to the case of Iran which the Shah's megalomania wanted to turn into one of the greatest industrial and military powers in the world at a time when the country's second greatest export was carpets. A dream which, at the summons of an Ayatollah from another age, foundered on the revolt of all the people of the towns, moved by the contradictory aspirations of a society in the throes of change; from the workers of Abadan to the petty bourgeoisie of the Bazaar, in a revolution in which conservative puritanism went in the beginning side by side with Marxism, progressive Islam, and western-style liberalism. The determined and coherent Algerian experiment during the Boumedienne era which used oil revenues to finance an industrialisation planned and operated by state-owned companies. But here the problems of socio-political balance (particularly between the new state bourgeoisie and the rural areas), the dangers of the model being warped by the privileged social strata of bureaucrats, the development of agriculture, and finally the terms of trade with firms from developed countries, will prove to be one of the critical factors of the long-term future. Reflection leads to the following observation: the average income of the region in the year 2000 – perhaps 3600 dollars per annum – is less important than the seismic upheavals which may have the area between Lybia and Iran, Turkey and Saudi Arabia as its epicentre, upheavals that could shake the world until the oil fever is cooled.

One final turn of the globe, for we shall end up in unfathomable China, the China of Peking, Shanghai, and Canton, but also that of Sin-kiang and Tibet: the China of questions. The China of whose population we only know about 15%, but which, by the end of the century, will be inhabited by around one fifth of humanity: some 1200 million men and women. Will it enter an era of political stability that will allow it to pursue an organised strategy of economic growth over a long period? Experts differ depending on whether they refer to the fragility of the ideological or regional balances at the heart of the Chinese Communist Party, or to periods of consolidation – Thermidorian reactions – that have historically almost always followed great upheavals. I cautiously propose a positive response. But if that is the case, how will the Chinese economy react? Here the prognosis is more favourable, for, in the past, this economy has shown itself to be remarkably adaptable at times when political confusion did not disorganise it. And the spectacular increase of Chinese agricultural output in recent years has just confirmed it. For all that, my son, China will not be the great country of your childhood, but of your adult years. And those who govern China know this very well. Their diplomacy never gives up the least bit of land that has been Chinese from ancient times, from the Siberian borders to the South China Sea; at the same time, they do not make any attempt to recover them. Because from the international point of view – both militarily and economically – today's China is nothing. It has the advantage of immense size, and it will need a quarter of a century at the very least to sort out its fundamental problems. Meanwhile, it must choose a model of development,[7] establish the acceptable volume of foreign debt, slow down and then halt population growth, face its food needs in an organised fashion, exploit its colossal mineral resources, its oil and coal, make teams of trained scientists and technicians, develop its iron and steel industries, transport, communications and its electronics industry, renew its armed forces, and bring up its nuclear arms to a level of retaliation which will safeguard its territory and free its foreign policy; in the meantime it must slow down Soviet expansion, forestalling an East-West détente and preventing an upsetting of the balance between the two blocs that would place the Third World under the direct or indirect control of the Soviet Union. This does not preclude coming to an agreement with the USSR in three instances: if the Soviet Union were to consent to an Asiatic Yalta and withdraw from the Far East, if the United States were to fa:l back on itself, or if there were to be a genuine East-West detente. China in the year 2000? Perhaps 10% of the world's revenue (as opposed to 6% in 1970), an income of around 900 to 1200 dollars per capita, industrial development mainly concentrated in the eastern provinces, especially those along the coast. And (who knows ?) with 100 million continental Chinese as productive as their cousins in today's Hong Kong and Singapore. A China which, at the dawn of the Twenty-first Century, will have created the conditions of its future strength.

Thus our imaginary voyage around the Third World of the year 2000 would come to and end. In a few moments we would have viewed the most extraordinary , colourful, moving, comical and terrible collection of human figures in history, that of the leaders of the South in the last quarter of this century. Within this collection, some of the greatest men that humanity has ever known, honest and courageous men, rub shoulders with sinister and bloodthirsty buffoons. In passing we would have recognised Mao Tse Tung, Nasser, His Royal Highness the Emperor Bokassa the First, Nehru, Castro, Evita Peron, the Ayatollah Khomeini, Allende, General Idi Amin Dada, Pinochet, Indira Gandhi, Ho Chi Min, Kadafi, Nyerere, and a good many more.

This voyage calls for a synthesis. Let us begin with economics.

Arbitrarily setting the upper limit for development at around 4500 dollars, the countries which (between now and the end of the century) will join the group of developed countries will have 760 million inhabitants – 12% of the world's population. This new middle class will mainly come from Eastern and South-east Asia and Latin America. Perhaps (but this is less certain) two or three from the Middle East-North Africa zone will join this group. All in all, with the OECD and Eastern bloc countries, they will constitute one third of the world's population.

At the other extreme, by choosing 400 to 500 dollars as the threshold o per capita income for the poor nations, the countries which would be found on this side would, together, have 1650 million inhabitants, 28% of the world's population. They would be found principally in the world's two great poverty zones – Southern Asia and black Africa. In an optimistic scenario, the percentage of human beings in these regions living in a state of absolute poverty would decrease between 1975 and th<

year 2000 by almost 50% (from 52% to 27% of the population) but actual figures would fall very little: from 630 to 540 million!

Between these two extremes would lie a large number of Third World countries: in Latin America, North Africa and in the Middle East (Algeria, Morocco and Tunisia, for example), in Black Africa (Nigeria, Ivory Coast), in Southeast Asia (the Philippines and Thailand), and in the midst of them, China. 38% of humanity would be in this group.

Politically, the map will have a totally different look. Apart from the United States, the Soviet Union, the European Community and Japan, the countries that will count will be the oil-producing countries of the Middle East, China, Mexico, and to a certain extent, Brazil... But too many pieces are still missing from the jig-saw for me to hasard an overall judgement. And before that we must bring the great zones of the North to life.

# The United States: from the power of regulation to the power of veto

For thirty years, we Europeans have lived with the reality of American power. Computers? IBM. Planes? Boeing. Satellites? NASA. Military protection? the US army. The organisation of big companies? McKinsey. A political model? Presidential democracy. A credit card? Diner's Club. Our industrialists, bankers and journalists have crossed the Atlantic seeking ideas that could be brought back to Europe, ideas which had not yet been put into operation by subsidiaries of American companies. Have not *L'Express* and *Der Spiegel* been inspired by *Time Magazine* and *Newsweek*? As for our scientists, the only ones who are known outside of their own countries are those who write in English for international journals which are nearly always run from the United States. We have been the generation of the American challenge.

Just a few years ago, a scrutiny of the press, administration, business or research, would have left one in no doubt that the superiority of the United States was both past and present fact. Then one day, with the help of Carter, and with the unpredictableness of European fashion, the decline of the United States made the headlines, to disappear just as abruptly with the coming to power of Reagan. But let us not be misled by the simple everyday repercussions and vicissitudes of politics. With some exceptions, our contemporaries on both sides of the Atlantic have not faced the real problem – a problem as important as the emergence of the Third World. What will become of the United States tomorrow, that nations which, over the last few decades, has been the avant-garde of the West, and incontested leader of the whole world, with the sole exception of the Soviet bloc and China?

But upon examination the question may be split into three. It could use as a point of departure the investigation of future objectives of American society as they are expressed by the different groups which make up this society; either a consideration of the ability of this society to attain its objectives, i.e. the probable internal coherence of its development; or a questioning , from the outside, of its long-term adaptability in a new international environment; or else the examination of the probable consequences for the rest of the world of changes in the United States. It is obvious that the answers are linked. Equally obvious is the fact that they are different. Is it necessary to recall all the the societies in history which stopped facing the challenges of the future at the very moment when the full blossoming of their maturity ensured their people an ephemeral and precious quality of life? All the same, in order to understand better the multipolar world, we must give priority to the last formulations of the question.

I put my cards on the table. The world is seeing the end of what Daniel Bell has called "American exceptionalism." Signs of ossification are becoming evident in American society. But it continues to hold trumps that are unparalleled in the world. This mixture of strengths and weaknesses will give rise to new relations between the United States and the rest of the World. The American will cease to carry the destiny of humanity on his shoulders at the very time that interdependence will prevent him from taking refuge in isolationism. So he will play bridge or poker with the rest. But a lot will depend on how he will view his interest. If it is a long-term view, it seems possible that new kinds of cooperation may emerge. It becomes more likely that the control deficiency on the international level will be mastered. If it is short-term (in other words, if the lack of national control in the United States becomes too significant) the multipolar world will become a world where it will be more difficult to confront the challenges of interdependence.

After the judgement comes the analysis, and first of all, an analysis of the trump cards. And they are considerable.

I shall begin with energy. The United States has about one third of the world's supply of coal. It has abundant resources of oil shales and asphaltic sand. As for its reserves (both proven and potential) of natural gas, they are as high as 23 billion TOE, and reserves of oil as much as 20 billion TOE. That leaves uranium: according to reliable sources, North America should have about two thirds of world resources of Uranium with an extraction price of less than 140 dollars per kilo. Do we need to be reminded of how these figures compare with US energy consumption? Around 2 billion TOE. The conclusion goes without saying. Compared with the majority of the other great countries, the United States is in an exceptionally favourable position as far as energy goes.

Agriculture? Trump number two, and a tremendous one it is. a few figures will be enough to convince us. The recent problems of American agriculture due to the exchange rate of the dollar should not lead us to forget that the Unites States is able to supply half of world exports of wheat, two thirds those of secondary cereals, and a quarter of rice.[8] In 1960 each American farm worker fed 26 people of whom four were foreign. In 1978 he fed 52 of whom ten were foreign.[9] In the future he will be feeding more and more Arabs, Latin Americans and inhabitants of tropical and equatorial Africa. An extraordinary schedule, but it owes nothing to chance. What are the principal causes?

Advanced genetic research, intensive mechanisation, an extensive use of computer technology, large-scale farms, and the birth of an agro-industry in which Ralston Purina produces 14% of all animal fodder, Sunkist Growers supplies 80% of California's citrus fruit, Iowa Beef Processors slaughter 10% of the national total of cattle, the presence of five companies which cover 90% of American grain exports, and a coherent government policy of supporting exports... Some people call it green oil, and in fact, a number of Third World countries will be increasingly dependent on American agricultural exports.

It would be tedious to list all the minerals. In the United States abundance rubs shoulders with shortages. It has 35% of the world's reserves of molybden, 25% of silver, 21% of lead, 18% of copper, 14% of zinc... but manganese, chrome, cobalt, and a good many other metals have to be imported. Does this imply a certain vulnerability in this area? Certainly. Although this is largely compensated for by the power of the mining companies. Companies which specialise in groups of related metals and which master research, extraction, and processing techniques, know the markets well, and are able to operate in all the countries of the world by bringing together the necessary capital. When one evokes these mining companies or big agro-food companies, one draws attention to a major phenomenon that the man in the street basically does not want to believe: the economic prosperity of a country is less the result of having natural resources, than of having the human and technical capacity to put them into operation. And there are countless examples to prove it: ancient Athens, medieval Venice, the Low Countries in the Seventeenth Century, Japan today, and Singapore tomorrow... So many spectacular economic successes without natural resources. The extraordinary blossoming of the American economy in the two last centuries is less due to its considerable natural resources than to the individual and collective attitudes of the men and women of the New World. There is a debate which is simply the economic version of the problem of a system's adaptability. Those who believe in the protective shell of reserves are answered by those who place their confidence in the ability to act, and who are of the same kind as those who believed in armoured divisions rather than in the efficacy of the Maginot line. To summarise: the developed countries will be even more vulnerable in the area of natural resources if they prove themselves to be unable to act in any sphere.

Hence the vital importance of another American trump card: their position in the high technology industries, those connected with satellites, launchers, planes, calculators, electronic components, solar energy, pharmaceutical products, combustible fuels, and the extraction of submarine nodules. A position that is reinforced daily by the close connection between science, research and development, and industry. Some precise details? Here they are, in two areas.

Electronics, the dominant sector of the future. In 1975 American firms were responsible for 41% of world production[10] With their foreign subsidiaries, they controlled 66% of the total market of semi-conductors in 1980.[11] As for the most advanced integrated circuits, an American firm (VLSI) alone has a research development plan comparable with the entire Japanese programme.

On the subject of energy, where the United States will ultimately meeting the challenge, the figures speak for themselves. Since 1973 American spending on fusion, geothermics, and solar energy was four to five times more than that of West Germany, and eight times that of France; for coal distillation it is nine times that of West Germany. Based on the decisions of a few years ago, it is possible to forecast considerable American progress in both solar energy and the liquification of coal when the demand for energy renders it necessary.[12]

The very size of the American economy favours these efforts. We all know that when one is dealing with research and development the absolute volume of expenditure is more significant than the percentage of the national income that it represents.

The great American banks? Twenty of them have established an unrivalled network of branches in Europe, Latin America, and Southeast Asia. To such an extent that their international operations account for at least half of their profits. Thanks to the extent of their own capital, strict management and high level of professionalism, they tap the greater part of oil surpluses, play a vital role in the financing of big projects, and starting a few years ago, become the creditors and advisors of the governments of developing countries. How many of these governments tremble at the thought of being considered to be an unacceptable risk for the international banking pools controlled by these banks? Banks whose influence allows them to dictate codes of practice for the the whole profession. Certainly, American dominance does not give any indication of declining in this area of activity. Did not English financing power reach its apogee long after British industry had passed its zenith?

Such a banking network could never have been set up without the parallel development of American industrial multinationals. In the case of Europe, no comment is necessary; the phenomenon is too well known. What we Europeans are less aware of is its importance on the American continent, from Canada to Argentina, or in the Third World as a whole. What we should also know is that because American multinationals have been obliged to come to terms with governments in Europe, they have not behaved here as they do in their fiefs – Canada and Latin America. Canadian government ministers have a lot to say on this subject. And so do the Latin Americans.

A spider's web of firms quoted in the New York Stock Exchange, and which consolidate their accounts in dollars. What backing for the privileged role of the dollar! Money... Is it an asset or liability of American power? But we are not yet ready to analyse the possible futures of the international monetary system. A few basic data will suffice for the moment. There is no doubt whatsoever that the international value of a currency reflects, above all, the importance of an economy, but when the relative position of this economy weakens, the institutional privileges of its currency begin by checking the decline before creating increasing disadvantages which finally force the country to abandon all asymmetric monetary functions. The pound has almost completed this cycle; the dollar has actually reached its peak, but we must not forget that the early Seventies saw the beginning of the 'de-dollarisation' of world economy. In the post-war years, the fact that the greater part of world gross product came from the United States, allowed other countries, whatever the state of the American balance of payments, to keep their reserves in dollars and to hold their dollar exchange rates steady (or at worst, from devaluation to another). Fixed exchange rates are dead. Stone dead. They have been killed by the *relative* decline of the American economy, by the *corresponding* ascendancy of Japanese and European economies, and by the oil cartel. These fluctuations in its currency mean the beginning of difficulties for the United States despite a few advantages. However, the dollar continues to be a reserve currency which allows the U.S. to maintain a balance of payments in deficit. What of its future? A multipolar world makes an SDR-style international reserve currency unlikely.[13] As for a national currency, in order for it to become a reserve currency, there must be a huge domestic financial market, precisely for investing these reserves. Whereas at present, if 20% of official world reserves were to go over to the D.M., this would represent 20% of German market capitalisation and 130% of Germany's public debt, an almost unbearable burden. And what of the European Ecu? An important financial market in Ecus would still have to be created. One conjecture: in the long term, the dollar will have a less significant role, but this contraction will be slow and will not exclude periods of sharp rises of dollar deposits. Towards the end of the century, more than half of world reserves will continue to be held in this currency. One conclusion: in the course of the next decade, the United States will continue to reap considerable profits from the role of the dollar, but the difficulties will gradually overtake the advantages.

A final asset (in the economic sphere) may be added to the easily identifiable ones that I have just mentioned, but only global models will really make it apparent. It is the long-term capacity of the American economy to maintain growth even in the face of widespread protectionism. Protectionism between North and South, or protectionism between North America, the EEC and Japan.

Finally we come to military power which, for a long time, will mask the gap between the two Greats and the others. For the moment, I shall confine myself to one obvious fact: what a weapon this is in all kinds of negociations with developed countries that feel threatened by the Soviet Union! And this is particularly true of their two biggest economic competitors – Japan and West Germany! Because, for the foreseeable future, the West will depend on the United States for defence.

As I bring this analysis to a close, I shall no doubt plunge my reader into a double perplexity. Does the question about the relative decline of the United States and the changing of its international role retain any meaning, bearing in mind the considerable permanent factors of American supremacy? How could one even debate the issue? And, in addition, why have I not mentioned in my list of assets that admirable American capacity for organisation that we Europeans have tried so hard to acquire over the past twenty years? This is a double perplexity that I shall attempt to dispel.

Obviously there is no indicator that allows us to measure relative power. Alfred Sauvy did indeed try at one time to relate power to the volume of national production after subtracting what would provide the basic needs of the whole population, but nowadays, everyone knows how vague this notion is. So let us simply consider the probable history of the percentage of world income held by the United States: 1970, 32 %; 1975, 28.7%; 2000, 18 to 20%. Thus the downward trend which began in the 1950's with the reconstruction of Europe and Japan's take-off, should continue until the end of the century and, no doubt, beyond. The per capita income of an American in the year 2000? Between 20,000 and 24,000 dollars. According to some pictures of the future, it should be the same as that of a Japanese person – 25% more than that of an inhabitant of the nine-member EEC. With the decreasing importance of the American economy, the regulating hold of the United States on world economy can only continue to weaken.

There are those who are of the opinion that we are dealing with a misleading decline. The fact that the index of the productivity of all factors has increased yearly from 2.7% between 1948 and 1966, by 1.6% between 1966 and 1973, and by only 0.7% between 1973 and 1977, simply means that the American economy is experiencing a qualitative growth in which 'production' is underestimated by the methods of calculating national income. But it is precisely this that gives the initial distinction its full significance. The ability of American society to influence the rest of the world is not to be confused with fulfilling the aspirations of American citizens. Those who are responsible for the American economy are not deceived. What concerns them is the fact that the low level of growth in productivity should be more marked in the United States than in other industrial countries. "The experts (J. Kendrick, E. Denison) give a number of reasons for this decline: a decline of the rate of growth in activity that cuts the profits that the United States gets from large-scale production and their capital stock; a reduction of research and development budgets; decreased mobility of men and capital on account of the small number of people in agriculture; negative repercussions of regulations on working conditions, protection of the environment, etc.; soil erosion and lower mine yields."[14] We must disabuse ourselves of one belief. For twenty-five years, we Europeans, we Japanese, have seen American productivity as a ceiling that we had to attain as nearly as possible. We have forgotten the lessons of history. When, in the Nineteenth Century, German productivity caught up with the British and proceeded to breeze past it unhindered, no bang betrayed this breaching of the so-called productivity wall. The same misfortune could befall American productivity during the last decade of this century. The sacrilege would be committed by Japan.

Back to the symptoms. And I shall focus on the economic sphere (research and development, and industrial trends) before attacking the heart of the subject: social organisation.

American technological advances in a few vital sectors are not in the least incompatible with the pessimistic picture of America's technological future sketched by analysts such as Boretsky, Gilpin, Holloman and Melman. Some signs? Government-backed projects apart, altogether Western European industry has, over the past fifteen years, devoted as much to research and development as American industry.[15] A study of the history of the percentages of research-development spending financed by industry in relation to national income even shows that American industry has ceased to be the leader since the early Seventies. It has been surpassed by German, Japanese, Dutch, and probably Swiss industry. Compared with the leading industrial countries, the American balance of patents is slowly worsening, and has become negative compared with Germany and Japan. Let K. Pavitt sum it up for us: "The United States is not lagging behind the other industrial countries in technology as is the case with Great Britain, but there are signs that this could happen in the future."[16] All the same we must recognise that recent developments lead to a less black and white diagnosis.

The link between technology and industry is obvious. What do we find in the long term? A steady loss of international competitiveness on the part of American industry. America will have to depend on agriculture and the services to pay for oil, because its industrial balance is in deficit: "The shortage of consumer goods has grown; the surplus of intermediate goods has become a deficit and, what is more disturbing, the surplus of equipment goods has shrunk."[17] The United States is beginning to meet competition even in the advanced technology sectors: today, the Franco-German Airbus and the Phoenix breeder reactor, tomorrow, perhaps Japanese computer technology... Other examples? Certain big American chemical firms are beginning to withdraw from Western Europe and concentrate on products, technologies, and countries where they can keep a large share of the market. That is what Chrysler has done in the car industry.

A purely economic interpretation of the situation is not enough. We need to dig down to the roots. Like any great society, the United States has built its rise on a Credo that our forefathers were already listening to in the years preceding the French Revolution. A Credo of faith in the individual, the source of all initiative, but an individual who, in order to protect his freedom, accepts and defends the rules of the community. There is a profound consonance between this conviction and the three forms of American social and political organisation: management, the market, and presidential democracy!

What do American-style principles of management tell us – these principles that we have tried to imitate (I almost said 'ape') for years?

That each person is free to act as he sees fit as long as he internalises the aims of the company and respects the bible of its organisation. Sanctions? A rise in salary or dismissal. Remarkably efficient principles, since they fit in nicely with individual attitudes.

The market, for its part, is the economic model of democracy, for here the appropriation of resources depends on the free vote through which each person says how he would like his income to be used.

Finally, the Constitution ensures that the rules will only be defined according to the wishes of the majority of the country's citizens, and guarantees the equilibrium of the system through the strict division of power.

This trilogy is one of the high points of history, but during the Seventies it teetered on its foundations with the symptoms of an American disease and its triple cause: the adverse effect of the normal functioning of social and political organisation itself, signs of the ossification of this organisation and a questioning of its validity, and consequently, of the Credo on which it is based.

The adverse effects? Let us pass over the muffled anxiety created by professional uncertainty, and linger longer on the inequalities generated by the market in the absence of compensating mechanisms. Social or ethnic minorities in inner city or backward rural areas were progressively eliminated from the economic circuit. Regions got caught in the spiral of underdevelopment. Despite its high per capita income, the United States undoubtedly had a higher proportion of rejects from growth than other developed countries. Rejects who indeed received considerable financial assistance, but lived on the fringes of the society of their own country. Faced with unconquered regions, the American economy was comparable with French Catholicism which once found mission fields at home. Added to the adverse effects of the market were the difficulties peculiar to the public services in a country where the cult of individual initiative holds sway. Nothing demonstrates this better than some of the big problems of American daily life: town development, the health service, educational opportunities.

After the adverse effects comes ossification. Originally, this was not a purely American phenomenon: the movement of society towards a social oligopoly[18] in which organised groups confronted each other; the blossoming of associations dedicated to the promotion of this or that interest, and which check the reallocation of resources. The result is an ankylosis that is all the more powerful because, unlike Japan or France, the United States has not experienced any shocks capable of shattering its structures since the Civil War.[19] If we were to confine ourselves to a single example, we would need only to mention the long march of the American trade-unions that brought them to the point where they became one of the most conservative pressure groups in the country. Hence a crisis of the American political system. Hence the obstacles that the market was beginning to come up against.

For some years – although Watergate made things worse – American political institutions were not able to come up with satisfactory answers to the country's big domestic problems: energy, new town planning, health care, the struggle against poverty, access to education. The shift in the balance of power in favour of Congress, something that had never happened since the days of Roosevelt, in other words, since the beginning of the United States' world role, limited the American government's room for manoeuvre in foreign policy. Because of the length of terms, Congress and the President exist in a quasi permanent electoral climate. Four years for the president! In the first year, he must organise his administration and keep electoral promises. In the second, if the House is due for renewal, he must avoid any initiative that might prejudice the reelection of his party's candidates. In the third he works, always keeping an eye on the presidential candidates. In the fourth, he must get ready for the elections! And don't believe that the president controls his administration. This absence of control is the other side of the coin of American-style management. It cannot be compared with French or Japanese management. Run by men with sound professional ability, the departments and agencies live like independent fortresses. Each one by itself for itself. And leaning heavily on this little world are the press and media – the most important pressure group in the country; to the extent that certain high-ranking officials prefer not to think, for fear of finding their questions in the next morning's *New York Times*.

Make no mistake. The American political system entered a period of instability; it was not to be changed in the short or medium term, and the more the interdependence of internal as well as external problems grew, the less efficiently the American system would function.

As for the market, its ossification was becoming apparent. The multiplication of regulations combined with administrative and legal decentralisation made it possible for any group of activists to block a decision for years. Here are a few examples from the sphere of energy alone: West Coast oil companies were unable to increase their capacity, due to objections raised by ecologists, and they could only process 2.6 million barrels a day, whereas demand stood at 3.1 million; oil companies were not given permission to build a terminal for oil tankers between San Francisco and Los Angeles; after four years of preparations,

Standard Oil of Ohio gave up on constructing a pipeline running from
the west to the northwest coast of Texas, because it should have
requested 700 authorisations from the authorities concerned; building a
nuclear power station takes eleven years... A point of information: my
aim here is not to criticise the aspirations of the ecologists, but to
underline the consequences of current procedures on the functioning of
the market.

And finally, a questioning of the Credo that was evident on two levels –
institutions and values. The federal state exasperates Americans, but
they have turned to it more and more to solve their problems. Lagging
behind the other developed countries, slowly but surely, the United
States was on the way to becoming a Welfare State, at the very time that
this institution was entering a crisis throughout the Western world. In
the home of free enterprise, did not Carter's program for energy indepen-
dance propose the creation of two state companies, to be funded by
taxing the profits of the oil companies? Big business, once the pride of all
Americans, became the target of much criticism, accused of corrupt
practices, and of meddling in the internal affairs of other countries... All
this against a background of shattered values, and the flourishing of
minority groups with divergent behaviour patterns. No longer self-
confident, American man has been questioning himself. Four years on,
the analyses above sound like ancient history. The individual, management and the market have been rehabilitated. Fashionable slogans
celebrate rediscovered American power. The big car-manufacturing
groups have been radically reorganised to confront Japanese competition. New industries flourish in the Southwestern and Western states,
far from the highly unionised areas. Many new jobs have been created in
a multitude of services. Taking advantage of its cultural diversity and
tremendous size, American society has rediscovered an unquestionable
adaptability.

Where will the America of tomorrow be, between the stigmas of
Carter's America and Reagan's America stamped with the mark of
restoration? This is a difficult question, for if the long-term trend is
towards a relative decline of the role of the U.S. in the world, the
adaptability of North American society and the difficulties of Western
Europe and Latin America will postpone the time of reckoning.

This is the country that will have to confront the multipolar world. As
it becomes aware of the influence of other countries on its everyday life, it
will in turn become mindful of the influence – both positive and negative
– that it has had on the rest of the world. Gone is the continent which, by
managing its own affairs ensured world economic growth, using a few

diplomats and soldiers to stabilise political situations. But news of the world, will now have to get through to the Mid-West.

The influence of others is already evident in three areas.

Firstly, in the military sphere. Faced with the improvement of the Soviet armed forces in every area, will it be able in the long term to maintain the strategic balance, protect its European and Japanese allies, and intervene effectively in the critical zones of the Third World? We shall deal with this subject later on.

As for energy, the United States will remain dependent in the short and medium terms until the shackles of foreign oil are permanently loosened.

In several industrial sectors, it will have to face double competition, from old and new industrial countries. Consequently, the debate over protectionism is being revived on both sides of the Atlantic.

The hallmark of maturity is a balance between opposing forces before old age sets in. American society, which has shown remarkable vitality in the past, and which gives daily evidence of its creativity, still has the means to overcome its present dilemma and adapt itself. Not by turning in on itself, but by joining in the multipolar world game and playing its many cards.

There remains one unknown factor, for the American nation has the choice of assuming one of two roles in its maturity; one characterised by the short-sighted defence of immediate interests resulting in intensified conflicts with its OECD partners, while increasing the chances of a fragmented world being created, or one in which it searches for a new long-term place in the world's politico-economic system, and the prospects of both greater independence and cooperation will improve.

Whichever choice is made, it will be affected by changes in geographical balance at the very heart of the United States itself. Let us consider Woody Allen's nostalgic look at *Manhattan*. Much more than New England and New York, Chicago and the region of the great lakes, tomorrow's centres of creativity in the United States will be California and the South-Western States: an America with its face turned towards the Pacific, Japan, and China.

We had better believe it. As far as we Europeans are concerned, the changed role of the United States, as much as the rise of the Third World, are the factors that will shape the end of the Twentieth Century.

# What news of the East?

If one were to sum up the history of the Soviet bloc from 1950 to our day, one word would come to the fore: continuity. Despite destalinisation and detente. In spite of the uprising in East Berlin, and agitation in Poland, the ephemeral Hungarian Revolution, the spring of Prague, and Romania's economic self-sufficiency. Despite Afghanistan, and despite Solidarity.

It is true that shaking off the dreary Stalinian uniform has helped the popular democracies to rediscover their personalities. It is true that they have developed widely differing planning methods. It is true that without the presence of the Red Army, they would move rapidly towards a decentralised socialism with a more human face. But when all is said and done, the Soviet bloc has been maintained, and everything would seem to indicate that it will continue along similar lines tomorrow if there is no upheaval. For the centre of power is to be found behind the walls of the Kremlin. The Politburo has controlled destalinisation as it saw fit. Neither too much nor too little. Khruschev's exuberance had its day. It was an intermediate period preceding the colourless days of Brezhnev. As for détente, it has continued to be strictly monitored: a few technical and commercial exchanges, but without prejudicing the constant reinforcement of Soviet military potential. And détente has never got in the way of opportunism: in Angola, Ethiopia, Yemen, and Kabul at the time of the 1978 coup.

The invasion of Afghanistan is less an indication of a radical change in Soviet policy than a reversal of naïve Western public opinion. Forty years on, Carter found himself in Chamberlain's shoes on the morning of

the invasion of Bohemia on the fifteenth of March, 1939. A miscalcu-
lation on the part of the Politburo? Perhaps. But it was also a defensive
move, because a spreading of the revolt of Afghan tribes was likely to
replace a neutral state that had traditionally been favourable to the
Soviet Union, with a turbulent zone on the border with the Muslim
republics.

But what can one say about Poland? A Communist Party that has
been forced to put up with the opposition of a free trade union for more
than a year! Is this not a harbinger of change? We really do not need to
use this as proof of the failure of communism in Eastern Europe. The real
question concerns the outcome of the experiment. The events of December 1981 show that Moscow has never accepted compromise, and that,
thanks to General Jaruselski's state of emergency, it has been able to
reabsorb the absess while avoiding the cost of direct military intervention, and getting the West to pay for the restoration of the Polish
economy. And since the protest was backed almost to a man by the
Polish people, the only way now open to them is passive resistance.

Will this continuity carry over into the future? Between now and the
end of the century?

With the death of Chernenko, we come to the end of the impressive
collection of septuagenerians who ruled the Soviet Union for so many
years. The nomination of Gorbachev marks the coming of a new
generation to power. Already, heads are rolling. What will this transformation lead to? Continuity or radical change? One cannot exclude the
possiblity of radical change; remember Parkinson's satire on the choice
of a company president, a satire in which he relates the misfortune of a
technostructure which goes to a lot of trouble to ensure that the
presidency goes to the most conformist, most unimaginative, conservative executive. Too late, they discover that he is a strong, creative
personality, who has hidden his hand for decades! Remember the
harmless John XXIII! Democratic centralism could have a similar
accident – reform from above. The future history of the Soviet Union and
the world would be changed by it.

But if things do no work out that way – and this hypothesis is
altogether much more probable – the strong trends will come into their
own again. What will they mean for the USSR and the popular
democracies? For the former, autonomous but slow growth, the continued rise of its military power for two decades, perhaps some crumbling
of its national and social cohesion, in the long run... In short, between
now and the beginning of the next century, it may have passed the peak
of its relative power. The popular democracies, on the other hand, will

see increasing tensions between the aspirations of their citizens and the forms of social organisation, along with the constant need to resolve crises without overstepping the limits acceptable to the USSR.

The USSR has abundant and varied raw materials. It is the world's second or first producer of coal, oil, gas, iron, copper, lead, zinc, chrome, cobalt, manganese, nickel, platinum, and gold; it occupies second to fifth place for the respective reserves. Nonetheless, one cannot be sure that beyond 1985 it will be able to cover both domestic oil demands and those of its socialist partners, while keeping up supplies to western countries (about 80 million tonnes of oil and oil products), but it should be able to cope almost indefinitely with its own consumption of energy, and continue to be more or less self-sufficient in mineral raw materials. With the help of Polish coal the USSR should be able to cover Eastern Europe's basic needs if it gives priority to supplying this zone.

But what about agriculture? Here, opinions vary more widely. A grain production that is very vulnerable to climatic fluctuations, and the maintenance, for political reasons, of an agricultural organisation of debatable efficiency are two factors that will limit the effects of government investment. Nonetheless, the USSR should gradually attain total self-sufficiency in food, apart from some non-essential tropical imports.

Thus we see that, unlike Japan and Western Europe, the USSR has the necessary resources for independent economic development, but the spectacular growth rates of the old Five Year Plans will be no more than a memory: a growth in the labour supply that will be divided by three (compared with the present decade), an increase of the active population concentrated in the republics of Central Asia, the need to invest in agriculture, housing, transport, arms, the continuing assertion of consumer needs. All these factors will force the Soviet Union to base growth on increased productivity of labour. Unwieldly Soviet planning has never been known for its shrewd management of available resources! What about turning to the West for technology? The slowing down of expansion in the West will limit imports from the East, and, in order to preserve its independence, the East will have to limit foreign debt. An annual growth of 2 to 3% would seem to be a maximum for the next decade. At least in the opinion of those who hold to the likely hypothesis that there will be no changes in social organisation.

This relatively dual economic situation will not prevent Soviet military might from increasing and, up to about 1990, reaping the rewards of its colossal past efforts in the years when military spending absorbed 11 to 13% of the national income! For all the signs would seem to indicate that the USSR is could very well move towards a military government, brought about by a rift between an inefficient and nonchalant civil society and a military society that absorbs the most dynamic forces of the country.[20] The number and precision of its missiles make it the greatest strategic nuclear power on earth, and it boasts the greatest conventional army in the world, uncontested military supremacy in Europe, a daily improving capacity for long-distance intervention, and a navy that is only surpassed by that of the United States. All this is what allows USSR foreign policy to take advantage of the slightest favourable local oportunity, revolution, coup or border quarrel. The only constraint? To ensure at each turn that the United States will deem the stakes too low to risk direct confrontation... True, one day they will have to contend with China, but that will not be for another fifteen years at least. Given such circumstances, what does it matter that the ideological power of Marxist-Leninism is in its death throes, that Third World uprisings are inspired by other kinds of socialism, or other messianisms, and that as far as practically all of the South is concerned, the Soviet Union is just another Northern bureaucratic bourgeoisie?

As for the Soviet people, they do not challenge the regime. The handful of scientists and intellectual dissidents does not herald any more imminent changes than the Decembrists did in 1825. As long as the party and the administrative hierarchy absorbs the most capable people, as long as the level of consumption improves for everyone, as long as a great collective design tones down national realities, the USSR will remain as it is today.

Certainly, the response to the difficulties of growth could be found in a *reformist path* which would be translated into a 'new policy' characterised by more flexible planning and administration, promoting greater productivity and increasing the international influence of the USSR. Within this context, and linked with an atmosphere of détente on the international level, Soviet participation in the 'new international order' would develop, and East-West exchanges would increase rapidly. The countries of Central Europe would gradually attain greater freedom in their choice of partners and modes of development.

On the other hand, another strategy would consist of side-stepping current issues and facing future difficulties by reaffirming *the originality of the socialist model*. Once more the Soviet Union would take charge of the future of a self-sufficient socialist world. Giving a new thrust to anti-imperialism, nationalist manipulation, and a hardening of internal attitudes, all these would be used to counterbalance internally imposed sacrifices. The USSR would thus be in a better position both to take upon itself the responsibility for its relative underdevelopment and the originality of its social system. Such a strategy would pose a greater threat to world peace.

However, *continuity* would seem to be the most likely strategy. It could not be combined with a simple opposition to progress, but would once more face foreseeable changes on the national and international levels without essentially changing the current balance of relations between leaders and led, between the Soviet state on one hand, and the rest of the world on the other. The same would apply to attitudes to the slowing down of growth which would be made acceptable by periodic – and relatively formal – revisions of the mechanisms of management by demonstrating the fairness of "socialist" management of natural resources compared with the difficulties being experienced by Western economies. In addition, the stepping up of regional transfers of capital would help to control tensions provoked by the demographic dynamism of the Asian republics. In the same way, a moderate increase of East-West exchanges would be compatible with the maintenance of a high military potential as well as the accentuation of an attitude of opportunism *vis à vis* the Third World... Thus, *vis à vis* the outside world, continuity would mean Soviet policies remaining the same with its mixture of prudence and adventurism, with its cocktail of Russian expansionism and support for world communism.

But continuity will not be the keynote of the USSR forever. The end of the century will be a time of uncertainty. A few decades of homogenisation will not have been enough to dissolve old ethnic differences. As has happened dozens of times in history, there will be a rebirth of national consciousness. The Georgians, Kazakhs, Uzbeks, Tadzhiks, Turkmen, and many others, will demand a new autonomy. Full of confidence because of their population of 80 million inhabitants – one third of the Union – made dynamic because of their demographic vitality, the Muslim republics of Central Asia will have no qualms about shattering this empire that is a heritage of Czarist colonisation. This will signal the awakening of all the non-Russion groups, and even of their confreres the Ukranians. But the danger will not end there. The increasing role played by the service industries in economic development combined with the diversification of specialities that will characterise the technology of the future, will accentuate the decentralisation of the economy and several centres of power will have been created. And so, finally, the social dissent so long predicted by Western thinkers will flare up. A double domestic crisis. And all this within a gloomy international context: China established as an industrial and military power; rivalry with the United States kept up; loss of the loyalty of Eastern Europe. American presidents are not the only ones who sometimes have nightmarish dreams. For anyone who accepts these conjectures, the path of the popular democracies is clear. Initially there is a risk that Eastern Europe will suffer from competition between socialist countries for access to the world market, and from differences of adaptability between the various societies at a time of slow growth. A contraction of the economic base of solidarity, the resurgence of nationalist reactions, the appearance of political situations that favour the diversification of internal systems... That is all that would be needed to create centrifugal forces. Poland on the brink of bankruptcy and rebellion; East Germany more sure of itself; a Czechoslovakia that has not forgotten Dubcek; Hungary with an already decentralised administration; Rumania locked within its own borders. Only the slender consolation of Bulgaria's loyalty will remain! And yet, in all likelihood, the system will last. In the shadow of the Red Army. As long as nothing happens in Central Asia.

Continuity at home and opportunism abroad. This is undoubtedly going to be the path the USSR will take, as long as the ripening of internal problems does not lead to a dilemma between reinforced caution and the temptation of adventure.

# The Rising Sun approaches its zenith

On board the *Missouri*, August 1946, the day of surrender, who would have thought that thirty years on, the Emperor Hirohito would rule over a Japan controlling 7% of world income and one quarter of the total income of the United States, bearing in mind the fact that the archipelago had neither coal, oil, nor raw materials, and that its agricultural prospects were poor?

But the past should have led to a bolder forecast: to come out of the Middle Ages in 1868 and beat Russia thirty-seven years later, to conquer Korea, Formosa, Manchuria and Eastern China within half a century, and hold their own for almost four years from Burma to the gates of Australia and the heart of the Pacific against the Anglo-American coalition, were already great feats. Imprudent and questionable, certainly. Banal, no.

The disaster of 1945 did Japan three favours: it shattered certain castes of its social oligopoly; it taught realism to a country that had never known defeat or invasion; it put the economy back into the free trade system of the *pax americana*. But this left intact the hard core which has been the strength and cohesion of this society, and at the end of the century, it will undoubtedly be to this cohesion that Japan will – despite its weaknesses – owe its position as one of the countries with the highest per capita incomes in the world.

Japanese cohesion? It has nothing to do with our parents' naïve image of the Japanese, which portrayed them as all looking alike, meticulous, disciplined, and lacking in imagination, only able to copy the West without paying patent rights. In this society, the first non-Western society to make a success of its development, the individual is active and creative, but for him his life is only meaningful if it is a part of the community. Decision-making is not the prerogative of the hierarchical paternalism so often described by Westerners. The more common pattern is for initiative to come from young people who propose and oppose in a lively, detailed and professional debate. The hierarchy? Far from imposing its views, it acts as a framework for the discussion and helps it to mature, until a consensus is reached; for each person wants to convince, but also wants to to be convinced and be a part of the collective harmony. The outside observer only sees the length of this phase of research in which there is less an opposition of logical constructions than the interpenetration of each person's exploratory research. Neither does he understand the ruthlessness and speed of execution once the time for action arrives. These ways of working are practised everywhere: at the heart of the MITI,[21] or the Planning Agency, among ministers, in big industrial and financial groups, and in relations between the government and the private sector. There is no comparison with American decentralisation in which each individual is free to make decisions within the framework of rules and directives handed down from above. We had better believe it. The more interdependence between fields intensifies, the more the Japanese method of research and decision-making will eliminate the risks and wastage associated with Western individualism. More than the United States, Japan is a society that is able to change and forget; a society in which a few big decisions amplified by exchanges of information and forecasts are enough to reorient the whole economy.

The seeds of the future are already sown: a level of investment that is one third higher than that of other developed countries, a considerable educational drive, much attention paid to research and development, swifter collection and processing of data, first class potential in electronics and biology, a government that encourages the closure of factories that will cease to be viable in five years... Ever attuned to the world market, able to sell, buy, and reorient production in line with developments which it sees long before others, Japan, in the economic competition of the next twenty years, will retain the remarkable aptitude that has been the foundation of its rise in the last quarter century – the ability to mobilise national forces.

If there are no major breakdowns of the international economic system, there can be no doubt about the result: a generally higher growth rate than that of other developed countries. Obviously, higher energy prices , the change in the content of growth, and higher military spending will prevent it from attaining the 10% level of times past, but a rate of around 5% would seem to be a likely figure – almost twice that of the United States. And towards 1995, the productivity of the Japanese economy could well break clean through the ceiling that American productivity seems to have set for a long time. Having redeployed their industry, multiplied their foreign investments, and developed services, the Japanese would then produce 10 to 13% of world income, and would be assured an average per capita income of around 21,000 dollars.

"But," some readers will protest, "your image of Japan in the year 2000 is no more than an extrapolation of the past. What do you make of the new aspirations, the violence of student protest a few years ago, the strength of the ecologist movement, and sharp criticisms of life in Japan's towns? Aren't the Japanese going to stop being workalcoholics, TV addicts and camera maniacs? As they have no example to follow, will they not lose their collective sense of direction? Won't their socio-cultural equilibrium be shattered? Will their political system be able to absorb a questioning of the dominant socio-cultural model?"

Behind these questions is the reading that sees past Japanese growth as no more than the result of productivist brigading. They forget that over these past twenty years, regaining self confidence has been more important to the japanese than multiplying cars, and they will no doubt find it easier than others to find ways leading to new growth. Besides, the dynamism and efficiency with which the public authorities have taken into account the issues of the quality of life, decentralisation, and the fight against pollution speak volumes. Let us not deceive ourselves: the transformation of the Japanese model of growth , combined with the improvement of housing and the development of services is in progress; it is a responsibility that should continue to be borne collectively. All the same, the mystique of work will not vanish so quickly in these islands devoid of natural resources, where everyone knows that the future will be the fruit of tenacity and adaptability.

Japan's weak points? They are in the sphere of international relations.

American military protection and the opening up of international trade have, thanks to the extraordinary growth of its merchant navy, allowed Japan to import oil, ore and agricultural products, and in exchange to step up exports of manufactured goods. The Japanese economy is dependant on Middle East oil, and should decrease its weakness *vis à vis* energy as soon as possible. It is turning to Australian coal and Chinese oil... But there is more: increased protectionism between the great zones of the North or between the North and South would seriously jeopardise Japanese growth, even if there is no energy crisis. Hence a change of attitude towards the Third World, a Third

World which from from the perspective of Tokyo, has quite a different image: not the Third World of poor African republics, but of young Asian states in the midst of an economic take-off. With Asia undergoing profound changes, adaptation takes on a new meaning. And Japan's roving gaze turns towards the limits of the great system of the Pacific's future economy. From South Korea it moves down towards their vast Chinese partner, towards the states that comprise ASEAN,[22] towards Australia, that source of agricultural and mineral raw materials, extends to Brazil on the other side of the Andes, then Mexico, and finally ends up in California – the matrix of US technical inventions and social innovations.

But the military and strategic vulnerability of Japan is not less clear than its economic vulnerability. Certainly, withing the framework of a reinforcement of military cooperation between the United States, Japan, South Korea and ASEAN, Japan could, by increasing its defence efforts, play a stabilizing role in Asia and become a real military power in the region. But relations with the Soviet Union are delicate, and marked by an important disagreement over territory. If American protection should come to an end, a fortiori, if a military conflict on the Asian continent were to widen to a certain extent, for example between China and the USSR, one cannot exclude the possibility that, forced to choose between destruction and conversion (to China or the USSR), Japan would choose conversion.

Few countries have profited as much from post-war bipolarity, which has permited Japan to combine extreme political caution with an amazing economic activism. But as it approaches its zenith, perhaps taking the torch of technological leadership from the United States, without, for all that, having the means to be a world regulator, Japan will have to learn from this multipolar world that its success has helped to create a world in which it will be one of the principal components of the future.

# European uncertainties

Why such a cautious title?

Because the 1974 crisis opened up an era of ambiguity for the EEC, the heart of Western Europe. Ambiguity on two levels: on the level of the Community as a whole, the revelation of handicaps that interfere with undeniable advantages; the emergence of national differences at the very time that the geopolitical evolution of the world is once more giving meaning to European unity from the outside. Hence a complex and contrasty reading that justifies a wide spread of possible futures.

Community handicaps?

Considerable energy dependence, in view of the fact that at best, energy imports will drop from 54% to 50% in 1990, and that at this time the Community will still have to buy between 470 and 570 million tonnes of foreign oil.

It is very vulnerable in the area of mineral raw materials, since European countries have neither resources of their own nor powerful mining companies. The degree of dependence for metals like manganese, chrome, cobalt, platinum, tungsten and vanadium, stands at between 99 and 100%, whereas the known reserves are held by Eastern bloc countries or by countries with a very uncertain political future.

Its security is basically in foreign hands, since the governments of Europe, backed by their people, no longer have the will to preserve their societies and are quite content to play at transparent stratagems with the United States: just enough military expenditure to calm Congress and maintain American involvement; the means and level of defence kept deliberately low so as not to frighten the potential enemy and, in the event of conflict, the intervention of American nuclear arms becomes vital; NATO forces which might be comparable with the French army in 1940; a constant plea for East-West détente combined with laudable efforts to prevent a Soviet-American condominium... All of which masks the half-suppressed deep-seated fear of being let down by the United States when the Crunch comes, and the unspoken fear of a Germany that would have become a nuclear power by the time of reunification. The single shock of the last quarter century? A man, General de Gaulle, when he gave France nuclear weapons. But in fact the state of the world mocks such subtleties. The strategic balance swings between the two superpowers; Soviet medium range missiles ensure the superiority of the Warsaw Pact in Europe. Secondary powers threaten Europe's communication and supply lines... If the future American space shield does not extend to Europe, the West of the continent could become an undefendable zone. That is all that is needed for the future of the Community to be marked by the precariousness of its defence.

After the weaknesses, we come to the challenges of adaptation.

Where will Europe stand in the new international division of industrial labour? Tomorrow or the day after, competition from the United States, Japan, and the newly industrialised countries will become more intense. In this competition, the Community seems to be in a less favourable position than its two great developed competitors. It is, in fact, less free from labour-intensive activities that will lead to competition from developing countries. Furthermoore, the structural tendency to an increase in taxes and social levies, and the burden of the agricultural sector will weigh heavily on the external competitiveness of European industry.

As for European agriculture, which yields 5% of the Community's income, it will undoubtedly be a bonus in the next century, but for the moment, it shelters behind the Common Agricultural Policy. The medium-term situation does not promise to be easy: saturated community markets, increasing Third World demand, though without a rapid rise in international prices, a growing need for livestock feed that the Community does not provide, an agro-food trade among the Ten that continues to show a debit balance (were imports in 1977 not at 43 billion dollars compared with 14 billion dollars of exports?). The Common Policy will be renegociated, for the slowing down of growth will throw national budgets off balance. The most likely hypothesis? A continued but rather slow reduction of the level of protection with compensatory measures designed to facilitate restructuring and make up some incomes. We should expect some sleepless nights and rowdy-dows ahead for the Strasbourg Assembly!

The Community will have to live through its vulnerabilities and adaptations – exaggerated by a two-tiered bureaucratic structure, and within a two-fold geographic context – in an environment of heightened inflexibility in the member countries. Between now and 1990, twelve million extra potential workers – an exceptional piece of luck. But beyond that date, aging followed by population decline. If current fertility rates continue, the population of the Community (258 million in 1975) should barely reach 268 million towards the end of the century, falling to around 243 million in the year 2050; by then it should include 50 million old people!

Thus, even if there are no cuts in oil supplies, the Community's rate of growth should fall (maybe to about 2.5% per year), and its share of world income should drop from 20% in 1970 to 14–16% at the end of the century.

But to limit oneself to this external vision of the Community, to forget that it is a conglomeration of countries, is to pass over essential dynamics. Already, faced with the 1974 crisis, as much its cyclical as its structural aspects, the various European countries whose economies had become increasingly complementary – at least within the Europe of the Six – reacted differently. And as they face the future, each one of them will also have to take up its own challenges.

It wasn't so long ago that everyone was marvelling at the German miracle. A negligible rate of inflation, flourishing export, a constantly revalued currency, and close collaboration between management and workers. Yes, West Germany benefited, industrially from the fact that its specialisations within the EEC had given it a structure that was well adapted to the intensification of competition between developed countries and the expansion of trade with Eastern bloc countries and the Third World. But over the past few years, it has also needed to make greater efforts to adapt, withdraw from activities precluded by phenomenally high labour costs in dollars, and concentrate its equipment industry on making electrical, electromechanic and electronic products. Because of this, West Germany is now, unquestionably the third industrial power of the West after the United States and Japan. As for the absence in West Germany of the great political splits which emerged between the two wars, it is hardly surprising, since this is a people that suffered cruelly from Nazism and Communism, and which sill lives in daily fear of the Red Army. A situation which helps the dialogue between the representative social organisations as well as the adoption of strict macro-economic policies.

All the same, the seeds of other futures are already apparent. Behind its evident consensus, German society has doubts about itself. Doubts about its technocratic, aseptic, political life which could do well with a breath of fresh air. It is uninterested in its demographic survival and allows its fertility rate to plummet.[23] It reaches confusedly after other values as the vigour of the ecological movement, hostility towards nuclear power plants, the intensity of pacifism and desire of a part of public opinion to negociate at any price with the Soviet Union over medium range missiles, all testify. West Germany has recovered prosperity, but, unlike Japan, it has not recovered its soul. And it suffers from this. Unconsciously. The more so, because German society has difficulty in finding its place in the international arena, torn as it is bewteen the United States which it has adopted as a model, France, which symbolises the European road, and the German-speaking community which prefigures reunification in the distant future. It is conscious of its military vulnerability, but it has become aware of the relative value of American protection, as well as the quasi impossibility of a complete European defence. Thus, deep down, the West Germans are at the same time searching for their own long-term path within the European framework, through Atlantism, or through a neutralism that would one day make reunification possible. They are less a menace to the Community due to the weight of their economy, than a source of uncertainty for the European structure they are a part of.

Bonn and London are two different worlds. London is indeed a European city, but it is also a pole of the Anglo-Saxon diaspora which makes it possible for a Briton to be almost at home in Ottawa, Boston, Canberra, or Aukland. Once one crosses the Channel, the face of the Community changes. It is demystified. For Britain, a late-comer, the immediate benefits are more important than distant objectives, because its personal history over the past half century has been the opposite of that of the Continent (which, be it French, German, Italian, Belgian, or Dutch, more or less lost the war, but won the peace), enjoying unprecedented economic prosperity. The British did indeed win the war, but lost the peace. Dignified and relaxed, they have descended the steps of relative economic decline and lost the will to make an effort, as well as the professionalism that had been their forte, trapped by ossified social institutions. Thus, faced with the 1974 crisis, the United Kingdom's adjustment of its productive structures was achieved with difficulty, because of the combination of ossified trade unions which rigidified social interplay and gave priority to wages, and the fact that significant proportions of the various social groups had become attached to new life styles. North Sea oil profits hide a grim reality: Britain's share in world trade continued to decrease between 1973 and 1977, and the fall in productivity has not prevented the manufacturing industry from losing 500,000 jobs over this period. It is therefore hardly surprising to witness the rise of protectionism and the temptation to withdraw from the EEC. Foreign policy? The attitude has been the same. To sum it up in the words of Henry Kissinger: "Great Britain still possessed the experience and intellectual resources of a great power... But with every passing year its leaders acted less as if their decisions mattered. They offered advice, usually sage; they rarely sought to embody it in a policy of their own."[24]

But should we extrapolate these tendances to the end of the century? Are we not currently witnessing a shake-up in one section of the nation? The policy of deregulating and denationalising a part of publicly-owned companies, the government's victory in the miners' strike, and the reorganisation of the iron and steel industry should help to restore flexibility to the British economy. However, the forecast is still a cautious one, because it is difficult to predict who will win out in this three-sided game between ossified unions, the twelve apostles of the 'new growth,' and Margaret Thatcher's liberal young troublemakers. If we were not living in a tough world, I might feel like exclaiming: "How sweet!"

Another country (Italy) has adapted itself to the crisis by lowering the productivity of labour and devaluing its currency. But the comparison with Great Britain ends there, for the political and economic evolutions of the two countries have practically nothing in common. Italian political life is totally controlled by the parties. A situation comparable with the France's Fourth Republic, but a Fourth Republic in which the shadow of Mussolini would prevent the emergence of a General de Gaulle. In addition, there is the heritage of the great time of questioning in 1968: with terrorism on one hand, and the richness and diversity of ideologies on the other. All this against a traditional background of weak central administration, strong regional autonomy, and extremely rarefied political discourses... But economic reaction to the oil crisis is no less interesting. It has seen the success of small businesses and a whole informal production sector that is more or less free of the fiscal and social burdens that weigh on the formal one. Is it not claimed by some that one quarter or one fifth of the Italian national income would thus escapes all national economic accountability? Be that as it may, Italy has been able to take up the challenge of competition with the young Third World nations in labour-intensive sectors. A miracle of control through decentralisation and self management.

Nonetheless, we must still ask: are we witnessing a recessive development which, in the long term, only leads to a dead end – the backyards of Napolitan houses that hide rag trade sweat shops that are merely a modern version of the miserable workshops of the Nineteenth Century? Or, is Italian society, with its creativity and adaptability, beginning to move towards forms of production that are more in harmony with the hopes of freedom and respect for tradition that are developing in European societies? What a contrast between Germanic Europe and Latin Europe!

And what of France, the last side in the square of the great European powers? Initially, it reacted feebly to the crisis. Lulled by prime ministers taken up with their Arab friends, its economy shaken by inopportune macroeconomic decisions, and torn by the battle between Right and Left, it turned in on itself. Then, once the 1978 elections were over, it opened its eyes to the world around it once more. It pursued the adaptation of economic structures, starting from an initially less favourable situation than that of Germany, in the midst of a heritage of manifold rigidities. At the same time, other specific areas were strengthened: the vigour of policies relating to nuclear-powered electricity, the existence of an independent military policy, and a consistently active foreign policy. When a socialist president came into power, the world asked: is this country, whose history over the past two hundred years has been marked by revolutionary incidents, going to pass through yet another period of instability? *Aggiornamento* or *fiesta*?. Will the result be a Europe that is destabilised at its geographical centre, a Germany even more confused, and a nationalised French economy incapable of adapting to a new international environment? The case is exemplary, for behind the changes in political direction, one perceives the confusion of a society whose internal aspirations come up against international pressures. Whereas Raymond Barre, seated on the lid of the boiler, had defended the priority of adaptation to the outside world, the entire socialist government of 1981–1983, with its budget designed to revive the economy and its social advantages, was driven by the steam of endogenous forces. Then, faced with the harsh realities of the world environment, they recognised the existence of macroeconomic constraints, and with exemplary courage, adopted austerity measures. Then, a year later, when the crisis of the iron and steel industry arose, it rediscovered – at least partly – the need for economic efficiency.

Let us complete the picture. Rather than looking at Belgium, which is still under the threat of political fragmentation, or Holland with its German economic structures and Swedish sensitivity, one should be turning one's attention to the southern members of the EEC. The recent history of Spain, Portugal, and Greece has been dominated by the movement from an authoritarian regime to democracy. They stand between the developed European countries and the new industrial countries of the Third World, and one of them (Spain) will experience a great industrial take-off and will make Europe's centre of gravity move southwards. As for the other two, the prospects would be better if they did not combine the rigidities of industrial countries with the weaknesses of underdevelopment. the situation of Turkey is quite different. This country threw away its post-war opportunities. Its bureaucratic policies have made of its economic history a long initiation into underdevelopment. A land of uncertainty with 72 million inhabitants at the end of the century. Henceforth, it will only add to the fragility of the eastern shores of the Mediterranean.

So, the crisis of these past years has accentuated the divergent paths of the countries of Europe. Like a developer, it has brought out the specific character of the obstacles that each one will have to overcome. We should therefore not be surprised at the threats that hang over Community solidarity. Threats to the Common Agricultural Policy which seems too costly at a time of slow growth, and which is not at all appreciated on the inside by Great Britain, and on the outside by North America, Australia and New Zealand. The threat to the Common Trade Policy; there are wide differences of opinion between the champions of free trade and those who support a certain amount of protectionism. The threat to the European monetary system if the national economies drift too far apart. The level of independence varies so much from country to country that it is impossible to formulate a common energy policy. It is difficult to develop an industrial policy at a time when the structures of production are diverging. As for defence, in spite of the happy installation of Pershing missiles, it continues to pose a problem, both in the medium term, with the imbalance of conventional forces in the European arena, and in the long term with Ronald Reagan's Strategic Defense Initiative.

The convergence of these analyses is impressive. Faced with the intensification of international competition, there will be a greater temptation to resort to non-Community paths. Firstly, because the Community will be harder to manage: as it gets bigger, there is a danger that the already striking internal disparities will weigh down decision-making structures that are already far from flexible; moreover, it will become harder to share a slow-growing Community product than a fast-growing one. The Community is thus in danger of discrediting itself at the very time when the temptations to follow national self interest are most likely to be reinforced: in fact, socio-political tensions will be all the more acute in certain European countries, given the splits in public opinion in some of the member states. On the other hand, the search for areas of action and more broadly based solidarities could also, in time, undermine the *raison d'être* and functions of the Community.

Is there now nothing left but to write a *Pavan for a dead Europe*, or an *Apologia for a declining Europe*? Can it be that the dream of Robert Schuman and Konrad Adenauer is on its way to being shattered at the very moment when the emergence of a multipolar world could make it come true?

We must go beyond this partial vision. Let us once more ask ourselves some questions about Europe; on what it means, its pluses.

Europe. So many of us see it with Eighteenth Century eyes! Federation or confederation? The echoes of the French election campaign for the first European Parliament must have made the American founding fathers turn in their graves. As if the process of creating a nation were being repeated in the extreme west of the Eurasian continent! What an error of historical perspective! In order to become a nation, the EEC would need to have a dominant culture that gradually assimilated the others; a federalising state on which to build unity; borders that filter foreign influences; and finally, it should last long enough for the areas of solidarity to be more tightly woven than all the particularisms. The foundations of the Community are quite different: the diversity and vitality of its national cultures, the balance between its great countries, the intensity of its relations with the world (Twenty years ago François Perroux was already speaking about a *Europe without shores*). As for how long it lasts, the evolution of the world and growing interdependence will not allow it. Fears that history will repeat itself with France being swallowed up by Europe as Languedoc has been immersed in France are the result of a picture of the present that is as archaic as being sorry that it is not so... Disoriented? That we are, for lack of a word to describe what is happening in Europe: the creation of a family of nations. The solidarity of its members excludes neither differences, nor individual relations with the outside world, but it does help the family to find its place in the world society as a whole. And those outside are not misled. They recognise the personality of the family, and, by projecting onto the members their perception of the family, they reinforce an awareness of solaridarity on the part of the nations of Europe. And we can see this happening every day: US policy shows the limitations of Atlantism to many Europeans; the constancy of the Soviet Union reminds them of the existence of the Iron Curtain; China, OPEC, and the Third World also recognise the specificty of the EEC within the world community.

Ridding the European debate of its dross and reappraising it realistically, does not rob it of its content. A family of nations is also a place for debate, a room for affectivity. And changing the perspective highlights Europe's trumps.

The first trump? Quite simply, the Common Market. With 14 to 16% of world consumption at the end of the century, it will continue to be the second largest market in the world after the United States. It is obvious that Europe is heterogeneous (does not each country drink different blends of coffee, and does not each government establish different standards?), but one fact remains: intra-Community trade represents *half* of the foreign trade of member countries, and each partner country can rely on the trustworthy behaviour of the others. Such a market, on its own, can ensure that European companies basically benefit from all the economies of scale.

As for the importance of extra-Community trade – the other half – it is not just a weak point. It also makes the EEC the turntable of international trade. While the United States has Canada, Latin America, and, to a lesser extent, Japan and the Far East as its fiefs where it is both the main customer and a significant supplier, the Community is asserting itself as the main customer and supplier of the other Western European countries, South Africa, Australia, New Zealand, Africa, the Near East, some European socialist countries, and the USSR. Moreover, Europe plays a vital role in the economy of these parts of the world, though the reverse is not always true.[25]

Neither should one forget the trump that is the power of the European productive machinery. The high costs of agricultural production should not obscure the long-term usefulness of a sound agricultural sector that is technically advanced and backed by a vast network of research centres. The weakness of the industrial fabric of some countries should not make us forget the extraordinary richness of the Community's industry, an industry which, by the end of the century should still represent 16% of the world's industrial added value. The dispersion of European research and development potential, the frequently inadequate implementation and commercialisation of its results, should not obscure the fact that European research efforts are roughly equal to those of the United States or Japan – about 2% of the Community's product. Gone are the days when European achievements were no more than scaled down follow-ups of American ones. Aeronautics, nuclear science, and chemistry are now spectacular proofs of this.

But let us make no mistake. The only surity of this situation, the only trump card that guarantees the perpetuity of the others, is Europe's human capital. The expression sounds very dry and technocratic, but its harshness sums up the extraordinary richness of the individual abilities of the men and women of Europe. Aptitudes that are a blend of knowledge, perseverence, creativity, and the ability to work and achieve together, but also abilities that are augmented by the existentialist anguish and diversity of European cultures. These are the real weapons of Europe, the weapons of a family, and not of a nation. Heterogeneity is transformed from a weakness into a strength; it facilitates the multiplication of experiments, the variation of social innovations, the juxtaposition of distinct forms of organisation, and the maintenance of intellectual climates which differ, but which nonetheless recognise each other... It is up to Europeans to make this richness bear fruit through Community exchanges that are not confined to wheat and machines. But here we must interject a note of caution: anxious for security, aspiring to a certain quality of life, inadequately educated, and lacking in professionalism, a part of European labour remains ill-equipped to stand-up to international competition.

Besides, due to its history, the part it once played in the genesis of this civilisation which (for better or worse) has convulsed the world, Europe has preserved an extraordinary network of international relations. In the New World, in Africa, on the shores of the Mediterranean, in Southern and Southeast Asia, and in Eastern Europe. There is hardly a country that does not have links at least with one member of the Community of 12, profound relations which are rooted more in a cultural community than in a convergence of geopolitical interests.

So, the analysis does not allow us to avoid the uncertainty of Europe's futures, its many possible futures. There is no doubt whatsoever that Europe's influence in the world is waning but this is of little consequence since Europe, unlike the United States, stopped being the world's economic and political leader several decades ago. As far as Europe is concerned, what matters is maintaining room to manoeuver, reducing its dependence, and mastering its weak points, so that Europeans may improve their quality of life in the freedom of pluralist societies.

A better use of its trumps within the framework of the Community is a possibility. It is not a certainty, for the past few years have weakened Europe. Weakened its economic strength, political dynamism, and military security. Extreme hypotheses rule themselves out: the achievement of a Supranational Union by the end of the century does not seem to be at all likely, as the serious external threat that would be necessary to accelerate the process of unification would primarily reinforce transatlantic links; as for the complete dissolution of the Community, this presupposes the disruption of the whole international system. To put it another way, the visions of Europe held by partisans of supranational integration and supercilious independentists should increasingly prove themselves to be ahistorical, even if this view should continue for a time to influence the way in which most of the debates on European issues are conducted.

There remain the three great moderate hypotheses. A stagnant Europe, almost reduced to a free trade area that digests the arrival of new partners very slowly and confines its common policies to superficial, secondary actions. It is a Europe of slow growth, rising unemployment, worsening budget problems, conflicts over the distribution of benefits and contributions. A reinforced Europe that complements the Common market with a sound coordination of cyclical and monetary policies, that develops its industrial and energy policies, that keeps a watchful eye on its position in advanced technology, and carries some weight in inter-national negociations. This reinforcement? It implies a convergence of life styles and a strengthening of ties between the peoples of Europe. It has to be built on Germany and France, and the geographic widening of the Community will not change this. As for the intermediary images, there are numerous sketches. Some think that it will be a Europe in which the various countries take part at different speeds, because not all member-states will be able or willing to keep up with the pace of economic and social cooperation of the more dynamic countries. For others who consider above all some common achievements with different participants each time, it will be Europe *à la carte*. Unstable images whose apparition could increase the chances of a reinforcment, but which risk dissolving in the grisaille of stagnation.

In modern *Volapük*, the future only exists in the plural.

# Splits in the multipolar world

The maturity of the United States, the take-off of Japan, the constancy of Soviet pressure, the slow awakening of China, and the increased differentiation of the Third world. What will multi-polarity mean in this context?

If there are no major breakdowns – and we cannot exclude this possibility – it will be a world far removed from the two structures whose functioning the economist feels able to predict: monopoly (or if necessary, certain forms of duopoly), in which the dominant actor controls the environment; or so-called perfect competition in which all actors submit to an environment that they cannot influence, and which derives its stability from the multiplicity of atoms that constitute it. A world that will be rather like an oligopoly in which the actors of different sizes modify their respective environments and are sources of unpredictability for each other. This oligopoly would in no way be comparable with the one that existed in Eighteenth Century Europe or following the Vienna Convention. Those were encounters between a few players with analogous objectives and equal power. It was also easy to analyse the coalitions and aims that they were proposing. It will not be at all like that in the future: the wide spread of national powers will be combined with the variety of weapons held by the actors and the heterogeneity of their objectives to produce particularly complex situations. Saudi Arabia will not be a scaled down model of America. The objectives of a future Khomeini will not be an Iranian version of the objectives of Mrs. Thatcher's successors... There will be many gaming tables where different governments will participate. Tables with greater or lesser risks, varying rules, and distinct coalitions, but with interdependent results, at which each player will try to follow more or less coordinated strategies. There will be none of the silence of bridge tournaments, for other actors, the common people, will try to overturn the tables, mix up the cards, smash the chessmen, or shout out their preferences villifying their champion or supporting him noisily...

The big centre table will remain unchanged: it will still be the one where the governments of the two superpowers (the USSR and the United States) have sat since 1945, but a third player will have joined them – China. It will start off with a poor hand, but this will gradually get stronger. And from time to time the countries of the Community, or Japan will appear there. Whenever the tension rises at this table, all the other players will hold their breath. Like today. There will however be one basic difference: the course of the contest at that table will be constantly disturbed by what is happening at other tables, tables that the big powers will be less and less able to control properly.

We know some of these tables: the Trilateral table – that of the OECD – at which North America, Western Europe and Japan play at independence within interdependence. Patiently, constantly, the United States will try to create the great coalition that would allow it to sit at the centre table as the sole representative of the West. Patiently, constantly, the Europeans and Japanese improve their own games, especially in the area of economics. And now (we have reached the last decade of the century), more and more often, certain new industrial countries will come to sit there. Next to this table will be that of the EEC with its endless debates. The COMECON will sit at the other end of the room. Meetings at this table will be very short, because they will simply consist of communiqués from Moscow. Then come the tables of the Third World regions. Here certain chairs are often empty, and things are prone to get broken. It is the table of the League of Arab Nations, OPEC, ASEAN, and the Organisation for African Unity, to name a few. And then that of the 77 with their 120 chairs. Voices are deliberately raised, and there is an increasing number of absentees. And to calm the atmosphere, much use is made of a little machine that is always within reach on the table, and which serves to add up all the different claims. Over the years new tables have appeared. Around them sit a few players from the North and South. The Three-way Dialogue table where the Africans and Arabs often prefer to take turns sitting with Europeans, a Western Pacific table where Japan and Australia meet the ASEAN countries, a New World table where it is hard to find a common language between English and Spanish... And finally, in a corner, two huge tables: the Southwest table (still damaged since it was first used at Avenue Kleber and not repaired by Cancun); and the United Nations table with its 150 places. These are the tables dedicated to rhetoric and peremptory declarations, at which, after endless debates and twenty years ahead of time, rates of growth are decided which none of the players has the power to fix. Tables of great illusions, but it is around these illusions that the myths of the future will be developed, the myths that one day will give a sense of direction to humanity.

Thus, the multipolar future may combine the Americano-Soviet duopoly, the Americano-Japanese economic bipole with a shrunken European appendage, and the varied circles of a periphery occupied by the different groups of Third World countries.

The functioning of such a system does not exclude the possibility of revolutions and wars. Doubtless, it will juxtapose breaks and continuities. For if geology has its faults, so does geopolitics. Everyone is familiar with those lovely maps of the world which show the oceans and continents crossed by great sinuous lines dotted with volcanoes and earthquakes. Unfortunately, geopolitical fractures shift more quickly than those in the earth's crust, and in twenty years more progress has been made in the prediction of earthquakes than in the prediction of international crises. Tracing the crucial frontiers on a map, hachuring the hot spots, and marking the prevailing cultural winds is a much more delicate operation than identifying the great economic basins of tomorrow. But for anyone who would restore the games of the great actors in a multi-polar world, these two attempts seem to be indispensible prerequisites.

The situation of the great economic basins? It may be described in a few sentences.

Where were the 100 dollars of world revenue produced and consumed in 1970? North America, 32 dollars; Western Europe, 24 dollars; Japan, 7; Eastern Europe, 16 ; and 18 in the Third World. What will become of this distribution at the end of the century? I make my forecast with all due caution, of course! North America's share will have fallen to 20 dollars, and so will that of Europe; Japan's will rise to 10 dollars; and the Third World will reach 32 to 34 dollars.[26] As for the income of the South, the 4.5 billion people in the developing countries, one third of it will come from Latin America, a quarter from China, one fifth from North Africa and the Middle East, 13% from East and Southeast Asia, and only just under 10% from the huge group comprised of Southern Asia and black Africa.

Let us read these percentages differently. Five great economic blocs dominated the world in 1970: North America, the EEC, Eastern Europe,

Japan and China. Just these countries alone accounted for 81% of the world's income. By the end of the century, their share is cut, but it still dominates the scene.

But however useful it may be, carving the world up like this overlooks certain great complementarities. The pieces do not show the vast Pacific basin which broadly overflows the borders of the old zone of Japanese co-prosperity, and in which from California to China, and from Japan to Indonesia nearly one third of the world's income will be produced. They forget the old Atlantic basin, from the Mid-West to the Iron Curtain, and from Spitzberg to Brazil, whence the second third of this revenue will come. They do not show trade betweeen Western Europe, Africa and the Middle East. Proof – if such a thing were needed – that there is no one correct economic sketch of the world.

As for the map of fractures, it is above all marked by two great faults that furrow the globe: the North-South fault which, from the Soviet-Norwegian border, rejoins the boundaries of the two Germanies through Finland and the Baltic Sea, then reaches Yugoslavia and the Mediterranean, branching off towards Yemen and Ethiopia on one hand, and towards Turkey, Iran and Afghanistan on the other; and the East-West fault which runs along the Rio Grande, goes by Cuba, crosses the West Indies, passes between the two shores of the Mediterranean, and reaches the Middle East and Iran; then it too forks, with the northern prong following the Sino-Soviet border as far as Khabarovsk, and the southern prong rejoining the borders of China and Vietnam through the Himalayas. Where do these two faults intersect? Precisely in the East Mediterranean and the Middle East. It is here and all along the two main fractures that we must look for the sensitive zones. The central core? It brings together Yugoslavia with its numerous ethnic groups, Turkey in the throes of shipwreck, revolutionary Iran, a poor Pakistan with its archaic structures, Egypt with its hopelessly entangled demographic situation, Lybia, the home of terrorism, fragile and rich Saudi Arabia, the Horn of Africa, and Chad in the centre of black Africa. The breath of Islam blows over this central core, from the Middle East towards the Soviet Steppes of Central Asia, towards the centre of Africa, towards the Atlantic coast, and towards distant islands of Indonesia. The Western zone includes Mexico, Central America, Cuba and the West Indies; the northern zone has its symbol – Berlin; this zone centres round the IndoChinese peninsula and Thailand. But there are other faults with more or less active volcanoes! Southern Africa up to the borders of Zaire. Various South American countries like Chile. Between Eastern Asia and Japan with Korea as a centrum... And one day the wind of Islam will be answered by the quiet strength of Chinese civilisation propagated by its diaspora.

Some will say, "Never mind that. Since a multipolar world is unpredictable, let us reduce the risks by limiting exchanges with the outside world, or by creating zones of intense cooperation relatively isolated from the rest of the world." But those who say this forget that tomorrow's world will also be one of strong interactions between nations and between spheres.

And once more we are up against the control inadequacies of the international system, but after having shown it using the poles as a point of departure, we must now deal with it by starting with relations, that is to say, by asking ourselves questions about interdependence.

# THE RISE OF INTERDEPENDENCE

"Nothing will be done anymore, without the whole world meddling in it."

Paul VALERY
*Regards sur le monde actuel*

# Weaving spiders' webs

Independence within interdependence? The French remember this brilliant formula aimed at paving the way for the end of the protectorate of Morocco. Let us resurrect it for a moment's reflection.

What does independence mean for a nation that would see itself embodied in a single actor? The ability to choose from the possible options. But what are the variables that one may select? What is, in each case, the extent of the options? From a legal point of view, the answer is simple, since each sovereign state is only bound (and then only if it so chooses) by past commitments. Its constitution. Its civil law. Its economic organisation. Its alliances. Its votes in the United Nations. The gauge of its railway tracks. In all this, it is free to decide. This is, however, an illusion, for the possibilities depend on the circumstances and the actions of other states, as well as the reactions of these states to one's own decisions. Ask Dubcek... That is where interdependence comes in. Actor B will be dependent on Actor A if A's decisions can modify B's range of choices. As for interdependence, it will proceed from reciprocity.

What does restoring the rich network of their actors to nations add to these commonplace statements? A considerable multiplication of the possibilities of mutual influence. By taking into account these interactions between national and international games which – if one is to believe Henry Kissinger - are what make the work of a Secretary of State or Minister of Foreign Affairs so attractive. For it is now possible for Pol Pot, on the day of his entry into Pnom Penh, to thank the *New York Times* for the part it played in helping to overthrow Lon Nol; for European textile manufacturers to complain to the European Commission about the prices that their American competitors are paying for naphta; for multinationals to extend the web of their subsidiaries beyond borders.

It is within this context that the above statement assumes its full meaning: the world will not merely become multipolar; it will also become more and more interdependent. In other words, for an increasing number of actors in an increasing number of countries, the range of possibilities will depend on the strategies adopted by actors from other countries. And these strategies will themselves be less predictable as the environment of the actors themselves becomes more and more complex. Let us look at a concrete example. Fifteen years ago, European economic policies did not depend on the policies of the Gulf States. But they do now. They had to take American policies into account, but these policies were predictable, because the United States, being the world regulator, could have fixed strategies; that is not the case today. However, the rise of interdependence does not only mean a limitation of room to man-oeuver, increased unpredictability and greater vulnerability; it also implies the possibility of influencing the situation of others, being a source of initiative and creation. And this is indeed the way the Third World leaders (who have for so long known nothing but dependence) see it...

The spiders' webs of interdependence are many and varied: endless human migrations motivated by work, tourism, or fear; the flow of information transmitted through books, scientific journals, radio, television, newspapers; streams of oil, grain, or ore; shipments of shirts or machine tools; the transfer of money from one account to another; arms deliveries and the movements of aircaft carriers; groups of alliances, accords, and pacts; underground terrorist or intelligence networks; corps of diplomats flitting from one world conference to another; participation in all kinds of intergovernmental organisations... Interdependence is multidimensional: cultural, military, political, economic and social... There is no longer a single activity of human societies that escapes its net. How does it manifest itself? In the fixing of a price, the increase of a flow, the creation of an institution, the change of a negociating procedure, the strengthening of a military superiority. Let us not try to unravel the intricacy of the plot bit by bit. Let us for the time being be content with observing its characteristic forms in order to understand the futures that torment us with questions.

First, we shall look at cultural movements, at mental habits, ideologies, religions, myths, and sciences. An impossible task indeed, but it is less bad not to be equal to a problem than to sidestep it quietly for the sake of convenience.

The second pole of reflection commands attention: military and strategic relations. At its centre lie some fundamental questions. On the survival of humanity. On the risks of nuclear war, local conflicts, revolutions, and widespread insecurity.

Then, and then only, will an analysis be able to concentrate on social and economic interdependence, an interdependence that expresses itself in terms of flows of patrimony and of institutions.

Asking ourselves questions on the prospective development of flows (flows of energy, raw materials, agricultural products, and industrial products) will be indispensible if we are to understand the economic situations resulting from cooperations and conflicts that will confront social groups, firms, and governments.

The patrimonial vision, on the other hand, emphasises the solidarity that will be needed to protect our inheritance from the past, and the future management of our common heritage, whether we are dealing with the restoration of Borobudur or the extraction of deep-sea metallic nodes.

Finally, the institutional approach will focus the projector on the mechanisms of interdependence, monetary system, or market regulation, and on international organisations, those structural translations of interdependence and foci of a greater interdependence.

But interdependence asks two fundamental questions:

Can we reject it, or at least loosen the ties? In other words, is it conceivable that the world could organise itself into semi-autarkies, like a colony of hedgehogs?

And even if this were possible, would it be in our interest to reject it, to withdraw inside ourselves in order to protect our ways of life, lessen our vulnerability, and bring a new social scheme into operation?

For the moment, I shall refrain from answering. But first, a diagnosis.

# Cultural cyclones and tradewinds

April 1980. American television viewers are watching live the demonstrations converging on the American embassy in Teheran following the announcement of the abortive attempt to free the hostages by helicopter. But the speeches that they hear invoke the name of Allah and boast of the strength that Iran derives from the purity of its Islamic faith. On the one hand, proximity, on the other, remoteness. A commonplace incident that could happen at any time, and which nonetheless contains the germ of many questions bearing on the cultural future of the interdependent multipolar world that is being born.

For, when it is put back into context, the anecdote carries several messages. It leads one to consider the crisis of the two great dominant cultures born of European civilisation: the liberal culture of which the United States became the torch-bearer, and the Marxist culture that the USSR embodies. It suggests the probable coexistence of more and more intensive information networks and an increasing resistance to cultural imperialism and social massification. It attracts attention to the cultural instability of Third World countries, while at the same time making us look beyond the difficulties of the United States to the cultural explosion of Western societies, and in rebound, the apparent slowness of Soviet cultural development. It gives a new relevance to the old debate between Religion and Science that, from the birth of the Buddha to the heyday of Cordova, from the appearance of Christ to the triumph of the Enlightenment, has punctuated the history of civilisations again and again... These are major themes, some of which will crop up later on when the time is right for asking questions about the peculiar dynamics of developed societies and about the deficiency of control on the national level. But we must tackle them now, in the interdependence file (even if they are far from being enough on which to base a prospective analysis of culture) remind us that culture is an independent area of creation that helps to mould the development of an international system.

It was not so long ago that the case seemed clearcut: two great cultures played, and would increasingly play a universal role in the world. In a grandiose manicheism they would throw themselves into a Titanic struggle over the division of humanity between them. On one side was the liberal culture, based on individual freedom guaranteed by pluralist democracy and the market, to a large extent reducing the societal to the economic, and giving priority to full employment by means of cyclical policies, to the raising of the national income through competition and technical progress.

On the other, revolutionary Marxist culture. As far as it is concerned, there is no freedom without equality, no equality without destroying beforehand capitalist and imperialist exploitation. There can be no economic development that benefits everyone without creating a classless society and the new man that would emerge from all this.

Striking twin sisters who, their mutual hatred aside, have inherited from their common mother, the Europe of the Enlightenment, their passion for the future, and their vision of rosy tomorrows. The strength of their proselytism? They draw it from the vigour of their prospective societies.

Let us listen to the liberal culture's speech. Its advice to the citizens of the Third World is: "Reproduce our history. Use technical progress. Invest. Get industrialised. Rely on the international market. Economic prosperity and political maturity go together, and soon, you will join Western countries in the harmonious concert of developed nations." It suggests to the citizens of industrialised societies: "Let us continue in the path of Progress and Efficiency. The industrial society will soon give way to a post-industrial society. It will mean a higher income, free time, and security for all. Mastery of the world will serve the blossoming of the individual."

Everyone knows the Marxist answer. The model that it offers to the Third World is that of the October Revolution, armed struggle against the local bourgeoisie and foreign domination, a workers' and peasants' dictatorship, and then once the existing order is destroyed, it may be replaced by socialist planning which makes objectives fit in with the aspirations of all, and avoids wastage through the reasonable use of resources. The future that it offers Socialist Man? A higher income than his Capitalist brother, with the bonus of the True Liberty and True Equality that take root on the tomb of exploitation.

These two cultures are passing through a crisis. Outside the United States, the image of (liberal) culture has been tarnished by the conjunction of the economic crisis (a slowing down of growth that is particulary marked in the industrial sector and a rise in unemployment), the difficulties of the pilot-nation (the United States) and increasing dissatisfaction felt by the people facing the excesses or the limits of productivism. The revolutionary culture has suffered from several things at once: from the internal evolution of the Soviet Union, from the exacerbation of oppositions within the socialist world, from the frustration of its attempts to put its theory into practice in different parts of the Third World, and, undeniably, from the fact that the competing model offers fewer footholds, since it has become less of a conquerer and consequently, more elusive.

Contestations in the Third World. Contestations at home.

Why should the elite of developing countries feel attracted to a liberal culture which must put up with local torture, disdain for human rights, corruption, a show of democracy, and extreme wealth living side by side with extreme poverty? Why should they identify with a revolutionary culture which, more often than not, takes the form of bureaucracies that are as brutal as they are inefficient? As for the Eastern European, he is no longer much of a believer in communism. He goes his way, indifferent to all ideology, or takes refuge in black humour, or, occasionally, like Sakharov or Solzhenitsyn, he revolts... That leaves Western Man. If he is American, his faith in liberal culture remains alive (though one should not attach too much importance to the evolution of political majorities). But if he is European, he questions himself, and sometimes, cannot see himself anywhere.

So, in all probability, tomorrow's multipolar world will no longer have the cultural simplicity of the post-war bipolar world. What a paradox! Just when interdependence is intensifying, when the theories of social massification look obsolete, and the possibilities of cultural domination seem limited.

Indeed, the standardisation and world-wide distribution of consumer goods continue to increase. Chinese restaurants patiently spin their spider's web all over the world, while the big international hotels will continue to be pallid propagandists of French cuisine. Parisian women will be able to dress Indian style, and Japanese women to decorate a room in their homes with reproduction Lévitan furniture... The dissemination of increasingly homogeneous imformation will turn mankind into a single world-wide audience. Through television, through the great networks of data banks, a wider knowledge of English, tourism, and an increase in business travel. Within the space of a single year, a company executive will have stayed in several countries, spent his holidays in Bangkok, been an armchair spectator of several revolutions in Latin America, and used his terminal to get data stored on a computer in another country. All this is trite prospective analysis, since it describes something that is already the present for a minority. It is also obvious that in the interplay of these powerful unifying forces, the relative influence of different countries will be far from identical. The assets of this cultural dominance? Modern language and means of communicating information, from press agencies to satellites, from books and films to universities. Despite the diffusion of power, these assets continue to be concentrated in a few countries, with the United States in first place.

Why then should we not expect a progressive massification of life styles due to imitation of the American cultural model which is the symbol of development and progress?

Firstly, because at the very heart of the Western world, in spite of the undeniable changes that have taken place in European life styles, the transatlantic and transpacific differences still run so deep that they are clearly not reducible, except later, in the very long term. Analyses of eating habits, the use of time, and leisure activities testify to this. The foreseeable disparities between rates and manner of growth will not favour the dissolution of these disparities, whether social or cultural. Then, because American culture itself has exploded. The current Western counter-culture of the 1980's was born in the United States in the 1960's, whether the issue is ecology, consumer militancy, women's rights, communes, drug addiction, religious sects, the ultraliberalism of sexual mores, or extra-institutional politics. Today it is even less realistic to speak of the imperialism of American culture, at a time when American society sees itself as a mosaic of life styles and ideas without any profound unity.

Even if American culture had preserved its homogeneity and its missionary spirit of yesteryear, it would never again find territories so open to imports in tomorrow's world. In fact, the dominant phenomenon in cultural attitudes will be the search for identity, and, to a certain extent, for specificity. No society will escape the need to define itself and understand its place in history and in the world. There will be various responses to this need; the revival of Christianity, the revival of Islam, the affirmation of the value of original life styles, whether old or new, the search for specific legal systems... The result will be clear: the disappearance of the single point of reference that once was Christianity, and then after secularisation, Western law. At the very moment when, for the first time, there is a single universal history, the dislocation of common points of reference will make communication by means of a common language more and more difficult, and will rather favour the development of differences rather than reduce them.

Cultural destabilisation in the South. Explosion in the West. Apathy and outbreaks of fever in the East. This could be the dominant cultural landscape of the next two decades.

The Third World will continue to be torn between its attraction to the West and the desire to rediscover its own cultural identity. A West whose literature, art and beliefs are less prominent than its science, technology, and economic power. A West that is better accepted because it will protect certain national cultures against other cultural influences: for instance the culture of African sedentary farmers faced with the Islam of nomadic slave traders, or Southeast Asian aboriginal cultures faced with the culture of the Chinese diaspora... But at the same time, each state, each nation, and each ethnic group will become the archeologist of its past, reconstuctor of its history, gardian of its language, restorer of its literature and art. Spoken languages will be transcribed and so become vehicles of literature and technology. The revival of traditional values will channel the evolution of family and community structures.

There can be no doubt about the result of the opposition of these two trends: strong inter-social, and intra-social cultural tensions, between town and country, between social groups, between ethnic groups, and finally, within the very soul of each person; with coexistences becoming more and more difficult to maintain, and marked imbalances in countries whose development is progressing very rapidly or very slowly. We already have examples of this happening. The Shah's Iran with its extreme westernisation which only served to underline efforts to seek its roots in the Persia of the Achaemenidae. The Indonesian blood bath which brought the economic stagnation of the Sukarno regime to an end.

Under such conditions, the leaders of developing countries will have very little room to manoeuver. Governments will often be unstable, with their successive revolutions of varying magnitude – from military coups switching dictators, to cultural changes that throw values into confusion. These revolutions will no longer be carried out in the name of liberal democracy or proletarian internationalism. They will be carried out in the name of the nation, in the name of its beliefs, in the name of the struggle against all forms of imperialism...

This cultural destabilisation of the Third World will often place Western countries in delicate positions. It will be up to them to find new paths for cultural exchanges. Perhaps the internal shattering of their own culture will make this creation easier. Having grown up in an environment of relative opulence, the younger generations of Westerners will attach less importance to the need for physical and economic security, and will attach themselves to other goals, such as belonging to small, exclusive groups and valuing the individual. This is a development that will not come about quickly or without contradictions, for the extent of cultural changes will vary widely from one social group to another. However, in the gradual movement from the "organic industrial society, to the polymorphous society of information... rivalries will no longer oppose two classes structured according to the way they fit into the industrial process, but rather, countless mobile groups conditioned by the diversity of their allegiances and their plans."[27] Fundamental uncertainty regarding the reasons for being together, and distress provoked by the absence of collective aims, will inevitably feed these centrifugal forces. The traditional dream of consensus will seem obsolete: within such a context, exorcising conflicts will be out of the question. Conflicts that will be all the more complex since the minorities attached to the new values will not be altogether indifferent to material things and quantitative demands, since the dissatisfaction of certain social groups could set off explosions of incomprehension and rage, and since the intensification of violence could make some people less socially tolerant, and increase calls for firmer authority. Consequently, a less self confident West will be ready to initiate a dialogue with other cultures that will no longer be characterised by condescension... Unless, terror-stricken in the face of world-wide contestation, it withdraws into its past in a reaction of cultural conservatism which, though unlikely, nevertheless cannot be excluded.

Finally there is the Soviet Empire where revolutionary marxist culture is no longer anything more than a corpse whose only legacy is a vademecum for interpreting the world used by Kremlin leaders, and where, under the faded paintwork of socialism, the colours of yesteryear are showing through once more (Toynbee's three civilisations): Western civilisation, reaching up to the Baltic countries and the eastern borders of Poland, Eastern civilization beyond that, and the Ottoman civilization in the Balkan Mountains. Behind the façade of the superstructures, Christian Poland, creative and decentralised Hungary, and a resigned but not submissive Czechoslovakia are more Western than ever. As for East Germany, everyone wonders whether its dreams of efficiency do not make it rather more an heir of historic Prussia than of Marxist-Leninism. The Soviet Union itself is still another world whose cultural development is slow, and where the individual lives space and time, resignation, boredom, patience and revolt differently. As for the dissidents, even if they are the bearers of a rich and diversified micro-culture, even if they rekindle the great orthodox flame or return to the variety of cultural currents of the last century, their message is not for tomorrow, but for the day after tomorrow.

With such a crisis of the two dominant cultures over the last quarter century, is it any wonder that the debate between Religion and Science should be renewed?

Faith in Science has been the foundation of the two dominant cultures. But its ethical legitimacy and concrete repercussions are now being challenged at the very moment when a new epistemology (which means going beyond the old way but not denying it) is being initiated, an epistomology based on the concept of system, of a group of elements linked by a group of relations. Whereas in the past Science depended on a passive Nature that was mechanical and submissive, totally predicta-ble and manipulable by whoever knew how to create the right condi-tions, tomorrow's Science will stress progressive development that leads, step by step, with wonderment, but without mystery, from the simplest systems with elementary attributes, to the most complex systems which, in their richness and diversity, can learn to organise themselves and to interact. What does Prigogine, winner of the Nobel Prize for chemistry, say? "The time has come for new links that had always existed (though for a long time unrecognised) between the history of people, their societies, their knowledge, and the adventure of exploring nature."[28] He explains: "The thermodynamics of irreversible processes has revealed that the currents that run through certain physico-chemical systems and moves them away from a state of equilibrium, can feed phenomena of spontaneous self-organization, breaks in symmetry, evolution towards increasing complexity and diversity. Where the general laws of thermo-dynamics end, the constructive role of irreversability becomes apparent; it is the sphere in which things are born and die, or are changed in a unique history that is the work of chance, fluctuations and the demands of laws."[29] But mankind does not yet know what the Science which is being developed has up its sleeve. And challenging the dominant cultures means shaking faith in Science; the Science that the Iranian mullahs think is hindering a return to the cultural roots of Islam and which is sometimes perceived by the Third World as the symbol of triumphant European civilisation; the Science that some Western phil-osophers believe is outside the control of Science itself; the Science which, in the opinion of many citizens of industrial societies does not exclude the coexistence of a growing rationality of our partial approaches with the absurdity of our holistic approaches.

Religion? The last century saw its decline. A dormant Islam. A moribund Buddhism. A Catholicism that was able to cut a fine figure as long as it could lean on the triumphant bourgeoisie and jump onto the bandwaggon of colonialisation, but the *aggiornamiento* of Vatican II exposed deep-rooted disease... Doubtless, the great religions of the world will never again recover their past glory; nonetheless André Malraux was probably right when he predicted that "the Twenty-first Century will be religious, or it will not be." Religious renaissance for some, the invention of a new religiosity for others. When the Arab rediscovers himself in Islam or the Japanese person in Shinto, he is searching for his cultural identity, whereas the Western Christian, through his many sects, is looking for an individual experience of the divine that wants to have nothing to do with dogmas and rites.

At first, this dual evolution of Religion and Science will set them against each other once again, but there are already signs of a future compromise between a more universal and open Science and a religiosity that is largely stripped of the weight of its history. For, beyond the cultural chaos of the multipolar, independent world of the decades ahead, the beginnings of a new world culture are already evident. The culture that A. Toffler tries to describe in *The Third Wave*[30] will not mean social massification. It will draw from the richness of interpersonal relations within real groups as well as from an awareness of the common interests of humanity. On the one hand, it will acknowledge the diversity of life styles, sexual morals, family ethics, and metaphysical beliefs. On the other hand, it will practise human rights, free itself from racism, and accept the existence of a common human heritage that extends over the whole ecosphere, it will encourage the discreet and prudent management of this heritage, will try once more to master complexity through self-organisation,and will be thoroughly reconciled with a Science that will have become systemics... Who will be the prophets of this culture? We know not. But they will not be Descartes, Marx, or Freud. Utopia? Perhaps. But we cannot be sure of that. Let us just take it as a provisional synthesis. On the other hand, it would indeed be an illusion to believe that we could eliminate the interim, the long years of transition ahead of us during which there is a risk that cultural heterogeneity will stir up both national and international conflicts, thus precluding any union based on a social and political adventure capable of transcending interdependence and multipolarity.

# In the shadow of rockets and missiles

The thought of war is intolerable. Like the thought of death. And more often than not, people repress it. Then speaking about it becomes awkward. It might seem shocking to quote General de Gaulle who wrote: "War creates and destroys nations; meanwhile, it hovers unceasingly over their existence." Then, overnight, the time it takes for a revolution in Teheran or an occupation in Kabul, the mood changes. The threat of war makes the front page of the weekly papers. Polemology is becoming a respectable profession once more.

And yet, whatever the climate of the moment, no book on prospective analysis can dodge the problem of war, especially at a time when mankind is capable of destroying itself.

Is war unacceptable? Yes. But for the man in the street, it is also incomprehensible. He is a pacifist. His neighbour is a pacifist. The merry-eyed Chinese people that he sees on the television seem to be pacifist, and so does the round-headed Moscovite who strolls around the squares. Who is to blame then? The kings, generals, capitalists, communists, and scape goats? Ah! If only all the young people... A ridiculous explanation. Certainly, no one can completely answer the question "Why is there war?" but of necessity the answer brings into play the three control deficiencies. On the individual level, the combination of a strong group identity with the projection of aggression on those outside. On the national level, the fact that it is possible for political systems to evaluate the risks and develop coherent strategies. On the international level, the absence of regulation in the relations between states. The interaction of these three levels has existed since the dawn of time, but for three decades the scale of the extent of their effects has changed. In the self-organised development of humanity in which large sectors are independent, science gave us the weapon of total anihilation before the international system could have the time to create regulations that would ensure its control. However, these regulations need much more time to develop, whereas nothing has changed the conditions which produce the explosions of collective aggression that continually generate war. Hence, the destruction of humanity by war is a possible hypothesis. It is not inevitable, because the national states can, by acting together, gradually overcome the third control deficiency.

It is useless to close our eyes or touch wood, to give ourselves over to incantations or proclaim our pacifism. We must get used to this fact: the multipolar, independent world of the next thirty years will be a dangerous world, a very dangerous world. Because of the volume of military spending, because of the delicacy of the balance between the two Greats, because of the spread of military power, because of the vulnerability of Europe, and because of the diversity of possible conflicts.

The overall figures for world military spending are absolutely staggering. For the world as a whole, it is the equivalent of the income of the poorer half of humanity. Out of the total, the United States and the USSR alone account for 59 %; the other countries of NATO or the Warsaw Pact, 18%; and the rest of the world, 23%. The figures vary considerably from one country to another, because expenditure ranges from more than 10 % of the national income (the USSR, China, Israel, Arab countries of the Near East) to less than 1% (for instance Japan)! The United States stands at between 5 and 10%, along with the countries of Eastern Europe and the East and a few developing countries such as Saudi Arabia, South Korea, and Pakistan. France and the European members of NATO, as well as many Third World countries stand at 2 to 4.9%.

However, one thing is almost certain. With the slowing down of growth and rising tensions, the proportion of world revenue assigned to military expenditure will increase significantly over the next ten years. On the national level, we cannot expect to see any reduction in the Soviet bloc, whereas it is likely that there will be rises in the United States, Western Europe, Japan and China. In the Third World, the continued wide range of national percentages will no doubt go hand in hand with a constant or higher average. These are predictions that give cause for alarm, but they only convey the reactions of states to the threats that they perceive.

For, behind the apparently unchanged backdrop of the ongoing competition between the United States and the Soviet Union, there has been a vital development over the last few years: the Soviet Union is now the world's greatest military power: both in strategic nuclear weapons and conventional forces.

What a change in less than ten years! By the end of the Sixties, the Soviet Union achieved parity with the United States in launcher numbers,[31] but the United States held the balance thanks to the reliability of their system and the number of nuclear warheads carried by their missiles.[32] The May 1972 SALT agreement? It gave the impression of institutionalising this balance: the definite banning of large-scale anti-missile defence systems left each adversary vulnerable to attacks from the other; the freezing of the number of Intercontinental Ballistic Missiles and Submarine-Launched Ballistic Missiles at July 1972 levels for five years gave the United States the hope of compensating for the numerical superiority that the Soviet Union had achieved in the meantime with technical quality. Alas, this attempt to fix strategic parity has been shattered, because the two adversaries have, in different ways, exploited the loopholes left open by the agreement. Consequently, we have witnessed a clear reversal of the situation. The catching up that the Soviet Union has done with the MIRVS and the accuracy of warheads, combined with the greater fire power of Soviet ICBMs, has radically changed the balance of power between the land arsenals of the superpowers. At least as far as these last mentioned are concerned, most experts today agree that the Soviet Union looks as though it will achieve a first strike capability against the American ICBMs in the 80's, while the less powerful American missiles will not have the same capability (they have an 'anti-force,' not an 'anti-silo' capability). Regarding the other two sides of the strategic triangle (nuclear submarines and bombers) where the situation is still in the favour of the United States, it must be pointed out that the rate of progress of Soviet capacity is more rapid than that of its rival. As a result, the Eighties are a period of particularly dangerous imbalance, the famous 'window of vulnerability' that the experts talk about. Until the United States can manage to restore a certain parity with the help of their new program. But will they be able to do it? We cannot be sure, for in the past, Westerners have always underestimated the speed of development of Soviet armed forces, believing mistakenly that a society that is incapable of making washing machines is unable to perfect aircraft carriers and missiles.

As for resuming SALT talks, this will become more and more difficult as the military and technical data of strategic confrontation become more and more complex: with the emergence of 'grey area' arms that fall somewhere between tactical and strategic weapons;[33] with the continuation of a gigantic Soviet effort in the area of passive defence, including experimenting with means of destroying enemy missiles, communication and warning satellites; with research into satellite-aided methods of detecting and destroying enemy submarines with the aid of satellites; with the maintenance of a Soviet military doctrine that stresses the use of nuclear weapons and strategic superiority rather than response and parity.

However, there are those who think that Soviet nuclear superiority does not make any sense. What is the point of being able to kill the same man several times over? If one wants to maintain the balance of terror, is it not enough that each protagonist be convinced that an attack on his part will not exhaust all the defence systems of the enemy, and will leave him the means to inflict intolerable damage when he retaliates? As long as American nuclear submarines continue to be practically invulnerable, the United States will undoubtedly retain a second strike capability. But we must push this reasoning a few steps further. Not only would an opening in the area of anti-submarine warfare become a risk of the greatest magnitude for the United States, but it is likely that it will have less room to manoeuver while the USSR will have more. For, in the uncertain world we live in, the way the United States and the Soviet Union behave towards each other will depend on their perception of each other's power. Other countries will not be insensitive to this development. It will reinforce their respect for the Soviet Union and lower their esteem for the United States. All the more so since in everyday life, the imbalance between the two Greats in the area of conventional forces is apparent. The Soviet Union has a clear lead in the air-land section; it has, over the past few years, significantly developed its long-distance intervention capability, and its navy which has seen a spectacular rise, is becoming capable of acting in the Mediterranean and in the Indian Ocean, even if it is still handicapped by the geographic configuration of the country.

The problem acquired a new dimension with the announcement two years ago of the American High Frontier Project. And 'Star Wars' has since been the subject of countless newspaper articles. The man in the street imagines that in the near future, the United States will be enclosed by a vast Maginot Line in space, a kind of science fiction shield on which wave after wave of Soviet Missiles will be shattered. The reality is less certain and more serious.

Less certain, because these projects pose tremendous technical problems, particularly as no defence system will ever give total immunity and the net will have the difficult task of stopping rockets with multiple trajectories... So the upheaval of world military strategy will probably not come before the beginning of the next century.

More serious, because the success of these projects may, in time, call European security into question. Will the umbrella cover Europe? That is not at all certain; for technical, economic and political reasons. Europe is so close to the Eastern bloc that the interception of Soviet missiles could well prove infinitely more delicate than would be the case for US territory. What then is Europe's defence if the Soviet Union is also protected by a similar system? One thing is sure: it is high time that the Hermes shuttle be used to complement the projects of the European Space Agency, and to set up a centre for European research on the militarisation of space.

At this stage, some readers, quick to turn the prospective analyst into a fortune-teller, would like to be able to ask me: "Do you believe that there will be war?" I shall tackle this question in a few pages. Not to give them an answer, naturally, but to try to judge all the factors that should be borne in mind. For future strategic development will not be confined to the movement of the Soviet Union from being a great regional power to being an imperial power; it will also be marked by a second phenomenon that is a corollary of multipolarity: the spread of military power over the world, which will mean that the two Greats will no longer be able to control the course of political events. Nuclear proliferation, the proliferation of conventional arms, the emergence of new powers. All these are aspects of the erosion of Americano-Soviet bipolarity. An erosion which could be stopped towards the end of the century by the installation of the anti-missile defence systems that are now being studied.

Firstly, there are the other nuclear powers. We begin with China, which has a nuclear submarine with five to ten strategic missiles, and maybe 500 nuclear warheads. By the end of the century, it may be the only one following in the wake of the two Greats. As for France, its strategic force is in danger of being below the level of credibility. Mirages and Plateau d'Albion rockets are no longer worth anything. As for submarines, it will need more of them if it is to be capable of ensuring an adequate sea presence at all times. Great Britain does indeed have four Polaris submarines, but the future of its military might will depend on the way in which it manages the modernisation of its forces. And finally we come to India, which by exploding a bomb in 1974 showed that a research reactor is enough to build a nuclear weapon. It could well have all the attributes of a nuclear power by the end of the century.

Who else will have the bomb? That is too simple a question, because there is a big difference between making a primitive bomb in a laboratory, perfecting it through real tests, and possessing vehicles that have a range of thousands of kilometres. And to pass from one stage to the other, one needs to have a combination of things: technological and financial means, political will, and the ability to resist international pressure. Many developed countries have the technological and financial means: Canada, Australia, Japan, West Germany, Italy, Sweden, Switzerland, Holland, Belgium, and soon Spain. But it is possible that neither West Germany nor Japan may have the political will in the future. Japan's situation is very complex. It certainly sees itself as being in an awkward position, but it has a tremendous psychological, political, and legal aversion to nuclear arms, and doubtless will not react except against the actions of other states in the region. As for vulnerable Germany, it knows that converting to nuclear arms could trigger a major crisis with the Soviet Union. We must look elsewhere for the risks of proliferation: Israel, Irak, Yugoslavia, South Africa, Pakistan, South Korea, Taiwan, Brazil, and Argentina. A likely conclusion? The proliferation of nuclear arms will come, and no country or group of counties will be in a position to prevent it. With two main corollaries: a questioning of the political and military status of present-day medium-sized powers, which, as they lose the quasi-exclusivity that was theirs, will see the range of threats to themselves widen; increased instability due to the heterogeneity of the nuclear powers, for, depending on whether it is the USSR and China, South Africa and its neighbours, or an Arab bomb against an Israeli bomb, the rules of the nuclear game, of the reaction of the Supergreats, and the balances or imbalances that these could create, will not be inscribed beforehand in any experience or in any theory.

   The spread of nuclear weapons will go hand in hand with the spread of conventional weapons. Contrary to common belief, the dealers are few and buyers limited in number. The United States provides 50% of sales, the Soviet Union 30%, France, Britain and Czechoslovakia together, 10%... The main buyers are Middle Eastern countries: Israel, Irak, Lybia, Saudi Arabia, Syria, Jordan... followed by the countries of Eastern Asia: South Korea and Taiwan, or Southern Asia, such as India. Sales of more and more sophisticated arms: tactical aircraft, ground-to-air missiles and anti-tank missiles today, precision-guided missiles tomorrow. An increasing mutual dependence of suppliers and their customers, the former because the arms industry has become an important sector of their economy, the latter because they need technical assistance. A rapid growth of arms production in the developing countries themselves. In short, a subtle game between deliveries of conventional arms and efforts to halt the proliferation of nuclear ones.

Tomorrow, like today, as regrettable as this may seem, states will continue to stockpile arms in keeping with their desire to increase their political influence and perception of national security.

As for the states that are now emerging, supporters of the spread of military power, we already know that their situation is so varied that (from Nigeria to China, and from Brazil to India) they will not be scaled down models of the superpowers . We must also understand the precise nature of the change that we are experiencing. Whereas up to the present the concentration of power has been so great that it could be measured by a single scale, in the future it will be multi-dimentional, with countries playing now one trump card, now another, depending on their abilities.

A swinging of the balance between the two Greats and the spread of military power. As far as Europe is concerned, the message is clear. It is entering a quarter century of growing vulnerability. Shipping routes that are susceptible to attacks, and these are likely to increase. Politically fragile countries that supply energy and raw materials, countries that the USSR or other radical countries may help to destabilise. A Mediterranean flank in the throes of a period of uncertainty. The ominous presence of Eastern forces along German borders. Is it necessary at this point to give a detailed account of NATO and Warsaw Pact forces? To contrast the 11,000 tanks of the one against the 27,000 of the other? To compare the 1153 short, intermediary or medium-range missiles of Eastern bloc countries with the 198 corresponding missiles of NATO?[34] All of this could only make sense in the first forty-eight hours of a conflict. Beyond that, Western Europe's territorial and political integrity depends on the United States. What does Henry Kissinger say? "No one denies any longer that in the Eighties, and perhaps today, the United States will no longer be in the strategic position of being able to reduce a Soviet response against themselves to tolerable levels... NATO is reaching a point where the strategic premises on which it has based its actions, the military structure that it has created, and the joint policies that it has developed are not sufficient for the Eighties... I would therefore say (something that I would not say in an official capicity) that our European allies should not continue to demand that we increase undertakings relating to strategic weapons which we shall not ,or should not wish to hold to, even if we were able, for if we use them, we may well destroy civilisation."[35] The case could not be stated more clearly. Today Europeans find themselves faced with a real choice: to shelter mainly under the umbrella of American strategic nuclear weapons which may well not open when the storm comes; to accept the installation on their soil of American Euromissiles (Pershing II and Cruise) whose mobility

could assure a relative protection for Europe; or to take on the responsibility of their own defence. As long as Bonn cannot become a nuclear
power without precipitating a crisis, and as long as London is not
prepared to build a Franco-British hard core, this last option is not at all
a simple one. Fortunately, the West German decision to accept Euromissiles means that Europe is guaranteed a minimum of security in the
medium term. In the longer term, if by one of those reversals so well
known in military history, the armour should become sword-proof, and
each of the two greats should manage to lock itself into a protective
bubble, each safe from the missiles of the other, Western Europe could
only have one of two statuses: that of a land sheltered behind American
ramparts, or that of a neutralised and undefendable zone , a sort of no
man's land between the two camps. Unless technology were to allow
Europe to have its own bubble.

The time has now come to ask the fundamental question, to move from
games of strategy that are a form of interdependence, to war, which is a
form of communication between people. It is too serious a subject for
prophecies, and too complex not to be tackled in successive stages.

In the first place I believe that the upheaval of the Third World will not
take place without revolutions, civil wars, or wars between neighbours.
Another long list will be added to the already long list of conflicts that have
taken place over the last thirty years, a list that we Europeans and
Americans forget so easily: the Indo-Chinese war, the wars between India
and Pakistan, conflicts between Vietnam and Cambodia, and between
China and Vietnam, the Arab-Israeli wars, the conflict between Algeria
and Morocco, Biafra, Katanga, Chad, the Falklands... to name a few.

Secondly, I shall hazard a guess: during one of these conflicts, the
nuclear taboo will be broken. Believing its survival to be threatened, one
of the Third World nations that will have acquired atomic weapons will
decide to use them. This does not necessarily imply a widening of the
conflict. A few million dead, but they will be millions of local dead...

Let us continue with another likely hypothesis: the heyday of terrorism is yet to come. For along the long road of an ever-growing human
population, along which each man is trying to realise himself, the cohorts
of those who ask themselves questions, do not understand, reject, and
wish to destroy, can only increase. World-wide oppression of all kinds
(ethnic, religious, political, and economic, which will become all the
more unbearable as the hope of escaping them appears) will be added to
the world-weariness of developed countries. As the Beirut suicide attack
on the U.S. Marines has reminded us, we should not forget either, that
terrorism is a weapon that is also used by states.

These observations only clear the path to the central problem: the danger of war between the Supergreats. In theory, there are three conceivable scenarios of the evolution of their coexistence:

A scenario of continuity. One in which strategic balance is maintained for a long time; East-West relations pass through periods of relative détente and relative tension, but Soviet-American crisis management techniques prevent both the widening of local conflicts and confrontation between the Greats.

A scenario of gradually reduced tension. The United States and the Soviet Union commit themselves to successive bi-lateral nuclear arms reduction agreements, and move towards cooperation capable of supervising the spread of military power in the world.

A scenario of confrontation. The Soviet Union continues to give priority to the reinforcement of its armed forces with the United States having the choice of either submitting or taking up the challenge by massively increasing its military spending, modernising its defence system, by taking the risk of confronting the Soviet Union in local conflicts: in Berlin, Cuba, the Mediterranean, the Middle East, Pakistan, and Africa, and by reinforcing the military potential of certain Third World countries.

There is no doubt that we are on the road to this third scenario. But war presupposes other conditions: that the wave of American public opinion (its crests and troughs exaggerated by the media) will break on the presidency in an outburst of fear and hatred of the Soviet Union, or that the Kremlin, obsessed with the future risks of the disintegration of the Empire, will fear the loss of a temporary superiority; that in the evaluation of the pros and cons, it may underestimate Western reactions as centralised regimes often do when faced with parliamentary democracies (Moscow should be aware that there is a bit of Chamberlain in characters like Carter), and therefore decide to smash what it sees as a circle around it.

One theory among many? One fine day in the Eighties, the Soviet Union decides:

1. To exploit the crisis in the Middle East and Central Asia and disturb Europe's supply of raw materials and oil when necessary by intervening with its navy off the coast of East Africa.

2. To launch a surprise attack on West Germany, taking advantage of the general commotion (while the people of Europe are worrying about how they are going to organise weekend transport).

3. To attack China.

4. To take over the smallest states that are the biggest oil producers in the Middle East, and even some of the bigger ones, if this has not already been done from the inside.[36]

No doubt all this reads like a novel. Everything would seem to indicate that the process of selection for the Politburo will continue to bring to power men who are cautious and realistic, but also men who are ready to exploit any local advantageous situation. Men of whom Nixon could say, as he said of Brezhnev: "They do not want war; they want the world," and who will be backed by the most formidable military machine of all time.

But we must look beyond all this. The great contest that has begun involves the way in which humanity frees itself from control deficiencies on the international level, and emerges from the contradictions of a multipolar, interdependent world. There are only two possible paths. Either war or a submission that will establish the dominance of one Empire; or else the gradual establishment of new methods of cooperation between states, brought about by seeking more and more extensive dominant coalitions in which each national society finds a certain satisfaction of its interests.

We must start off along the second road, but this demands that we remain clear-headed; the defence of peace is an active art, in which tactics are just as important as strategy, and naïvety is costly, for our horror of war that makes it inconceivable for us, is not enough to rule it out. Two hundred million dead would mean a delay of two or three years in the demographic growth of our species. A small blow to the ascending curve of world population.

# The markets for natural resources: between scarcity and abundance

The problem of physical limits may have often been dealt with naïvely, but that does not justify a reaction that obscures a harsh reality: in a world of sovereign states in the throes of demographic and economic explosion, many conflicts will be created by the differences in geographic distribution between the supply of, and demand for, natural resources. Scarcity will rub shoulders with abundance. People will suffer and some will die as a result of it. It is therefore pertinent to return to the subject of energy, food production and mineral resources. This time under the aegis of interdependence. A new perspective demands a new typology: there are too many features shared by minerals, whether metallic or not, and agricultural products such as coffee, sugar, jute, rubber etc., for us not to group them under the name of 'commodities' according to custom. Clearly a second category must bring together the agricultural products that constitute the core of human diet, especially grain. Finally there is a third group, that of major energy exports – oil, gas and coal.

Just as poor people have only their children, developing countries have nothing to offer but commodities and often (especially in Africa) must be content with having one only. Peanuts account for practically all of Gambia's exports, while coffee accounts for the bulk of exports from Burundi, Uganda and Ruanda; Zambia, Zaire and Chili are almost entirely dependent on copper, Bangladesh on jute, and Mauritania on iron.

We should therefore not be surprised if we find that, like the workers of the Nineteenth Century, the poor of the Third World should strive to change the marketing conditions of commodities, while at the same time pulling the chestnuts out of the fire for the rich or semi-rich who, like Brazil, also figure among the great producers. What can an exporting country really hope for? A stabilisation of markets to avoid having its development plans left vulnerable to the erratic fluctuations of the price of their exports. That prices hold steady or rise through agreements between producers to limit supplies, or through the acceptance by buyer countries of a price-pegging clause. Free access to the markets of importing countries, and finally, the possibility of transforming its own resources into manufactured or semi-manufactured products. Let us examine these four issues more closely.

There is a simple explanation for the instability of the prices of commodities: according to the commodity, either production depends heavily on the climate whereas consumption varies little as a function of the market, or demand varies widely with the economic circumstances whereas the supply is inflexible in the short term. Resulting in both cases in price swings which, over a long period, are as unfavourable to consumers as they are to producers. Perfect, you think: all that is needed then, is to come to an agreement. However that is where the problems begin. Regularise the market through a storage system that buys in a bear market and sells in a bull market. Fine. But is it effecient and whom does it benefit? Political pressure from governments, some speculative manoeuvres, and *voilà*: badly chosen intervention prices resulting in the creation of a chronic stock and higher average price... The cost of storage and transaction, administrative and financing charges should be subtracted from the gross profit. On the whole, a very mixed result: according to certain studies, stabilisation would only benefit developing countries as a whole for a few products (doubtless, coffee, cocoa, jute, wool, wheat[37]) and the great beneficiaries would the the main suppliers of products with an unstable supply: Brazil for coffee, Malaysia for rubber, Ghana for cocoa.

What should be done then? Start off along another road and stabilise the export earnings of each country by granting loans that are repayable in the good years? It is a simpler method. It leads to different distributions of advantages: regionally, the profits of the African countries become twice those of Latin America and Asia. It is basically the scheme adopted a few years ago by the International Monetary Fund, and by the European Economic Community. And there should be nothing to stop it being applied to all the exports of certain countries.

But one would have to be naïve to believe that the problem is as simple as that. What do Third World negociators really hope for when they recommend the creation of buffer stocks financed by a common fund? A gradual change in power relations that would allow producers to counterbalance buyers and to orient storage policy towards higher systematic price rises. This is just one step away from the demand for the price pegging of basic products in relation to industrial products. That is as it should be, some will say. Are wages not index-linked with the cost of living? But they forget that price is not only an index of income, but also of rarity. Scarcities, surpluses, artificial substitutions and wasted investments would be the inevitable result of such a measure. And the logic of the distributive effect is not apparent: if the aim of the exercise is to transfer financial resources to the poorest countries, why should Australia, Canada, South Africa or the Soviet Union benefit from it? It is therefore obvious that, even in the long term, the chances of intergovernmental indexation agreements emerging are low.

There remains the path that OPEC has followed: cartelisation. The minimum requirements are draconian: a heavy concentration of production, homogeneous raw material, a demand that is not much affected by the price, and a supply that is; a market that is independent of substitutes and recycling; the real ability of cartel members to agree on rules governing prices and quantities and the distribution of gains and losses... Conditions that would seldom be satisfied as long as Third World producers do not find allies among Western or Eastern bloc exporters... The chances are slim unless the whole trading system collapses.

The argument of the developed countries against indexation and cartelisation is sound... But only their unfairness makes them oppose the liberalisation of the international trade of commodities, for their import restrictions are far from negligible: although the nominal barriers against mineral and agricultural raw materials that do not compete with their own products are flimsy, these barriers get higher once it is a question of competing raw materials (sugar, meat, vegetables, dairy products) and they are raised even higher for manufactured goods, thus protecting the processors of developed countries.

A liberalisation of the international commodity trade would produce considerable benefits for the consumers of developed countries, for the countries of Latin America, for Third World producers of meat, vegetables and sugar. But why bury our heads in the sand? Farmers contribute more to the stability of Western political majorities than industrial workers in distress. "And what about processed products?" you ask, thus voicing the Third World's last criticism. Let us restrict our answer to the basic isues: on-the-spot processing of agricultural products would create a perceptible increase in Third World employment, and could affect around one million jobs in developed countries. In the case of the treatment of ore, the effect is less clear because of the more capital-intensive nature of the techniques used. One thing is sure however: producer countries will tend increasingly to process raw materials themselves, with wide differences between one ore and another. This is already true of tin foundries. In the case of copper and phosphate fertilizers, this development is already taking place.

Commodities. Is there a better example of the games of multipolarity and interdependence? Trade restrictions, domination, unreliable supplies, the struggle for the control of stages of processing, the whole panoply of the shortcomings of markets are to be found here... So the conflicts are not about to die down, even though the stakes are not as great as when human malnutrition or the scarcity of energy are the crucial issues.

The successive oil shocks constantly steal the headlines from any mention of interdependence in the area of food, but the awful pictures of Ethiopia or the Sahel that disturb the tra⊇quility of our television programmes from time to time should be enough to remind us of its importance. The first half of the Twenty-first Century will no doubt be the grain era, as the current half century has been the oil era.

On the high plateaus of Bolivia, on the edges of the Ivory Coast's tropical forest, the Third World peasant produces 20 to 60% of the national income of his country, and often provides half of its foreign earnings. Between 1971 and 1978, he has managed (often with meagre means and despite droughts and floods) to increase his production of wheat annually by 3%, and that of rice by 2.3%. But success is patchy, since per capita production in black Africa, Southern Asia, and certain Central American countries has risen very little or has even fallen.

Will this peasant be able to meet his own demand and that of his fellow countrymen between now and the end of the century? And we still have to know whether we are dealing with a solvent demand including subsistence farming, or a demand ensuring that the minimum food requirements of each person are covered: the first generally depends on long-term economic growth and income distribution; the second is brought about by standards that are very difficult to assess. Nonetheless, here are some figures by order of size: between now and the end of the century, solvent demand for grain in the Third World (apart from China) could rise at the rate of 3 to 4% per year to reach between 740 and 980 million tonnes in the year 2000. For China the figure could stand at between 300 and 380 million tonnes. We should not be misled by these figures: a consumption of 740 million, for instance, only allows Third World per capita consumption to go up by 20%, and even according to optimistic estimates 10% of the population of Asia (excluding China) and 25% of black Africa – some 350 million people – would still be malnourished.

But we must go beyond this global view, because the diagnosis varies radically from country to country. The best production prospects are in Latin America. Thanks to Argentina, and, according to some scenarios, to Brazil and Colombia, it should become a big exporter of grain. Another area with promising prospects and which could increase its exports – Southeast Asia with Burma and Thailand as its rice granaries. Against these exporters, the import zones fall into two groups of countries.

● Those (OPEC countries and countries that are in the process of being industrialised) that will be able to pay for their food with oil, shoes or refrigerators. They are basically found in two large regions – North Africa and the Middle East on one hand, and Eastern Asia on the other. With different weaknesses in the very long term, for, once the oil is used up, how will the Iranian and Arab feed themselves if their agriculture continues to be in such a poor condition?

● Those that have nothing to offer, low revenue countries in Southern Asia and black Africa, countries that are subject to infrastructural, institutional, and climatic constraints, that cannot be quickly overcome. For them, the projected deficit is generally no more than 5% (15% in exceptional cases) of anticipated production. Presently, due to rats, insects and damp, losses in distribution and storage are often as high as 10 to 40 %. And a draconian effort to reduce these losses would generally help to reduce the deficit. However, black Africa and Southern Asia will continue to be two sores in the world's flank.

Hence, for years, the recurring theme of all the reports on the Third World has been: give priority to the development of agriculture to promote social equity and reinforce political stability! The agricultural strategy of many developing countries is caught in a dilemma: a food production that is largely covered by small holdings and a policy that is often unfavourable to them. Whether the issue is the conditions of access to credit, legal systems relating to use of land, the weakness of marketing networks, the lack of roads for the distribution of crops, or the distortion of prices in favour of the urban masses, the result is well known: the reinforcement of the dual structure of agriculture, the profits of productivity concentrated in the large farms, a worsening of the terms of trade for traditional agriculture, many small farms pushed onto the fringes, and greater rural poverty... Where can higher production come from under such circumstances?

From an extension of cultivated areas (this accounts for two thirds of the growth between 1950 and 1970)? This is still a viable option in Latin America and certain African and Asian countries, but in the short and medium terms these vast resources will be more apparent than real.

Higher yields per unit area (responsible for the other third of growth between 1950 and 1970)? This is the only way open to many countries that are short of food and which have a high population density. As long as they take an interest both in the potentially irrigable areas and arable areas that are made fertile by natural rains.

But, in both cases, higher productivity will be the result of two major changes: the elimination of restrictions imposed by the lack of roads, wells, storage space, systems for distributing seeds and credits, the development of techniques adapted to certain crops such as millet and manioc, or to certain geographical zones such as tropical forests, deserts and semi-deserts.

As for China, despite the remarkable advances that have been made in the last two years, it has not permanently won its agricultural battle, which is inseparable from the demographic battle. If it does not win on this front, industrial investment will be threatened.

But let us continue our world tour. Let us leave the empire of hunger behind. Let us leave the developing countries, and move on to the Soviet Union and Socialist Europe. Here, rises in consumption may well be even more marked: from 300 million tonnes between 1973 and 1975, to more than 450 in the year 2000. Let us leap the Berlin Wall. A change of landscape. The obese people who fill the streets of New York munching their pop corn remind us that we are in the kingdom of 'junk food' and those who "dig their graves with their teeth." Processing losses apart, the rise in volume of food consumption should be very modest.

What is the meaning of this panorama? Between 1977–1978, Third World countries imported about 40 million tonnes of grain, or on average, 10% of their consumption. If supply and demand trends remain constant between now and the end of the century, these figures could reach as high as 80 to 100 million tonnes in 1990, and 140 million in the year 2000! 18% of Third World consumption! However, we must be cautious: it is a question of striking a balance between supply and demand that must perforce be very much affected by the hypotheses made, and other studies lead to much lower figures. However, let us accept these figures. They carry a triple message:

• The impact of Third World food shortage should not be significant till the beginning of the next century. At this time, Europe and the USSR should have very little need for imports. If we assume a steady increase in demand and no climatic changes, North America and Argentina (for wheat and corn), and Burma and Thailand (for rice) should be in a position to increase their production to meet the import needs of the other developed countries (20 to 30 million tonnes) and to contain or make up the Third World shortage (80 million tonnes). As for prices, rather than an explosion, it seems that we should expect a slow increase.

● It is misleading to speak of the strategic dependence of the Third World in the area of agriculture. Are not the big importers OPEC countries, the new industrial countries , and the and exporters of commodities whose economies are closely interwoven with those of OECD countries? There is no real dependence except for a certain number of countries in Africa and Southern Asia that are very much in need of food aid and agricultural exports, and whose exports are not essential to OECD countries. In these cases there is no doubt that food aid should be stepped up (whatever the adverse effects) to fill the widening gap between solvent demand and nutritional needs.

● It is not true that the importation by developed countries of food products from the South is a source of vulnerability. For the OECD, none of the food products (whether raw or processed) generally imported from developing countries is of strategic importance from a nutritional point of view.

Thus the main lines of the future worldwide agricultural game are clearly outlined before us:

● The United States will continue to be by far the principal actor on the international market, because it seems to be able to increase its production without raising costs significantly. It should provide the greater part of world exports of secondary grain, soya beans and oil cakes! *A contrario*, it will continue to be a major importer of coffee, cocoa, sugar, tobacco... Even though the present rise of the dollar and slowed growth of the Third World has brought the farmers of the Mid-west to the brink of bankruptcy, the American government is likely to try to manage the export of cereals and food aid in the long term so as to maintain the income of its farmers.

● Canada, Australia and New Zealand will make up another group of wheat and secondary grain exporters, while Australia and New Zealand will continue to be big exporters of beef and dairy products. In these countries also, there is the intervention of export policies and national regulations governing the organisation of markets.

• The same may be said of the EEC, that other vital actor with its very complex situation. Despite being a big producer of wheat, it will not cover its own consumption. Despite being a considerable producer of secondary grain, it will nonetheless continue to be one of the prime importers, and will account for half of world imports of oil cakes, as well as buying massive quantities of soya. Hence its self-sufficiency in meat will hide a serious shortage of animal feed.

As for Europe's Common Agricultural Policy, surely everyone knows its main principles (the free internal circulation of products, priority given to the Community above the outside world, financial solidarity...)? And everyone knows its problems. But what matters here is the interaction between this policy and the functioning of the world market. Need we recall the soya war with the United States, the debates surrounding the enlargement of the Community to twelve members, and the Lomé Agreement that granted Third World countries (mainly African) preferential conditions for the imports of their agricultural products?

• From the agricultural point of view, Japan is basically an importer country,[38] but it will find it easy to cover its future needs by buying from the United States, and, to a lesser extent, from Australia and New Zealand.

• Let us pass from West to East: apart from erratic imports of grain (which should not bring their strategic independence into question), Eastern Bloc countries should be importing considerable quantities of products like sugar, soya oil cakes, coffee, cocoa, citrus fruit... The rise in household consumption should mean an increased consumption of meat, vegetables, fruit and beverages, but they will be curbed by the need to contain the overall volume of imports.

There remain the Third World actors: OPEC countries that are rapidly increasing their food consumption (between 1970 and 1986, the North Africa – Middle East area could multiply its wheat imports by 3.5, accounting for 8% of world imports of secondary grain during that time). Countries in the process of being industrialised may be divided into two distinct groups: countries in Eastern or Southeast Asia which will easily cover their needs of agricultural products thanks to their exports of manufactured goods; large Latin American countries like Argentina which will also be major or significant agricultural countries. Other developing countries, countries that export certain products (Thailand and Burma for rice, Cuba for sugar, Ghana for cocoa, Ivory Coast for coffee, etc.), or countries which must, with a great deal of difficulty, set aside a large portion of their meagre foreign currency resources for food imports. And finally China, which we know has recently improved its delicate agricultural situation. But agricultural interdependence is not limited to products, as its upstream aspect is coupled with a downstream one.

Without the use of pesticides, world agricultural production would be greatly reduced, but present-day pesticides, produced in the developed countries by multinationals, are still formulated to suit the technologies, parasites, and crops of these countries. From now on, the formulation of pesticides and methods of use adapted to the different regions of the Third World should be a priority task.

European countries and Japan are dependent on Third World phosphate for fertilizers, and the Third World is in turn dependent on the grain that the OECD produces with this phosphate; in the other direction, a good many developing countries resort to the nitrate fertilizers that OECD countries make from OPEC oil, a situation of dependence that is being reduced by the development of Third World ability to produce fertilizers.

Finally, world agriculture would be severely affected by major cuts in OPEC oil supplies, because in the short term it would be difficult to replace oil with other sources of energy or to maintain fertilizer consumption. Still, there is a solution: make agriculture a priority since its requirements account for only a small percentage of total energy consumption.

Thus, the analysis leads on very naturally to the third of the great interdependences in the area of natural resources – energy. This problem that has already been mentioned, but we now need to look at it less globally, scrutinising consumption region by region, pondering the developments of the next twenty years, and focusing on the great international flows of energy products.

1976! The world is consuming a little over 6700 million TOE.[39] Of this, 10% is still non-commercial energy: firewood, wood chips, chaff, and other vegetable and animal waste. Those of us who rely on the electric switch and have fuel oil delivered to our homes find it difficult to conceive that the African woman must walk several kilometres each day to collect wood, and that non-commercial energy provides 70% of the consumption of the Black Continent. As for the four great sources of commercial energy, oil accounts for 42% of total commercial energy, coal 31 %, gas 19%, and primary electricity 7%. Three quarters of all consumption (including non-commercial consumption) is concentrated in the industrial countries. The structure of trade may be described in a few words: if we divide the world into three regions, industrial countries, OPEC countries, and the rest of the Third World, the flows of net exports corresponds to a quarter of world consumption, with OPEC exports alone accounting for 21%, and those of the rest of the Third World, 4.6%. Within the industrial countries , which as a group import one third of the energy consumption, the USSR is an exporter, and all the other regions, importers. Nothing demonstrates this better than a map showing oil trade flows: Western Europe looks like a new-born baby attached to its Middle Eastern mother by an enormous umbilical cord. Did it not import 665 million tonnes of crude oil in 1978 (80 from Algeria and Lybia, 475 from the Near East, 40 from black Africa, and 70 from the USSR)? At the same time, Arab countries and Iran exported 1105 million tonnes (555 to Western Europe, 255 to the Far East and the South Sea Islands, 215 to North America, 60 to Latin America, and 20 to Eastern bloc countries). If there is a sentence that every citizen of Europe should know by heart it is the following: in 1978 Western Europe got 83% of its oil supply from the Arab East and from Iran, while sending it 50% of its exports.

After the present comes the future. Let us forget for the moment the debate on life styles, rates of growth, the energy content of national production, energy savings (whether due to price rises or not) and the coefficients of conversion from primary energies to final energies... Whole rooms in libraries are piled to the ceiling with voluminous reports on world energy consumption in the years 1990, 2000, 2020, and 2030. Let us be content with a reference point for the end of the century (it corresponds to moderate growth and big energy savings, without radical changes in life style): a consumption of 10 to 12 billion TOE of commercial energy (to which should be added about one billion TOE of non-commercial energy). These figures hide two essential facts:

• Between 1976 and the year 2000, developing countries have moved from one quarter to one third of world consumption. Twenty years later their share will be more than 40%.

• Contrary to what the layman expects, the replacement of oil by other sources of energy is far from completed. Oil still covers 35% of world requirements of commercial energy, the share of nuclear energy is no more than 10%, hydraulic, solar, and other new sources of energy only 8%.

In other words, ten years hence (and in so far as we shall exploit all the natural gas we find, the data of the energy problem are surprisingly simple for consumer countries: they have only three cards, three aces that must be played simultaneously if they wish to maintain moderate economic growth: coal, nuclear energy, and energy conservation. All the rest is mere talk. Then it becomes possible to unravel the intricacies of energy interdependence: the oil game with the recycling of petro-dollars, the probable resurrection of coal, the advantages and risks of nuclear energy, transfers of capital and technology with the aim of helping the Third World develop its own energy resources...

There is nothing easier to understand than the oil game if one is aware that for economic and political reasons, "the oil problem is not a reservoir problem, but a tap problem,"[40] but the elements of the problem change with the times.

At the end of the Seventies world growth was reasonably steady. Under such conditions, producer countries are inclined to cut production deliberately, especially since the Iranian Revolution. Between December 1979 and June 1980, OPEC production fell by 150 million tonnes per year, or 10% . Of this, the unintentional drop in Iranian production accounts for only 4%. There are reasons for this reduction. The Iranian Revolution showed the social dangers of hasty industrialisation. The sparsely populated countries of the Arab-Persian Gulf (which could cut down their production considerably without suffering) wish to reduce their financial surpluses in currencies that lose their value yearly, and to keep their 'black gold.' A reduction in production accompanying the drop in demand makes it possible to put up the price (the aim of the producer countries is not to strangle the West, but to obtain the best price, if we can believe the declarations of OPEC in Caracas in December 1978, or Algeria in June 1980). Perhaps the producer countries want to negotiate on the basis of "oil capital against development capital" (technology, investments, access to the markets of industrial countries), but they would like to do it on better terms.

From 1982, the recession generated by the second oil crisis and American anti-inflation policy plus energy savings, have reduced demand. But OPEC strategy has not changed: it has fought to avoid a reduction of revenue from collapsed oil prices. Nonetheless, this policy comes up against the interests of producer countries that are in debt and would like to increase their total share of delivery. For a better understanding of these reasons, let us change our perspective for a moment. Let us stop being the European who until recently noticed his heating bill rise month after month. Let us put aside the image of the nouveau riche Arab world and realise that the consequences of the energy crisis affect those countries more seriously than the industrialised countries: it increases the risk of war and revolution; it forces them to move within a few decades from a principal (and in some cases sole) source of national revenue to other sources of revenue!

The last factor: the growth of OPEC countries will push up their domestic consumption of oil. And it would not be realistic to expect exports from these countries of more than 900 to 1100 million TOE, and, of this total, OECD countries may expect (at most, and taking into account the imports of the rest of the world) from 900 to 1100 million TOE.

There is a strong possibility that between 1990 and the year 2000, the price of a tonne of crude oil could go up by half, despite the recent fall in real prices. The level will depend on the stringency of the energy policies of industrial nations. Certainly, appreciable savings have been achieved in the last few years. However, the question still applies to the part of the savings that will be lost once more, should there be an economic recovery. And the crucial period will undoubtedly be the final years of the century. But there is a serious risk that prices will rise erratically, which would be disastrous for growth and employment.

Furthermore, the oil game is coupled with a monetary and financial game. Following the first oil shock, "according to the lowest estimates, the accrued surpluses of the current transactions of the thirteen countries of OPEC increased by a factor of five in the space of one year, moving from 6 billion dollars in 1973 to 67 million in 1974."[41] Many an expert predicted catastrophe. It never came. Due to the explosion of goods and service imports by oil producing countries, the following years saw a gradual reduction of the annual surplus. Overall, the balances of the current transactions of OPEC countries even showed a deficit of 1 billion dollars in 1978. As we already know, these surpluses were invested in the form of short-term bank deposits, transferrable securities, and to a small extent, in long-term shares and real estate. 1979–1980: history seemed to be repeating itself with the second oil shock. On a grander scale: in two years, OECD countries accumulated a supplementary deficit of 61.5 billion dollars, and the Third World (apart from OPEC) 107 billion! A deceptive similarity. Because the banking system, saturated with short-term deposits like a drinker gorged with water, was loath to increase its risks. Because the producer countries wish to control their growth, and under these conditions they prefer to reduce their production while investing their surpluses in the only available options: American or British Treasury Bonds, or in direct loans to the governments of developed countries. Then 1982 brought a turnabout, but it brought no comfort, for it plunged Mexico and Nigeria into difficulties, left the banking system very fragile, and held the big non-producing borrowers on the brink of bankruptcy. The thing that must be preserved at all costs is Third World access to credit borrowing. The trouble spot is still the situation of the new industrial countries: economic take-off guzzles energy like the locomotives of yesteryear. Raymond Barre was not wrong when he said at the time of the June 1980 meeting of the OECD Council of Ministers financing the future deficit of current transaction balances and refinancing existing commitments when they fall due is the greatest challenge to the economy in peace time. The conclusion is obvious: the more quickly developed countries reduce their dependence on oil, the greater their chances of mastering the formidable oil-finance game that is being played across the world. It is very important that the present drop in the price of crude oil should not lead to an end of energy-saving efforts in every direction: the insulation of housing, reduction of the specific consumption of cars, recovery of heat lost in industry, development of nuclear power, and taking an interest in new forms of energy even if they have no more than a top-up value. And finally, the revival of coal, at the risk of creating new dependences.

The good old coal of our grandfathers! It will have to supply between half and two thirds of the increase in world energy consumption in the next twenty years. OECD countries alone could consume 2 to 2.8 billion tonnes of it by the year 2010.[42] For the production of electricity, for the steel and iron industry, for industry in general, and to a small extent, for the production of combustible liquids. As for the world as a whole, it will use up 5 to 6 billion tonnes. Is this possible? Yes. From the United States (2 billion tonnes), China (1.45 billion), the Soviet Union (1.10 billion), and o a lesser extent, from Australia, the EEC, Poland, India and South Africa. But it will bring about a considerable growth of international trade in coal. Between 1977 and the year 2010 world imports could be increased by a factor of three or four. The two main importers will obviously be the European Economic Community and Japan, the big exporters, Australia, the United States and South Africa. It will be, however, a colossal task, because a whole coal-centred *system*, from extraction to ultimate combustion, will have to be created. By perfecting new production techniques (perhaps underground distillation one day); by solving many environmental, health, and work safety problems; by developing the overland transport of coal, by extending harbour terminals, by spreading new combustion techniques, the expansion of liquification and distillation... And to our young children, the coal of the Twenty-first Century will seem to be a source of energy that has nothing in common with the coal of the Industrial Revolution. As the way opens, other dependencies will be created. What will the day after tomorrow be like for the non-Communist world if American ecologists desirous of protecting the landscape oppose the mining of coal for export? One more reason for taking an interest in nuclear power.

Nuclear power shatters dependence. In four ways. Firstly, by reducing the pressure of developed countries on the oil market, it will lighten the load of the Third World. Secondly, the great sources of uranium to be found (apart from Eastern bloc countries) in the United States, Canada, Australia, South Africa, Niger, Namibia, France and Sweden are more evenly distributed than oil. Thirdly, under present circumstances the cost of natural uranium represents only 10% of the cost of the kWhr obtained (against 65% for coal and 80% for oil). So, who cares about its cost levels! Finally, the move to breeder reactors almost permanently frees the producer from the sources of supply.

But nuclear energy creates other chains that are already potentially forged. It will make a part of Third World production dependent on the technology of developed countries. It will threaten the present military balance because of the fundamental ambivalence of nuclear technology and raw materials: are they peaceful or military? An ambivalence that all the non-proliferation treaties in the world (however useful they may be for a time) will not be able to change. History is strewn with the corpses of such policies. From Lars Porsena who, six centuries before Christ, wanted to forbid the use of iron for the production of arms by Rome, to the Chinese attempt to keep the secret of the silk worm and gunpowder, or Venice, where desertion by glass-blowers was punishable by death! The problem is political rather than technical: following the 1977 Washington Conference, the experts from several countries tried for two and a half years to evaluate the risks involved in the proliferation of the various cycles of nuclear fuels. Their conclusion is unequivocal: all cycles (with differences of degree only) are capable of allowing the move from peaceful to military use. And this is not the only way. Is it not true that the Chinese military program dates from 1964 whereas the non-military program is only just beginning? For several Third World countries, a refusal to pass on the techniques of enriching uranium means institutionalising the technical monopoly of a few developed countries, and menacing the surety of their supply for civil requirements. And as for going back *sine die* to the reprocessing of waste from nuclear power stations to extract plutonium, that means delaying the advent of breeder reactors, and thus renouncing the real benefit of nuclear power. Which is all very well for the United States with its huge reserves of coal and natural uranium, but much less reasonable for France and Japan.

There remains the third constraint that nuclear energy will impose: the problem of radioactive waste. One must perforce point out the division over this point between large minorities of public opinion, and almost the whole of the technical community. The technicians believe that it is possible to place waste into containers and bury them, absolutely safely, for several millenia. Public opinion is afraid. Fear may be respected as long as it is willing to bear the consequences. But what are we to think of politicians who let themselves be dragged along by public opinion and shirk their duty as intermediaries between citizens and specialists ?

But we need one last brush stroke to complete this outline of world energy interdependence, because it is not enough for the developed countries to solve their problem. The Indian or African peasant, and the Brazilian or Malaysian worker need energy. Finance and technologies from the developed countries must be channeled to the Third World so that developing countries may harness their own resources, have access to new forms of energy, and loosen the noose that threatens to strangle their growth.

Commodities, food production, energy. Abundance for some, scarcity for others. A present day La Fontaine might write the fable of the Beggar, the Cobbler and the Arab merchant thus:

"Give me something to eat and teach me to become an artisan like yourself so that I may be able to stop digging my meagre soil with my hands," the Third World Beggar asks the Cobbler.

"I should like to," replies the Cobbler; "I spend hours with my arms crossed waiting for customers . But what will you pay me with? You have nothing to offer me that you have not already sold to me. Go to the Arab Merchant and beg him to lend you a few pieces of gold. Then I will work for you gladly."

"My gold, my gold," replies the Arab. "This Cobbler is a fine fellow; I have only the jars of oil that my father left me to survive on. Now, every year you already plead with me to sell you some of it to give you light. When I am old I shall have no more oil, and I shall have to give you my gold for you to give me some bread. If I lend you my gold, what guarantee do I have that you will return it?"

All the hope and tragedy of interdependence is contained in this fable with its three protagonists. Nonetheless the story is simplistic: It forgets that the Beggar's poverty is not due to a lack of gold, but also to the rules which he promised his father he would observe; it presents only one Cobbler, whereas there are several, each of them afraid that their Beggar-customer will go to his neighbour; it does not say that the Cobblers rise when the sun is already high in the sky, but stop working in the evening so as to avoid lighting the oil lamps in their workshops; it does not point out the fact that the Arab Merchant has already extended credit to the Cobblers to allow them to illuminate their evening parties; it does not remind us that the Arab Merchant was poor for a long time because the Cobblers used to come and dip into his jars in exchange for a few copper coins.

Thus modified, the fable would become realistic, and gradually it seems that managing interdependence is not an easy thing; even more so because in the course of the Great Transition rare commodities will change hands many times.

# The great industrial game

The subject confuses the layman who finds it difficult to come to terms with the complexities of the industrial fabric, the diversity of actors, and multiplicity of actual situations. The crisis of the steel industry, the flood of Japanese cars and shirts from Hong Kong, the contest between Boeing and Airbus, the problems of the European data processing industry... How does one fit these scattered facts into a realistic and coherent perspective of the evolution of world industry? How does one calculate the conflicting risks that low wages in the Third World and Japanese high technology represent to the United States and Europe? Interdependence is self-evident in the areas of oil, raw materials and grain. That is not at all the case with industry, although recent trends will perhaps make this area the core of world economic interdependence. Moreover, attempting to propound the global reality of the great industrial game in its dynamics over the next twenty years in a few pages is a risky business. But such an undertaking is worth the effort: and it is no doubt possible as long as we proceed step by step. By describing the present situation; by analysing the strategies of the actors and factors of change; by identifying probable developments, and illustrating them with examples from the various sectors.

When the rapid growth of the post-war period came to an end in the early Seventies, world industry added value was even more unequally distributed than national incomes, with 68% coming from OECD countries, 19% from Eastern bloc countries, 4.2% from China, and 7.7% from the rest of the Third World. It becomes even more lop-sided if we limit ourselves to the production of machines. Then the share of the

OECD passes the three quarter mark, while that of the rest of the third World is no higher than 5%. This picture of sharp contrasts is the result of very different patterns of development in the various parts of the world. The explosion of Japanese industry, the development of European industry, the weakening of American industry... These are the prominent facts within the OECD. Some figures? Between 1965 and 1974, Japanese steel production went up by 200%, that of the EEC by 35%, and that of the United States by only 10%. Between 1960 and 1976, Japan's share of the chemical production of Western countries more than doubled, while Europe's share only increased by 20%, and that of the United States diminished. The phenomenon is repeated in other divisions such as the car industry and ship-building. These real upsets were made possible by two decades of American technological transfers and intensive investments. Upsets that have had their actors: American multinationals, and the big Japanese and European projects.

During all this time, no comparable phenomenon has been seen in the Third World. True, between 1960 and 1976, exports of manufactured goods from the Third World to Western countries went up by 15% per year in real terms, but at the end of that period they accounted for very small percentages of the markets of developed countries, and the Third World's share (excluding China) of value added by industry to the world economy (excluding China) trailed badly: 6.2% in 1952, 8.5 to 9% in 1976! Moreover, a closer look reveals some curious things. Half of this share may be attributed to only four countries: Brazil, Mexico, Argentina, and India. In 1976 only five developing countries exported more than one billion dollars of manufactured products per year[43]: Hong Kong, South Korea, Yugoslavia, Mexico and Brazil. Mini-China (the little island of Hong Kong) provided one fifth of Third World exports of manufactured goods! And Third World exports of manufactured products are still concentrated on a small number of groups of products: clothing, metal products, food products, shoes... American multinationals and British marketing companies have played the key role in this development. Does not an EEC study record around 16,000 branches of multinational companies in the Third World? Branches which are to be found in the same countries: 10% in Brazil, around 9% in Mexico, a little over 4% in India, Argentina and Malaysia... These few facts are enough to reveal the extent of the industrial problem of the developing world.

1973. The World Conference of UNIDO[44] was held in Lima (with China absent because it had not yet been admitted). And confronted with this problem, what did it do? It makes edifying reading. Take a few well-intentioned international officials. Get them to multiply Africa's share between now and the year 2000 by five, that of Asia by three, and that of Latin America by two. Add a further 20%. Make a South American delegate stand up because he finds the percentage for that continent unacceptable, and asks that it be increased. Make all the African and Asian delegates get up in turn and demand that the proportions be respected. Once more, add 25%. A final vote. And... *voilà.* All the Third World countries have decided that in the year 2000, the Third World (excluding China) will provide 25% of the value added by industry to the world economy (excluding China). Poor Raymond Barre! According to him, a simple rate of growth cannot be decreed. What does he think of a decree on the distribution of world industry twenty years hence? Perhaps the delegates, lovers of French literature, have remembered the La Fontaine fable in which a tumbler who has just received a large sum of money in exchange for promising a king to teach an ass to read in three years, replies to those who are surprised: Between now and that time, either the the king, the ass or I will be dead." But let us postpone the debate on the role of international organisations and continue with the outline of the industrial situation of the world at this time.

In Lima, the Eastern bloc was dumb. Not being capitalist, it did not consider itself to be an exploiter, and declared that it was not concerned with the industrial backwardness of the Third World. However, its own industrial rise is also one of the great facts of the post-war period, since from 1953 to 1973 (twenty years) the economic share of the centrally planned economies has moved from 15.2% to 24.3% of the world total. With, of course, specific choices, because the traditional heavy industries take up a greater proportion of this total than they do in the West.

At the end of the first stage, it seems clear that the future upheaval of industrial structures will be nothing new. It has been one of the principal characteristics of the post-war period. To a great extent, the expansion of the European and Japanese industries has been to American industry what the growth of Third World industry now means to OECD industry. For two decades, industrial policies, often linked with national development policies, have figured among the main concerns of the governments of developed countries. Tomorrow, like today, technical progress, the growth of demand, the relative cost of different factors, the strategies of the big groups plus government policies will continue to shape the future industrial landscape of regions, states and continents. Tomorrow, the same actors, the same forces will be operative, but the scale of the scene will have changed. Competition between manufac-

turers of North America, Western Europe, and Japan will fit into a much
wider game between West and South, West and East, South and East.
A world-wide game. With three kinds of actors.

Companies (small and medium-sized companies or multinationals)
stretched in their constant struggle for survival, innovative, cautious,
launching products, developing markets, closing down some activities
and cutting down expenses. Ever maintaining an unstable equilibrium,
never out of danger from disaster. Custodians of that specialised and
perishable knowledge known as professionalism. Spiders at the centre of
extraordinary webs of information towards which customers, bankers,
suppliers, and researchers gravitate.

More and more sensitive to all markets, wherever they are, the major
ones will be trying to become truly international so as to secure the
loyalty of their employees and get a more firm footing in their markets;
but they will find it hard to elude the cultural grasp of their countries of
origin which has stamped their leaders, their structures and their
procedures. Prime movers without peer, but condemned to ambiguous
relations with governments. The governments of developed countries
protect those that issue from their soil as a national asset, but would like
to fit them into their regional and social policy. The governments of
developing countries reject them in the name of socialism, or attract
them as tools that they would see used only to serve their development
plans...

Next come governments. The governments of Western countries are
aware that they personify national sovereignty, but worn out in their
struggle against inflation and unemployment, forced to maintain their
position as short-term arbitrators between social groups, torn between
the political will not to increase their responsibilities, and the tendency of
their bureaucracies to dominate the other industrial actors. Playing a
major role in the industrial game by the rules they decree, by the
contracts they grant, by the financing that they make possible, and by
the international agreements that they negociate. Eastern bloc governments, capable of turning economies of scale to account, planning
heavy investments, and controlling international trade, but obliged to
struggle with the shortages created by a blend of rigidity and laxism; ever
seeking ways to stimulate innovation and to make an acceptable compromise between centralisation and decentralisation. Third World governments with their widely varying means, parading the haughty
nationalism that is the protection of the weak, crushed beneath the
weight of development problems, under the watchful eye of the property-
owning bourgeoisies, and at the mercy of urban masses, clinging to

industrialisation as a symbol of success, torn between the desire to export and the will to reconquer their domestic markets, between their preference for state-owned companies, and evidence of the efficiency of multinationals.

And finally, the unions. Organised nationally, and disoriented by games that no longer stop at national borders. On the defensive almost everywhere. In developing countries where they represent the interests of the relatively privileged minority of industrial workers. In developed countries where they either become conservative and protectionist as in the United States and Britain, or, like the French CFDT[45] pondering the choice between the strict defence of their members and the fight for a different society.

The strategies of these actors vary infinitely from one country to another, from one sector to another, depending on economic, political and social realities. However, the same factors of change crop up again and again in different guises.

Let us begin with technical progress. Whether it is brought about by the developments in scientific research, or by innovations of firms that are striving to escape constraints or to take advantage of opportunities, it has lost none of its vigour. Even if the cut-back of investments slows down its application. The great poles? They are well known: from now onwards, electronics, around which the whole technical system of developed countries is reorganising itself. Whether we are dealing with the automation of production, or computer-assisted design, the incorporation of micro-processors in many products, the reshaping of the office or of communications by computerisation, or the explosion of data banks... Tomorrow, biology will transform the role of fertilizers and the battle against pests; it will invent new animal and vegetable species, make possible the emergence of sources of auxilliary energy, change the conditions of animal feed, revolutionise chemical catalysis, and completely transform the pharmaceutical industry and methods of safeguarding health. And then, new sources of energy, the conquest of the sea and of space. But there are other pressures that also bring about significant technical progress: the search for clean (or in other words, non-polluting) technologies, efforts to save energy, the desire to obtain materials with predetermined properties, the will to develop measuring instruments... And let us not forget the technical progress made in the Third World: the improvement of traditional technology, discoveries that make it possible to utilise local resources, the adaptation of the technology of developed countries to new economic, social and cultural conditions. The picture is not yet complete, for it omits that which is beyond the blurred line between technical progress and economic and social progress: the methods for better combining the factors of production, for improving education, the search for organisations that would allow them both to create and cooperate... The time is right for reflecting on Jean-Jacques Servan-Schreiber's brilliant thesis:[46] will the microprocessor become, as he believes, the redeemer of the Third World, the leaven that will give billions of people access to the real life of development? In my opinion, yes and no. Yes, because Third World industrialisation will not be a reproduction of Europe's. The Cameroon peasant replaces his earthenware pots with aluminum saucepans, and not with cast iron vessels. It was with cassettes, not pamphlets, that Khomeini carried out his propaganda against the Shah. No, because development is a complex social phenomenon, of which technical progress is only one component.

A second factor of change? The development of final demand, of investment needs, of household and administrative consumption. The aim of this book is not to describe detailed trends; it is enough to be aware of future imbalances. It is possible that in twenty-five years the revenue of the Third World may be multiplied by four. Never before in history has there been an industrial market of this size; for consumer goods, intermediary goods, and hard goods; for the building of transport infrastructures; for the construction of housing. Unquestionably the precise nature of this market depends on Third World development strategies and the resulting distribution of incomes, but this does not change anything as far as size goes. On the other hand, the demand for industrial products will grow much more slowly in OECD countries. Because world revenue at the end of the century will hardly be double 1975 figures. Because this income will be spent differently. And finally there are the Eastern bloc countries – already largely industrialised. Here, there is still a considerable potential demand for industrial consumer goods. Hence the transformations in volume and composition of world demand will surely play an important part in shaping the physionomy of future industry.

But the worldwide redeployment of industrial activities will also depend on the relative production costs in the different zones and their development. What does economic science (with its successive theories that fit into each other like Russian dolls) have to say about this? At the centre is the smallest doll: the theory of comparative advantages, that economic *pons asinorum* that goes back to Ricardo. Its message is simple: if work is all that is needed to produce wine or cloth, and if for the same number of hours, the ratio of the quantity of cloth to wine that an

Englishman produces is more than the same ratio for a Portuguese person, it is in the interest of Britain to specialise in textiles, and Portugal in viticulture. The second Russian doll? It adds the costs of transport as well as the reduced returns that are likely to occur if every one in Portugal were to become a wine grower. So it shows that countries will only be partially specialised. Now comes the third doll. It introduces the assets of each country in factors of production (natural resources, equipment, different grades of labour...), sanctions the production of a great variety of goods, and makes a double prediction: in each country, the less rare one factor is, the lower its relative price will be. The more a country has an abundance of the factors necessary for making a product in relative proportions, the more this country will tend to specialise in making this product. One more Russian doll – the fourth. It now sanctions the movements of factors of production and declares that they will be moved from zones where they are abundant to zones where they are rare: Turkish workers to Germany, and American capital to Brazil. But I am particularly fond of the last Russian doll, the fifth. Because it introduces the differences of ability between the various countries *vis à vis* combining the factors of production. Because it stresses the gradual learning of these abilities that makes specialisation or training possible. There is no longer anything that predisposes the Portuguese to viticulture, and the English to weaving. Each one will be able to learn the trade of the other, but the more the English will have perfected a complex technology of weaving, the tougher the task of the Portuguese will be. With the learning process, trials and errors, successes and failures will crop up again and again.

Good old Russian dolls! You help us to understand a whole aspect of industrial redeployment. In the Third World and in the developed countries.

Yes, the industrialisation of Third World countries is indeed being achieved, to a certain extent in relation to the comparative advantages, that is to say, it centres round productive processes that make an intensive use of resources that are locally plentiful and cheap (notably, unskilled labour, and, in certain OPEC countries, available capital) or which suit a potential regional market; but there is nothing more incorrect than seeing the situation of comparative advantages as being stable in the future. Technological progress, the development of "human capital," and changes in the relative costs of factors will constantly modify it from one country to another. A significant portion of these transformations will be the result of the process of industrialisation itself, for it cannot be separated from the education of people, management training, and the mastering of techniques. It constantly recreates some advantages while destroying others, especially through the rise in wage costs that it permits.

Yes, the relative costs of the factors of production, labour costs, the price of energy, and the costs of protecting the environment will intervene in the competition between the developed countries.

Yes, the theory of comparative advantages also explains the easy rise of the least developed countries of Europe, and especially of Mediterranean Europe: Spain, Portugal, Greece and Yugoslavia.

Yes, but... The poles of attraction of costs and markets are distorted by political forces. Changes of government in the Third world that modify the rules radically and set off waves of nationalisation. The actions of governments desirous to maximise their share of world industry and to reduce the vulnerability of their economy to external actions. In Western countries: by financing research, granting preferential loans, assisting reconversions, and subsidising regional development. In Eastern bloc countries: by modulating the prices of their exports, and paying for imported factories with future deliveries. In developing countries: by granting tax relief, protecting their markets through customs duties, and sharing in the building of infrastructures. The multinationals fit into these poles, ever cautious in their calculation of risks, ever ready to benefit from the advantages of the three worlds. From what is often their perspective – short term calculation.

The consequences of such strategies? a world-wide wastage of capital and labour; a badly oriented industrialisation that gives priority to equipment and is unfavourable to employment, because of the tacit collusion between OECD governments, the multinationals, and Third World governments. The first of the three must square their balance of payments at any price, and in order to do this they must export. And they do not hesitate to subsidise the sale of capital goods by granting low interest loans. To the point that real interest rates became negative. As for the latter, they are content either to export or to buy shares. In the first case, it is hardly surprising that they propose durable goods that have been devised for developed countries, the fruit of a long technical evolution that has sought to economise on the costly factor – labour. And for the latter, what is more normal than that the gradual adaptation of their subsidiary to the relative costs of factors be restrained by their cultural habits and by the desire for international coherence in their methods of organisation. Finally, the third party works towards the same aim, because the most recent technologies have the support of officials, local capitalists, and sometimes, the unions. Because of the prestige they give, because of the personal security that they offer in case of failure, because of the standards of quality that they guarantee for export, because of the importance of the share of profits that they imply, because of the relative indifference that they permit with the wage levels of their employees...

And this is why we find completely automated brick works in Algeria, textile mills in Korea that employ fewer people than French textile mills, industrial enclaves in Indonesia that are entirely oriented towards export and keep down the number of workers in a country where 63% of the population is in a state of utter poverty.

Now let us get this straight. We are not proposing a return to the textile machines of 1870, nor carrying fuel to nuclear power stations in wheelbarrows, but rather using the enormous potential of science and modern technology to create techniques adapted to the relative rarity of equipment and work in the Third World. Techniques which take the economic, social and cultural environment of developing countries into account. *So that hundreds of millions more people may have access to dignity.*

Technical progress, the development of demand, the transformation of comparative advantages, and the industrial policies of governments. These factors will work for all goods, and all services, but they will act differently for the various categories. But to understand the plot we must go further. As far as the intimate reality of the games as played in each sector. Some readers, overwhelmed by the problems of industry, will think that this is a subject for specialists. How wrong they are, for they will be experiencing the industrial battle throughout the coming decades, and if they want to understand it, they must see it (if only for a moment) through the eyes of an IBM executive, a director of Volkswagen, the president of U.S. Steel, or a small textile manufacturer... And they will find that from electronics to steel, passing through the car, chemical, textile, or shipbuilding industries, the battle conditions vary widely.

First things first. The strategic importance of the electronics industry is greater by far than the place that it occupies percentage-wise in the industrial production and employment of developed countries. In the future it will have as much of a major impact on the productive structures and organisation of work as on the evolution of economic relations between nations.

There are five major characteristics of this huge movement:

1. The speed of technical progress, one that moves quickly from laboratories to products or production processes; technical progress that brings about miniaturisation and big cost reductions.

2. The lowering of barriers between sectors, which like telecommunications, data processing and general electronical appliances were still totally separate a few years ago.

3. The gradual creation of a world market, economies of scale being such that national barriers can only become more and more permeable.

4. Extension of the policies of deregulation which originated in the US, but which are being adopted with variations by other developed countries.

5. The growth of markets; it will be twice as fast as that of industry as a whole.

Where has technical progress mainly occurred? Essentially in the area of basic components and associated computers. The main result? The current upheaval in the conception of capital goods, from machine tools to furnaces, while goods destined for personal use such as cars and washing machines will be transformed before new generations of products such as telecopiers come into being. Thus, the game of competition in this sector will be dominated by the development of technology. A development in which the process of innovation will tend to become more and more expensive, and will necessitate increasing state participation. A development in which the techniques which have made it possible to create increasingly efficient integrated circuits could reach their limits at the end of the century, and a considerable effort in basic research will be needed for them to be overcome. A development in which hardware conception and system design will be increasingly at stake. The first result of this would be the accentuation of a process of integration, with the big electronics groups trying to cover several sectors; from components to telecommunications, from professional and medical electronics to data processing, from general electronics to computer-aided production. A second consequence would be the continued preponderance of the five principal producing countries (the USA, Japan, West Germany, France, and Britain), countries which alone account currently for more than 80% of world production (excluding countries with centrally planned economies). A very heterogeneous group besides, in which the United States would continue to enjoy an unquestionable superiority, in which Japan would attain total technological independence, in which the position of West Germany would be consolidated within Europe. On a global scale? Tri-polarisation seems likely. An increased concentration in developed countries on those activities that demand great technological capacity, or whose production processes may be generally automated. The pursuit of the delocalisation movement in a new periphery of the Third World (the Philippines, Malaysia and the Caribbean...) for products that are widely used, or which have high labour costs. Finally, in the case of products for mass consumption, a more or less independent development of conception and production capacities in intermediary countries that already have a domestic market and a certain level of technology (Korea, Taiwan, Brazil, Mexico and India).

Let us change theatres. Let us move on from electronics to the car industry. Here, one is totally disoriented, for not only is the scenery different, but also the plot. Confronting a swarm of small and big firms that have set off to conquer the electronic West are the fifteen or so independent car manufacturers that there are in the world. Confronting the explosion of demand for microprocessors is the gradual saturation of the stock of private cars in developed countries. The level of this saturation will vary from region to region as a function of population density, attitudes to cars, other available means of transport, and government policies: perhaps around 600 to 700 cars per thousand people in the United States, 500 in Western Europe, and 300 in Japan. And the rate of growth of demand will gradually decrease until it practically levels off towards the end of the century in North America, Japan, Central and Northern Europe. Altogether, the share of world demand for cars accounted for by the markets of traditional producing countries will drop while that of the Third World will climb. Just one figure: it is estimated that between 1980 and the year 2000 the annual demand for private cars in the world will go up from 29 to 49 million vehicles. (in other words, an annual growth rate of 2 to 2.5% on a global scale, but the figures for North America and Western Europe should not rise above 0.7% and 1.4% respectively. What will the General Motors, Fords, Renaults, Fiats, and Toyotas do...? There are three complementary options open to them to face the severe competition ahead: a gradual transfer of production to the regions where demand is increasing more rapidly (the edges of Western Europe, Southern Europe, Latin America, and certain countries in Asia). The search for technologies that are adapted to new rules or new user attitudes (an economic use of energy and raw materials, the limitation of pollution and noise, and the reduction of accident risks, etc.). Greater efforts to improve productivity and keep up international competitiveness. By automating production, by the joint manufacture of certain components, by delocalising the production of certain sub-assemblies.

The automobile and chemical industries having been the great generator of industrial growth in the past, the chemical industry is gradually maturing in the developed countries. A sure sign: its rate of growth tends to become similar to the average rate of growth of industry. Whether it is ethylene plastics, cellulose or non-cellulose fibres, synthetic rubber, nitrate fertilizers, soaps and detergents, or paints and varnishes, rates of growth are going to slow down (with infinite variations, naturally) in the markets of developed countries. In the other geographic zones, on the other hand, heavy chemical industry will be central to several investment projects. Rubber and ethylene should increase substantially. We should also expect that these countries will acquire a significant proportion of areas like methanol, aromatics, fibres and common plastics. How will the big chemical groups of developed countries react, the Hoechsts, the Bayers, the Rhône-Poulencs and the Dupont de Nemours? They are still capable of considerable innovation. With brilliant prospects in areas such as the search for synthetic materials, the chemistry of natural substances, interface technologies between chemistry and biology. Their probable strategy? They will turn to technology; they will develop light chemistry; they will concentrate on those products for which they can retain a large share of the market; they will make manifold agreements with Third World firms, but they will not create more jobs... What exactly will it be like in Western Europe? The chemical industry is currently (compared with the other zones of the world) the principal producer and principal exporter. Mainly concentrated in the EEC, the position of the heavy chemical industry will become vulnerable when faced with competition from Eastern bloc and developing countries. The substantial reduction of investments in petrochemistry will be precipitated by present surplus production capacity and the slowing down of demand, and it is not impossible that cartels of producers and protectionist barriers will appear. The situation of light chemistry is quite different. Growth rates in this sector (including pharmaceutical priducts and cosmetics in particular) will remain steady, with biotechnology permitting spectacular advances. In Europe, Swiss, German and (to a lesser extent) British firms, enjoy a strong position in the world market. They should improve it.

The fourth case. Textiles. Yet another theatre. For many, the play that is being acted there has become the very story of industrial redeployment; is it not true that the reallocation of trade flows can, to a large extent, be explained by the respective costs of the various factors? In the clothing industry, capital intensity is very low – around one fifth of the average for industrial activities. For the textile industry as a whole, the capital-labour ratio is no more than half the average for industry. A higher proportion of production workers and a higher percentage of unskilled workers is characteristic of this sector. This is a fair but simplistic picture, for we should not forget that many developing countries have invested in extremely modern equipment, to the point that variations in productivity are much closer together than wage variations, and we must remember that not all developing countries have made it. Those that have become significant exporters owe it to the assimilation of the industrial process as a whole, especially the marketing phase. In the future, the supply coming from developing countries will be growing faster than their domestic demand with the appearance of new producers and the declining profitability of that sector. Competition between Third World countries will be stiff. As for the developed countries, any analysis that dodges the differences between sub-sectors or the successive stages of the channels of production is useless. It is in industrial products, non-woven carpets, upholstery fabrics and articles that are very closely linked with fashion that these countries will maintain some advantages. They will also try to take advantage of labour savings made possible by computer-aided production (automatic design and cutting, for instance). The gaps will grow wider between the big companies that are able to take advantage of the international division of labour and the marginal companies that find it difficult to hold onto their slot in the market.

Why put shipbuilding after textiles in this brief panorama? The answer is simple. There is no better illustration of the consequences (in a sector that is expanding very little) of the interaction of economic factors and government intervention. The growth of sea transport will decrease appreciably, for many well-known reasons: the probable curbing and modification of the growth content of developed countries (especially Japan, which in the past created more than half of the growth of bulk transport and more than three quarters of the sea transport of raw materials); the processing of raw materials in their country of origin: a slight increase, followed by stagnation and decline in the transport of crude oil (the transport of coal and natural gas, providing only a partial compensation); the development – but only to a limited extent – of the other forms of transport... And it is within this framework that the factors of the localisation of shipbuilding will act: (1) The absence of international companies; (2) Different economic conditions depending on the various vessels. At one extreme, standardised constructions like those of oil tankers and ore ships (here conception and development costs are low, mass production possible, and sub-contracting easy; in the long term, the importance of labour costs, and the relatively low level of necessary skill will give developing countries unquestionable advantages); at the other extreme, the specialised vessels: methane tankers, research ships, lighter carriers, etc. (their construction calls for a highly skilled labour force and substantial research and development efforts; the developed countries should therefore retain a definite advantage in this area); (3) Various political measures, within both the OECD and developing countries. A veritable museum of government arms: equipment and supply subsidies, help in the promotion of exports, support for national shipyards, and captive markets. In the case of Eastern bloc countries, the security of supply and the acquisition of currencies seem to be behind the efforts that have been made. The result is foreseeable: a significant boom in Eastern Europe and in certain Third World countries like South Korea which at one time aimed to satisfy one third of world demand, or like Brazil, which has reserved 96% of the growth of its commercial fleet for its national industry.

A final example? The iron and steel industry. A sector whose development has long been the very symbol of industrialisation, whose owners still retained the pride and confidence of the ironmasters of yesteryear, a sector that is experiencing the greatest crisis in its history. Are these problems attributable to the combination of circumstances or to structural transformation? Both, obviously. As is the case with many other sectors of industry, steel and iron did not anticipate world economic development accurately. And the reversal of circumstances hit it in the midst of a period when it was increasing its capacity. But (and here we are dealing with structure) because of their different levels of productivity, the various national iron and steel industries were not all able to withstand the strain. The greatest competitive pressure came from the best performer among them – the Japanese steel industry, whose net exports rose from 2.7 to 23.4 million metric tonnes in the Sixties. It is within this context that long-term trends came into play: the gradual reduction of the steel content in the future growth of developed countries, and the rise of Third World steel. Countries like the United States, Japan, Britain, Germany, France and Italy will continue to be important producers, but they cannot expect a significant rise in production in the coming decade. By the year 1995, of a world production of crude steel of 745 Million tonnes (against 681 million in 1976), the developed countries with market economies will still provide close to 44%, but with a bigger share coming from Canada, South Africa, and Spain. Substantial increases will take place in Brazil, Mexico, Venezuela, China, India and South Korea. The Third World, including China, will reach about 30%.

These analyses help us to go straight to the living reality at the heart of the industrial game, and they confirm some rough figures that would otherwise be no more than a repetition of Lima. Within a hypothesis of moderate world economic growth, the rate of growth of industrial added value over the last twenty years of the century, should range from 3.4% for OECD countries to a little over 7% for Third World countries, but with a wide spread: 4.6% in black Africa and perhaps 7.5% in Latin America and China. Percentages? OECD countries should account for roughly one half, China around 10%, and the rest of the Third World from 16 to 17%, with a more limited redeployment for the production of machines. The famous Lima objective would not be reached, but new industrial countries would have been born – in Latin America (almost 10% of world industrial added value), in Eastern Asia and China. Once more we come up against this truth: when the first day of the next century is celebrated, mankind's great transition will only be half completed.

What lesson do we learn from this rough outline, despite its brevity? What images of world industry in the year 2000 does it evoke? The answers to these questions are all contained in a few propositions:

To think of the industrial sector as a line or column of coefficients on a matrix of inter-industrial relations, is to bypass the main point, omitting the actors which create, invent, attack, and defend themselves. Industrial redeployment? One must conceive of it on the level of basic cells, on the level of products, on the level of the elementary markets. There, games are played day after day: games of infinite variety, or with different rules, constraints, nature of actors, and possible range of strategies.

It would be a mistake to be hypnotised by the industrial competition of the South. For two reasons. Firstly, because the industrialisation of the Third World, if well managed, is a tremendous boon for world economy... And secondly, because the major industrial war is being waged within the West. A war like the feudal wars of days gone by, in which alliances are made and annulled, in which conflicts and cooperation coexist. A war that draws in the countries of the Third World, countries that are striving to stop being stakes and become sometimes partners, and sometimes opponents, and whose presence increases the complexity of the whole system.

To conceive of tomorrow's industry in terms of the driving activities of yesterday, is to forget that slowly but surely, the great sectors of the post-war period whose development supported this extraordinary growth (the car industry and heavy chemical industry) are nearing their maturity. The pathways of the future revolve around electronics, biology, the sources of renewable energy, and tomorrow around biology.

A portrayal of developed societies as future post-industrial societies in which the service industries take the place of the secondary, in which services take the place of industry, is based on an ambiguity, for many of tomorrow's activities will combine the supply of goods with the supply of services, and they will involve both secondary and tertiary employment. And technological and economic ups and downs will be constantly shifting the boundary between hardware and software. Is not the giant IBM both the world's foremost service company and one of the biggest producers of goods?

To underestimate the role of science and research and development in the industrial game of the developed countries is to overlook the crucible in which technologies are developed, technologies that are sometimes carried by big multinational groups, and sometimes by innovatory little companies created by defectors from laboratories. Tomorrow, the economy of a developed country will derive its vigour from the efficiency of its research system and the quality of the interface between this system and its productive structure.

To give the geographic distribution of world industry in percentages as in Lima, is to be impervious to the opposing trends that coexist. Whereas on one extreme, mastering advanced technology is no longer within the reach of more than a few countries (the United States, Japan, West Germany, France, Britain and Italy – end of roll call!), the spider's web of industrialisation is gradually reaching every state on the planet. Everyone will be playing industrial football, but only a few will remain in the first league.

And finally, to see each country as an independent industrial pole, is to be unaware of the double transformation that multinationals will bring about in the production processes. First of all, a fragmentation of these processes, making it possible to delocalise only segments of pathways... for the delocalisation of whole pathways may prove impossible for technical reasons, inefficient for economic reasons, and impractical for social reasons. And secondly, a greater concentration of production capacities at each stage, in so far as the extension of markets world-wide could bring large-scale markets fully into play.

Should we accept this industrial interdependence in the hope of increasing world revenue more rapidly? Should we reject it and become self-sufficient in case of trouble, or in order to escape from the competition of the Japanese and Koreans? Happy are the militant champions of liberalism or protectionism, for theirs is a simple faith. I believe that the answer must be more subtle but before proposing one, let us complete the picture.

# An increasingly common heritage

Private goods, public goods. For a long time, economists, basing their thinking on a closed national economy, have accustomed us to this distinction. They have even refined it, differentiating between public goods such as parks and gardens (which all of us are free to use), and 'goods' like national defence (which must perforce be collective). They have separated private goods used by a group (such as housing) from those which only concern individuals (such as fruit and vegetables). Academic quibbling no doubt; but on a global scale, in the multipolar interdependent world that is evolving, it describes tremendous political stakes and cultural changes.

For the benefit of the initiate, the usual term is 'the preservation and management of the common human heritage.' A felicitous expression, because it comprehends generosity and hope; a useful concept, because it draws attention to an area of conflict in the international system.

And what do we find in this area?

Firstly and paradoxically, private goods, but private goods that are geographically localised and hard to replace. Non-renewable resources such as oil and raw materials. Renewable resources like shoals of fish in territorial waters or the produce of some agricultural land. While it is obvious to some that one is dealing here with a common heritage, others find this idea incomprehensible. But these two attitudes are understandable when one takes into account the very real nature of the stakes involved: a problem of equity between successive generations, or between contemporary national societies. By exhausting the oil reserves, is not Twentieth Century man jeopardising the income of his descendants of the third millenium if they fail to come up with a viable alternative source of energy? Do not some countries risk contributing to the spread of famine in areas incapable of producing enough food for themselves when they refuse to share their agricultural surpluses? I can see heads shaking: "The bottle is new," some will say, "but it contains nothing more than the old wine of discourses on the unequal distribution of man's common heritage. Collective appropriation of the means of production. Yes. A familiar tune." Granted. But they overlook one dimension: the higher the annual rate of extracting a resource in relation to its world reserves, the greater the inequalities likely to be created between human groups. The fact that I am less pessimistic than some about the likelihood of long-term shortages does not mean that there will not be an intensification of conflicts in this area. And naturally, national societies will choose one or another of the two possible strategies.

The first option is to extend the appropriation of resources, taking them away from those who presently own them, transforming public property which belongs to all humanity into national property. This is, secretly, the favoured option, and every day we see examples to prove it: the nationalisation of deposits of raw materials is at its height, and one of the main outcomes of discussions on the law of the sea has been the extension of territorial waters for ocean exploration to 200 miles.

If this strategy is impossible or ineffective, there remains the other alternative: that is, attempting to make public property of other people's private property, or preventing others from appropriating public property. Abstract language perhaps, but it describes concrete realities as long as the West claims free access to OPEC oil, and as long as Third World countries ask for the free availability of the technology of industrialised nations, or call for an international agency to take on the responsibility of exploiting the oceans in order to avoid having their mining revenues appropriated by large multinational companies.

What is certain is that throughout the numerous conflicts towards which interdependence will lead nation-states, the flag of common heritage will be waved in turn by one or another group in the course of tough negotiations over private property which is localised and difficult to replace.

But it is obvious that common heritage is more than barrels of oil or fishing grounds, because world goods are as varied as the things which it comprises are numerous. Here are some examples:

● Interplanetary space, the atmosphere that surrounds us, the great oceans that separate and unite the inhabited world, the regimes of climates and tides... all the areas in which international actions take place. From the measurement campaigns of the World Metereological Association to the definition of air routes; from the distribution of radio wave-lengths to regulation of the use of telecommunictions satellites, from negociations over the law of the sea to debates on air and sea pollution.

• The genetic heritage of the species. Man was not a guardian of this heritage until humanity acquired the ability to destroy itself, to manipulate its stock of genes, or to produce mutations unwittingly.

• All of the existing species. They are a constant testimony to the diversity of the branches of evolution and life's varied responses to the numerous problems of adaptation to the environment; a whole that is less the juxtaposition of isolated species than the symbiotic relationship between groups of species in their natural environment, from the tundra to the steppes, from the lofty Alps to the Everglades.

• The history of man and of life on earth. From dinosaur deposits to Neanderthal caves; from the ruins of Catal Huyuk to New Guinea systems of kinship; from the Indian languages of North America to the first Sumerian texts; from the Veda to the Koran; from Ikhnaton's 'Hymn to the Sun' to the Bible; for in his desperate struggle to escape death, modern man likes to think of his life as one episode of a tremendous adventure series running through the continents and centuries.

• Our aesthetic heritage, natural and man-made. From the Grand Canyon to Along Bay, from the frescoes of Ajanta to those at Saint-Savin, from the temples of Nubia to the Mexican pyramids; from the sculptures of Chartres to African images; from the *Iliad* and the *Odyssey* to the *Genji Monogatari*... All these are proof of the fact that Beauty (whatever the criteria of judgment) is an essential dimension of human existence.

• As for scientific and technical knowledge, it is public property par excellence. Once a step is taken, a discovery made, a theorem proven or a data bank set up, then using it only requires having access to, and understanding it.

• And lastly, moral values. Though the great civilisations may have lived differently, and even if morality is interpreted differently in Moscow, Santiago, Washington, Kinshasa, Delhi or Teheran, the majority of mankind is not indifferent to famine, torture, mutilation, political imprisonment or extermination, whatever the conditions or the place.

This is an impressive list which interdependence will make more and more pertinent, and which for many reasons will prove to be the cause of thorny arbitration *vis à vis* human conduct.

Whether consciously or unconsciously, we shall be obliged to *strike a balance* between the production and destruction of these items of public property and the consumption of others. (Up to what point can the government of a European country increase taxes in order to fight famine in Africa? What should one do if obtaining oil in the Middle East means propping up a government which tramples on human rights?).

Then there is the need to make irreversible decisions which destroy this public property (for example constructing a hydroelectric plant which completely alters the countryside; sacrificing an archeological site in order to make way for the development of a new town; increasing tourism and thereby threatening the survival of an ecosystem.)

Long-term risks which are not easy to assess, whether you are dealing with nuclear waste, the possible consequences of the extended use of toxic chemicals, or the disappearance of certain species.

Interference in the manifold problems of 'equity' (for example: does Khomeini have the right to prevent non-Shi'ites from visiting Isfahan mosques? How long does one justify encouraging the government of a poor country to turn down lucrative investments and maintain its architectural heritage instead? At the end of the century, how will we go about choosing those who may visit the Sistine Chapel from the sea of human candidates? Shouldn't a child's ticket be reserved at birth?)

And, as it develops, the concept of common heritage will inevitably be the focus of many conflicts. Conflicts between preservation of the past and creation of the future; this will be aggravated by the fact that the emerging societies of the Third World, preoccupied with pulling themselves out of poverty will find Western society's dream of turning its environment into a permanent garden-museum totally incomprehensible. Conflicts between raising the living standards of present generations and reducing long-term risks for the generations to come. Conflicts between the conservation of heritage and the pursuit of their own private interests by limited human groups. Conflicts between the international community and governments which may seem ready to sacrifice ethnic groups, works of art, or archeological sites. There is no simple institutional answer. On the contrary, it will be by feeling our way, choosing organisations that reflect current needs and relationships, and by tolerating pluralism that we shall have a better chance of improving the management of this common heritage. UNESCO is indispensible; the innumerable scientific associations are no less invaluable. If a new President Carter were to emerge speaking of human rights (with less naïvety), all the better. That would not negate the usefulness of Amnesty International. It is absolutely essential that visits to places of interest be regulated, and at the same time it is vital that each tourist feel personally responsible for the damage which he does to the environment.

Though it is betrayed daily and invoked without conviction in political discussions, the concept of common heritage will establish itself slowly but surely as nation-states disintegrate. Bearing this in mind it would surely not be a waste of time for moralists, biologists, and economists to devote some serious thought to it, and explain to us how and why the heritage of all mankind is more than the sum of its individual or national parts.

# Monetary chaos – until when?

After flows and stocks, come mechanisms, and first of all the one that regulates the working of this mysterious stage on which the monetary shadows of streams of oil, wheat or textiles move about. With each real exchange of one thing, its double moves in the opposite direction. The more familiar the first one seems, the more puzzling the second becomes, both by its nature and the laws which govern it. Moreover, although the crisis of the international monetary system is on everyone's lips, that is often where the debate ends... It is too technical, dull, and abstract a subject. Nonetheless, if it is limited to the basics, analysis proves more simple than it appears. The functions of the IMS (as the experts call it) are two-fold. Providing those who make foreign transactions with means of payment that are acceptable to their correspondents. Allowing the central banks to stock means of payment in anticipation of future transactions. The first of these functions opens onto the problem of exchanges, and the second onto the problem of reserves.

Shortly after the Second World War, the Bretton-Woods conference gave a simple answer to these two questions that was based entirely on the difference in size between the American economy and that of the other national economies:

1. Currencies would be freely exchanged into dollars at fixed rates, and each country would strive to bring into operation macroeconomic policies that would ensure full employment, stable prices, and an equilibrium of its balance of payments. Should this balance show a persistent deficit, then it must devalue its currency. If it was merely

experiencing temporary difficulties, it could overcome them with the help
of loans from a new organization – the International Monetary Fund.

2. The reserves of the central banks would be held in dollars or gold.

This system worked for about twenty years in the shadow of American
predominance. A predominance which produced manifold effects: indifference to the foreign balance deficit of the United States, tolerance of the
surpluses of other countries, and a steady energy price. On the national
level, it facilited the short-term regulation of economies through fixed
rates of exchange. In return it was consolidated by low national rates of
inflation. Let us pay tribute to the Bretton-Woods decisions, for it is
thanks to them that the current productive structures of developed
countries were created, and that international trade has experienced the
greatest expansion of its entire history.

So, whence the IMS crisis?

From its two shortcomings and its success.

The first shortcoming: it did not impose any restrictions on the United
States' foreign debt which could be constantly financed by printing
money. "An extravagant privilege," to quote de Gaulle. The result? The
creation of huge international liquid assets, further accelerated by the
multiplying phenomenon of credit, a credit based on the dollars held by
non-Americans (the famous Euro-dollars). Hence a reinforcement of
world inflationist tendancies. Long before oil prices went up. What a
paradox! Whereas in the past, in the days of the gold standard, the
volume of international liquid assets was under control and governments
had rather to find means of regulating the issuing of money by their own
banking systems, the development of international liquid assets was
getting out of all control at the very time when national methods of
containing credit were being perfected.

The second shortcoming? The system did not force countries with
surpluses to reevaluate their currency. Consequently, by slowing down
the adjustment of the rates of exchange between the various currencies, it
helped to create increasing disparities in economic performance and
artificial distortions in the productive structures of different countries.

As for its success, it resulted (as we already know) in the lessening of
the relative economic influence of the United States. The consequences
towards the end of the Sixties were a worsening of its trade balance,
growing nervousness on the part of the economic agents about the
American balance of payments deficit or the surpluses of other countries,
and the increasingly difficult task of making the dollar play an asymmetrical role.

Under such conditions, one of the pillars of the system was bound to give way. In the first stage, it had to be exchange control. Its death was announced in the Azores[47] and confirmed in Jamaica.[48] Fixed exchange rates were no more. Long live floating exchange rates! But at the same time a period of decline of the dollar as a reserve currency (in other words, the collapse of the second pillar) was beginning.

It was on this ramshackle monetary system, characterised by an absence of discipline in the regulation of exchange rates, the fragility of the principal reserve instrument (the dollar), and the weakness of the constraints imposed on national adjustment policies, that the tidal wave of oil shocks crashed twice. Hence an upheaval of the landscape: a state of relative equilibrium of all balances of payments (except that of the United States) was followed by an enormous surplus held by OPEC countries, offset by an equivalent deficit among importer countries, whether developed or not. This surplus meant that a huge mass of floating capital what was increasing by the month was loaned to the developed countries, sometimes in one currency, sometimes in another, depending on expected exchange rates, and the developed countries in turn had to lend a part of that stock to the Third World to enable it to buy what it needed to survive. It was as if the old ship of the monetary system, tossed by the storm, was constantly taking on great quantities of water with each roll. The instability of the international monetary system was thus tremendously increased.

Nothing demonstrates this more clearly than the double development of the Eighties.

1982. Faced with the growing debt of the Third World in the context of a world economic recession, the commercial banks took fright and balance of payment crises spread like wildfire: Mexico, Brazil, Argentina, Venezuela, black Africa, Southern Europe, Korea... to mention but a few. Were these crises of liquidity or solvency? The answer is not definitive. However, it would seem that the period of acute danger is past.

During the same period, the combination of American budgetary qnd monetqry policies made US real interest rates rise, resulting in massive flows of capital to the United States and a regular rise in the value of the dollar. A dollar which began to move towards a more realistic exchange rate from the beginning of 1985. But there is no proof that the landing will be a smooth one, and that an overly-sharp fall might not open the way for new fluctuations.

That was the past. Now let us move on to the future.

There will be no international monetary system in the near future. Let us say it less forcefully and more precisely: because of the political and economic upheavals taking place, it will be difficult to set up in the next decade a world-wide monetary system that would be stable, and which would not create major negative effects.

The difficulties revolve around four poles: exchange control, the coordination of economic policies, the creation of international liquid assets, and the reorientation of financial flows.

We are free to lay wreaths on the grave of fixed exchange rates. They will not rise again. Henceforth, and for a long time, it is inevitable that exchange rates will be variable and (even if governments change their behaviour) will fluctuate needlessly, because of the wide spread of national rates of inflation, because of the short-term arbitrages of the holders of capital between the different currencies, because of reactions that are difficult to foresee and which could bring about variations in the American balance deficit, and because of non-monetary phenomena: the considerable volume of oil imports, the value of which depends on a few price decisions, the rather varied sensitivity of different countries to imports and exports in relation to exchange rates, the slowness and inefficiency of the mechanisms which tend to restore trade balances in response to variations in exchange rates. The time when devalution easily restored the equilibrium of a country's balance of payments is long past: a devaluation of the franc or lira will push up the oil bill, does not always boost exports, and is not attractive to short-term capital investments that depend on interest and profit from future exchanges.

This instability of exchange rates has a negative impact on economic growth, since it reduces investments because of the uncertainty of future profits from any export transaction, reinforces protectionist trends, and produces inflationary tendencies when prices rocket. And full 'market' solutions may not prevail in the future. Governments will try to control the swings, to separate the wheat from the tares, and medium-term trends from transitory fluctuations. It is doubtful that they will succeed without attacking the mechanisms which create liquidities.

But here the problem of exchange links up with that of national macroeconomic policies. How? One does not need to be a great economist to understand it. If the balance of payment deficit is not easily absorbed by exchange fluctuations, governments have only one other alternative: to reduce national production and consumption levels so as to reduce imports. I hear you ask: and exports? Certainly. But increasing their share of the market requires time and effort since every country is trying to do the same thing, and as for increasing the volume of world-wide exports, this presupposes a coordination of the economic policies of the bigger countries. And that is where we are now! Over the past few years, the developed countries have, in fact, replaced the search for a cooperative solution with national policies through which each one strives to find the best strategy given the behaviour of the others. Recent history is full of examples: in 1977 the United States, Germany and Japan did not agree to be the locomotives of a recovery; in 1981 the Reagan administration maintained a policy of interest rates that pushed Europe deeper into depression. Why has cooperation between these countries become so difficult, and why is there a danger that this trend will become more pronounced tomorrow? The answer is contained in several complementary proposals:

Firstly, the decline of the U.S hegemony deprives the system of an accepted leader.

Secondly, the interference of circumstances and structural elements complicates the task of governments enormously.

Thirdly, within each country, the multiplication of the national governing bodies concerned already makes arbitration difficult on a national level, and this limits freedom of action in the intergovernmental arena proportionately.

And lastly, conflicts between internal political imperatives and international needs are getting worse. Governments with small majorities, subject to short terms, besieged with conflicting demands, and hampered by their own bureaucracy, find themselves with less room for manoeuvre. Thus, on both sides of the Atlantic, Ronald Reagan and François Mitterand, elected within a few months of each other, proposed radically different macroeconomic policies to their respective electorates.

In any case, the result is obvious. And this is one of the sequences that are helping to reduce world economic growth.

However, the real Gordian knot of the crisis of the monetary system concerns the creation of liquid assets. Let us listen to one of the world's leading monetary experts: "Neither stable exchange rates nor floating exchanges rates can work satisfactorily if there is no restrictive international control of the incredible explosion of international liquidity raised for the market in the past few years by the monetary authorities and the commercial banking system."[49] Here are some startling figures: calculated in dollars at current market prices, world currency reserves tripled over the six years between 1973 and 1978. They went up from 191 to 571 billion dollars. An annual growth rate of around 20%, naturally bearing no relation to the possible expansion of world production and international trade! One third of this growth was due to the accumulation by central banks of dollars and Eurodollars as international reserves; almost all of the remainder resulted from the increase in the price of gold which created surpluses in the accounts of central banks. As for American engagements with official foreign holders, by the end of 1978 they reached 194 billion dollars, fifteen times total reserves at the end of 1972. Result? The combination of floating exchange rates with the dizzy expansion of world reserves suppresses a major restraint to inflationary national policies. Whereas all the textbooks of political economy explain that on the national level, governments have had to perfect procedures for regulating the amount of money issued by the banks, economists can only verify that the same mechanisms that cause a multiplication of credits have reappeared on the international level. The second negative effect: whereas on a worldwide scale investment needs are enormous and meeting them should be the object of rigourous selection, the laxism of financing contributes to waste in the use of world savings and facilitates the improper recourse to equipment-intensive technology.

There are three solutions:

• Create a sort of world central bank vested with extensive powers over the issuing of international currency (the experts' special drawing rights), the monitoring of exchange rates, credit grants to governments experiencing difficulties with payments, and the control of their economic policy. Marvellous! On paper. For there is a long road ahead before cooperation between governments becomes close enough for such a system to work.

• Form regional sub-systems each with their own reserve currency and rules for adjusting exchange rates. An intermediary stage that could then lead either to the first solution, or to fluctuation of groups of currencies in relation to each other. This is the path of the European monetary system and the Ecu.

• Seek the constant approximation of an acceptable solution, produced by the self-discipline of each country. In short, voluntary cooperation without any constraint.

Bearing in mind the configuration of political power relations, the most likely solution will be an uncertain exploration of the third option, tempered by a reinforcement of the European monetary system. Within this context, the principal asset of the dollar will be the fact that possible substitutes do not seem capable of widely developing their role. Certainly, in a world marked by political and economic tensions, gold will continue to play a significant role. National currencies or Special Drawing Rights have very little chance of seeing their position clearly reinforced: in fact, it is hard to see what coalition of countries could today impose on others a significant increase of Special Drawing Rights, especially if international liquid assets are abundant. On the other hand, the international role of certain currencies may well develop: the diversification of the reserves of central banks, and an increase in the number of transactions in currencies other than the dollar will lead to an extended use of the currencies of strong economies (West Germany and Japan). But the international supply of these currencies will not be unlimited: very dependent on the outside world, the countries concerned do not wish to see their foreign balances grow too much, for they are a source of potential instability in the exchange market; besides, the absorption capacity of their monetary and financial markets is limited. So both public and private diversification is bound to be slow. As for Europe, it will not be able to have a currency that is truly common and therefore capable of being used as a reserve currency by others except at the end of a very thorough, and inevitably long process of integration. Altogether it is most likely that the dollar will continue to be the world's principal payment and reserve currency, but in the future its relative influence will be clearly lessened...

Is the stack of cards not in danger of tumbling? Is the present crisis, cruelly, only the prologue to an extensive catastrophe? The sequence has been described many times; recalling it should be enou ;h. But not without presenting beforehand the last component, the reorientation of financial flows.

When oil prices shot up in 1973, the whole world wondered: how will the holders of capital in OPEC countries find borrowers? It seemed impossible. Different people came up with different solutions. Some suggested that the IMF should be the one to borrow and reloan; others thought that it should be governments. None of that materialised, because it required cooperation between governments. And there was a very simple solution. One that had the tacit backing of the United States: leave it in the hands of the big international (mainly American) banks. And quietly, with remarkable adaptability, acting on the basis of unwritten professional rules, the international banking system – about twenty banks – reoriented financial flows to an incredible extent. The rough and incomplete estimates recorded by the Bank of International Settlements show a net increase of around 330 billion dollars of private loans between 1976 and 1979. Of the net total of the foreign financial resources of developing countries, loans from private banks accounted for 3.4% of the total in 1970; by 1977 this figure had reached 27.2%. An amazing balancing act!

Then came the second oil shock. Before the non-oil-producing developing countries could have the time to absorb a part of their deficit. For 1980 alone the extra debt inflicted on these countries was more than 4% of their GNP, and the total amount outstanding reached 25% of this same GNP in spite of previous debts being lightened owing to the depreciation of the dollar. In that year, for each 100 dollars of Third World export, 24 went towards paying debts, as opposed to 10 only in 1973![50] As for the banking system, it became increasingly hesitant about accepting from oil-producing countries short-term loans that it must reloan to countries that were almost insolvent.

The present functioning of the system is therefore extraordinarily fragile. Because they all go together: the creation of international liquid assets, the money market, the volume of national currency masses in circulation, and the international financial market. One understands the fear that for the first time, gripped bankers at the Toronto meeting of the World Bank in 1982. The fear that other developing countries might follow certain Eastern bloc countries and Mexico and renege on their debts, placing the banks in a difficult position, that economic agents might begin to withdraw their deposits, setting off cumulative waves of panic. The last bulwark being a collective guarantee given by governments to the lenders. This hypothesis is however less likely than an (almost equally gloomy) alternative – the banking system's refusal to finance the development of a part of the Third World, with the result that these countries are forced to reduce their growth sharply, with the shadow of a terrible recession extending over the whole world.

All the same, some progress has been made in the last three years. Both with the banks and the governments of debtor countries. The Authority of the IMF has grown, and this has resulted in control of the international volume of liquidities. Even though the conditions imposed on debtor countries are very harsh, the IMF may at least be credited with forcing banks to keep up their loans to these countries, and to extend them in certain cases.

Few areas illustrate the systemic nature of international relations so well. The crisis of the Bretton-Woods system is the result of the crumbling of the econmic and political foundations on which it was built and which its functioning helped to undermine... But the crisis has not prevented the system from developing degraded modes of operation. Modes which more or less ensure the redistribution of liquid assets. A precarious adjustment that could collapse at any time the way a front crumbles in wartime, or it could be consolidated little by little as cooperation in a multi-polar world progresses.

# Free or organised trade?

The regulation of monetary flows is counterbalanced by the regulation of real flows, and economics had not yet been christened when the debate between the supporters of state control of all foreign trade and the partisans of the free movement of people and goods began. A debate that was listened to sometimes attentively, sometimes absent-mindedly by statesmen and high officials who were compelled to apply themselves empirically to day-to-day administration. Depending on the times, the conflict either raged or smouldered under the ashes of the dominant ideology. Twice since the end of Eighteenth Century, Britain, and then the United States, imposed a measure of free trade and proclaimed the superiority of the market as a manifest truth, but within the same time period, the October Revolution had given birth to the first economy in which the state had a monopoly of all trade. On the threshold of the great post-war growth, the United States entrusted the OECD and GATT[51] with the task of keeping a vigilant eye on the treasure of the official doctrine: Long live the market! The coals seemed to be almost extinguished.

With the recession, they have begun to glow again, setting fire to the twigs and overheating the large logs. Voices are raised in defence of protectionism. The voices of manufacturers, and of trade unionists when factories close. The serious voices of academics, secretly glad to have something new to write. Meanwhile, the politicians get going: acting furtively when dealing with other countries; and with great pronouncements at home. Application feeds the flames of the debate.

But there are obviously two sides to the question. A question of doctrine that bears on the advantages of this or that institutional framework within tomorrow's multipolar, interdependent world. An issue for prospective analysis that concerns the likely development of the rules which currently govern international trade.

Everyone is familiar with the argument of those who support free trade. The market, which ensures the best allocation of production and factors, allows the greatest growth of all participating countries. Unfortunately, pure unvarnished economic theory, true economic theory, does not agree. It is content with stating that with 'perfect' national and international markets, incomes are such that it is impossible to increase the income of one country without reducing that of at least one other country. The fact that all benefit from trade must be demonstrated case by case... And there is nothing to make the resulting distribution of national revenues acceptable to us. Furthermore, markets are never perfect. They are non-existent when trade is no more than internal flows between factories of the same group; often dominated by a small number of buyers or sellers, states or transnational groups, they do not take into account in their functioning secondary effects on the social structure, technological development, or the education of the people of a country or region. More basically, they disregard national societies that are struggling for their economic development.

Should we therefore cry: "Long live protectionism?" This is a double error. Firstly, because protectionism, with its quotas, customs duties and regulations, is not the only way of influencing the working of international markets. Regional aid, subsidies to investment and employment, the financing of research, the manipulation of State markets, foreign loans at favourable rates, the use of ambassadors as commercial travellers, these are all actions that interfere with markets by more subtle means.

And, because protectionism (which is supposed to facilitate the development of new activities or the reconstruction of the economy sheltered by a defensive wall) often leads to ossification. It gives new life to the hackney carriages and sailing ships of the day. It makes one lose the habit of playing economic tennis in the top class. It sanctions laxity in cost control. It is extolled as something that facilitates change, but it sounds the death knell of adjustment. The easiest thing in the world to get into, but much more difficult to get out of.

Besides, beyond protectionism itself, all government policies pertaining to interaction with international markets raise two problems: the validity of their objectives and the efficacy of their measures.

Maintaining stock, facilitating the disappearance or contraction of declining activities, increasing future competitiveness. These are the objectives. The first of them is illusory because in a world in upheaval, society ends up rejecting the growing cost that it generates. Let us smash the smokescreen of their justifications and ask our British friends: how sweet must be not to modify one's habits while others must! How bitter not to have done it when others enjoy the higher income that they have created by taking the appropriate steps. The second objective is a legitimate one. Why should a worker from Lorraine be the cruel victim of the competitiveness of Japanese steel? But an iron hand is needed to prevent the groups that should adapt from exploiting the management of the transition in order to perpetuate the present. As for the third, it is the only truly creative one, but there is a great risk of diverting it from the gaps of the future, and to salvage doomed activities in the vain hope of a miraculous diversification that will make it possible to graft healthy, vigourous, new activities onto the worm-eaten wood of declining firms. The fact is that these three objectives are rooted in a deeper one: that of satisfying (in a political market that is even more imperfect than the economic one) group after group of minorities that have a great deal to loose, and which know how to organise themselves to negociate.

The objectives of state action are often debatable, and from the point of view of efficiency they are clearly not above reproach. Let us beware of facile sarcastic remarks: the incoherence of successive or simultaneous decisions, slow procedures (is it not true that IBM was able to design and launch a new generation of computers before the French state could manage to resolve the first Bull affair?), the unwieldliness of created institutions, the inability to do away with existing organisations... Here is where the real superiority of the market lies: like Revolution in politics, it is the Great Destroyer, but an anonymous destroyer that the anger of its victims cannot burn in effigy for it has thousands of heads. Have you ever seen the workers of a factory that is in difficulty smash up the offices of their customers because they do not make enough orders? How much easier it is to turn on a minister, that controller of the omnipotence of the state which has refused to act!

This backdrop is common to almost all times and all countries. But it should be given new colours – suited to the world that is being created. With an American economy that is discovering foreign competition, Japan in top exporting form, middling European economies that want to hold on to their freedom of decision (West Germany, France, Britain, Italy), small developed economies (like Finland) that have played the open economy game and are pondering their future, Eastern bloc countries that are seeking to benefit fully from the advantages of their state-run trade (the disadvantages cost them enough), new industrial countries that are both exporters and protectionists, countries that produce mineral and agricultural raw materials and which are disturbed by the fluctuations of their market, poor countries that are fearful of having the timid candle of their nascent industrialisation blown out by high winds... And most of them absolutely must buy oil and food products.

In all these cases the balance of institutional strategies is different, but the preferred solution is hardly ever either free trade or protectionism.

For a long time, it will be in the interest of the strong ones (OECD countries for industrial products and grain, OPEC for oil) to favour the market, apart from limiting or organising its functioning. They have established business concerns, and their governments have no desire to hand over their power to international bureaucracies. The weak ones (mostly in the Third World) would gladly favour, not protectionism, but trade control organisations, hoping secretly that with one seat per country in councils the price of their products would go up and their trade would no longer be at the the mercy of the Greats.

As for the extent to which economies are open and the form that government policies take, the situation is equally varied.

In the cases of the United States and the EEC, the size of their domestic markets is so huge that there is little to be gained from waiting for economies of scale in production (through trade). Specialisation, so as to take advantage of the range of prices throughout the world? Yes, as long as they retain the ability to regenerate the activities that have disappeared. And, as far as the EEC is concerned, excluding the leading activities that control the future, and excluding agriculture, that gardian of present political stability and security for tomorrow. Furthermore, industrial policies must inevitably differ. The United States is well represented in the high technology industries with which each of the great European countries is determined to keep up, strengthening its only champion if necessary, while the small countries of the Community can only count on their patchy collection of transnationals. The United States is not really forced to square its foreign balance while European countries must export industrial goods in order to import energy and raw materials.

As for Japan, its strategy is clear. Abandon those sectors whose disadvantages are too great. Perfect innovations on the domestic market, and then make huge exports in gaps where large sections of the market may be conquered. Guarantee its imports of energy, raw materials and food products through the flow of trade and investments. Limit its industrial imports through the structure and performance of its economic agents without having to resort to protectionism. Negociate compromises whenever its exports threaten to provoke retaliation and endanger the openness of international commerce.

But for developed countries, measuring free trade by the yardstick of economy would mean having a blinkered view of the world. The stake is a social one, for the opening of economic frontiers is part of the battle against ossification. To be modified only when there is a risk that the limits of social plasticy are in danger of being overstepped. It is also political, for there is a need both to be prepared for future revolutions in the Third World, and to consolidate the international system by fully incorporating the new industrial nations.

And as for these countries, they would adapt very well to an asymmetrical situation: the partial closing of their economies and opening of the economies of developed countries. They have strong protectionist traditions. And as is the case with Latin America and India, they have even endangered their industrial development for a long time by allowing the emergence, and then the maintenance, of inefficient concerns with exhorbitant manufacturing costs... Their (justified) fears? Sudden changes in the import policies of developed countries, changes that can ruin overnight ten years of patient effort to build an industrial sector. It should be possible to come to a mutually beneficial agreement with OECD countries: the latter would open their frontiers wider and make a medium-term pledge not to change their rules in exchange for a diversification of exports and a reduction of protectionism on the part of the new industrial countries.

As for the poor, sparsely populated countries, they often over-estimate the value of the international trade of industrial products. With domestic markets that are (and will continue to be) small, and competition with other developing countries for OECD markets, they are in danger of finding more disappointment and bitterness than success on the road to industrialization. What is really at stake for them? We already know it: their exports of minerals and agricultural products. They mainly hope for prices to stabilise and go up.

What answer can one give to the first question? That in an interdependent world without a regulator, the different groups of countries will not have the same immediate interests regarding the way in which international trade is organised. Worse still, that each nation will find itself constantly in a series of *squeezes* as far as the institutional framework of international trade goes. *Squeezes* that will be all the more tricky because the effects of the policies of one country will depend on the policies of the others. The first *squeeze*: the opening or closing of frontiers, but opening them means forcing oneself to make certain adjustments, containing local falls in income, risking repercussions of unpredictable foreign events; closing them means starting off along the road to inflexibility and accepting a relative fall in the standard of living. The second *squeeze*: developing international trade by means of bilateral agreements or by a general liberalisation; but bilateralism destroys the advantages of free trade while free trade makes it difficult to eliminate market imperfections. The third *squeeze*: filling in the gaps (or not) in the general liberalisation of trade by national support measures; but 'filling in the gaps' means risking a return to indirect protectionism and not doing it means suffering the unmitigated effects of international competition.

However this is too narrow a vision. We should not leave the debate on the regulation of international trade up to the specialists. Just like industrialists or trade unionists, they are too insensitive to what determines the long-term future of a nation. And my opinion is based on a comprehensive interpretation of the international system. I believe that the industrial societies of the West will have to reduce their vulnerability in the vital gaps such as energy, but it will be in their interest to struggle to maintain, and even extend, international markets in order to protect themselves from themselves and contribute to the future political balance of the world. And this will exclude neither efforts to correct the shortcomings of the market, nor national industrial or agricultural policies aimed at getting themselves in shape for playing the game.

Let us turn over the page of doctrine and consider prospective analysis. But in order to evaluate the range of options, we still need to know the point of departure.

On the whole there is no doubt that there has been a recent rise in 'neo-protectionism.' Indeed, international trade has continued to be dynamic, but this expansion means deceleration compared with the rhythm of the last quarter century. Above all, it is taking place within a framework that is increasingly characterised ( appearances notwithstanding) by protectionist practices: though only a few countries have adopted mechanisms for limiting their overall imports, measures for protecting different sectors have been adopted by a great many (especially in the case of traditional industries such as textiles, steel and shipbuilding, shoes, televisions, and certain mechanical items, as well as high technology sectors such as the electronics, arms and aerospace industries); these measures vary, ranging from bilaterally negociated

trade restrictions to the erection of non-tariff barriers such as administrative regulations for certain products; perhaps more significant than
the development of measures closely linked with trade is the multiplicity
of government interventions aimed at strengthening the position of
concerns in the worldwide competitive game (sale or employment
subsidies, tax exemptions, capital shares, preferential credit for exports).
Similarly, the balance of the latest multilateral trade negociations
(Tokyo Round) confirms the impression that the international community is becoming rather breathless in its effort to liberalise international
trade. The importance of questions relating to tariffs in these negociations is already an indication of a certain gap between the aim of the
mutual concessions secured and the reality of the problems. The predicted reduction of customs duties by 25% (spread over 8 years) is not only
small, especially compared with its effect on the international price of a
product that can be caused by fluctuations in exchange rates; it bypasses
the problem of exceptionnally high tariffs in countries like the United
States and Japan. But it is above all in the non-tariff area that the results
achieved, though not negligible, fall short of initial ambitions.

   Also to be taken into account is another major trend of internationql
trade – the increasing role of the services in trade: banking and insurance
services, the supply of computer software, patent royalties, engineering
services. Even within the Common market, the problems they pose to
free trade are still far from being resolved. This gives some inkling of the
difficulty of the task related to this issue that awaits the next GATT
conference.

   Is this diagnosis accurate? We may well wonder, for at the end of six
years of economic difficulties basic international trade does not seem to
be threatened. Certainly, the probability of protectionism escalating is
not zero. American trade unions, a good proportion of the Congress,
Lord Kaldor and other Labour economists, a section of French
Socialists, and the farmers of the Community strongly recommend
protectionist measures – against Japan and the Third World. But many
other forces are acting long-term in favour of retaining a liberal trade
framework. The industrialised countries are increasinly adopting
industrial strategies that presuppose world-wide markets and build their
units of production accordingly. The countries that are in the process of
being industrialised demand free access to the markets of developed
countries. Transnational companies practise the international division
of labour. The international banks commit themselves heavily to
countries which must be able to export in order to remain solvent...
Finally, a growing dependence on imports (of raw materials, agricultu-

ral products, energy, and manufactured products) constitutes the most effective initiative for expanding exports, and consequently, for the struggle against protectionist temptations.

Hence the range of options remains wide, but everything would seem to indicate that in the multipolar, interdependent world that is coming into being, the institutional framework of international trade will be neither simple nor stable. 'Free or organized trade?' was my question. I should say 'free *and* organised trade' because they will coexist. Affected by many contradictory trends. The competition between the United States, Japan, and the EEC will be stepped up. More and more frequently, the governments of developed countries will devise industrial and commercial policies, and at times, they will take over the control of their exports through intermediary actors. They will strive to create zones of preferential trade around them (Europe in Africa and the Middle East, Japan in Southern Asia). Industrial Third World countries will seek to develop intra-South trade, while at the same time trying to obtain a redefinition of the framework of international trade. There will be friction between OECD countries and Eastern bloc countries that have the power to use the centralisation of their economies to fix export prices which bear no relation to manufacturing costs, and which have destabilising effects on the producers with whom they are competing. Within such a context, partial and successive reforms of the institutional framework of international trade may well see the light of day: supervision by a new institution of GATT and UNCTAD,[52] The two international organisations that act in this area, the former being intellectually close to the Western World, and the latter to the Third World; the organisation of the markets for commodities (coffee, cocoa, cotton, copper, tin...) with stabilising funds for each product and an overall federal fund; the introduction of compulsory consultative procedures and time for reflection before the adoption of any protectionist measures; every country being able to appeal to a court of arbitration if it believes that its interests are endangered by indirect protectionist action... But the road will be long and confused, for any progress in the regulation of trade must go hand in hand with a consolidation of the international monetary and financial system, and greater political cooperation.

It would have been much easier for me as a writer to proclaim the triumph of liberalism or the inevitable rise of protectionism, but the tea leaves and crystal ball do not give such clear signs.

Young officials, if you have a passion for the intricacies of trade regulations, if you dream of nothing but widespread preferential systems, if lowering customs duties on Indian hockey sticks, or stemming the flood of Mauritian handkerchiefs gives you the shivers, do not be alarmed: in ten years, there will be room for you.

# The institutions of interdependence

The institutions of interdependence are just one step away from the regulation of trade, a step that both liberals and socialists make cheerfully, transferring their quarrels from the theme of protectionism to that of international planning.

Happy to find at last a worldwide arena. Happy also to escape from the mire of their doctrinal debates on national levels. Long live a Worldwide New Socialist Order! shout the young technocrats of the South who have been educated by the socialists of Western universities; only a form of planning can redistribute resources. Some American professors, on the point of apoplexy, hurl back above the din, "The market! The market! Is it this totalitarian, inefficient socialism which has failed within the narrow confines of national borders, that you want to extend over the whole world?" Planning? For whom? The nation-state is strong, and there is nothing more misleading than comparing the parliament of a democratic country with the General Assembly of the United Nations.

These are pointless debates, for apart from the market, interdependence is in the process of creating institutions. Weaving a web that is far more complex than the cramped schemes of theoreticians. A web in which the 'whatchamacallit' ("machin"), as de Gaulle once called it, despite its importance, is only one element. We must also reverse the perspective, start from the bottom, discover the extraordinary richness of the institutional melting pot in which we shall be living, and only move up very slowly towards the heavy, multipurpose intergovernmental machinery that seems to rise above the fray.

The priority? International associations made up of individuals. We do not often reflect upon the fact that every scientific and cultural elite in the world (and even to a certain extent, including totalitarian countries) is involved in an association that knows no frontiers. Science, that major phenomenon of our time is basically run by a host of independent international republics, each of which has its president, government, elections, newspapers, rules governing naturalization, its Legion of Honour... The defence of human rights is taken care of by Amnesty International and the League of Human Rights, to cite only two examples. The restoration of certain monuments is made possible by friendly associations that are financed by funds from all over the world. Development aid for Cambodian refugees and the starving people in Ethiopia mobilises the efforts of a multitude of associations.

Ah! If only governments, rather than believing their administrators or their permanent delegations (selfish guardians of their interests in intergovernmental organisations), would entrust a part of their aid budgets to independent foundations! They would make a great contribution to the solution of certain problems of our day: foundations for research in the Third World; foundations for adapted technologies; foundations for agricultural development; educational foundations...

Need one recall the role of the Churches here? Whether they proceed from one or another of the three great monotheistic religions, whether they are growing or passing through a crisis, they play a tremendous part in interdependence. The Pope is a bond linking the Polish worker in Gdansk and the inhabitant of Recife. The Marrakesh believer and the Afghan who is felled by Soviet bullets belong to the Islamic community. In both cases this creates a loyalty over and above the national one.

Mentioning transnational companies in passing does not mean that we have a taste for scandal: they too educate men, by training them in business life and making them take part in strategies that transcend nations. The fact that a large majority of their top staff presently come from their countries of origin should not obscure what they are working towards: a gradual internationalisation of their technostructures. They demand of each person more and less than a church does. Less because they do not impose a monist vision of the world and they do not examine the heart and soul. More, because they demand the daily pursuit of precise aims through adaptive and creative behaviour.

The climate changes with the international technical organisations. Whether one is dealing with the International Postal Union, the World Meteorological Organisation, or the International Railway Union..., it is now functionaries who sit in councils and commissions. The defence of national interests and respect for orders are beginning to emerge. Nonetheless these men feel close to each other in two ways: they share the knowledge (and often the love) of the same technology, and what unites them also separates them from others within their own country. They have concrete problems to solve: measuring campaigns for the meteorologists, tariff agreements for the post office and railway employees and the distribution of frequencies for the telecommunications people. Because they are cautious and wary of the media, because their debates tend to be dry, the considerable part that they play today and will play to an even greater extent tomorrow in the organisation of interdependence is too often unappreciated. Another path to explore? That of the regional clubs of governments which join forces for specific tasks. An example? The Sahel Club: around the table are eight African countries suffering from common problems, and a few developed countries prepared to help them to realise clearly defined projects. It must be obvious that by defining objectives and reducing the number of members, such formulas are less likely to be swallowed up in the quicksand of generality and abstractions! They should prove effective for encouraging cooperation between developed and developing countries within the Balkanised areas of the Third World such as tropical Africa or the Caribbean.

Broaden the objectives and a step is made in the direction of complexity. Multi-purpose regional organisations prove to be much more difficult to create and above all, to keep alive: the Arab League, ASEAN, the West African Economic Community and the Andean Pact. What a lot of corpses for a few successes! The lack of a federator, centrifugal forces, the political instability of member countries, and the unwieldliness of bureaucracies have often emptied of all meaning projects that were over-ambitious from the start. But so great is the hope of reducing the vulnerability that goes with interdependence by creating huge economic zones with self-centred development, that they will always rise from their ashes. But for them to have at least some chance of success, those who promote them should at least ensure that several minimal conditions are met: a hard core of two or three countries whose political continuity and common interests will serve as an anchoring point for the whole operation; the ability to resist outside pressures; the absence of internal obstacles that are so powerful (transport costs, for instance) that they prevent any emergence of an embryonic common market...

And here we are, halfway through. Let us stop for a moment. A clew is already appearing: for one or two decades, the international system has been experiencing an *à la carte world*. In the sense that Louis Armand and Michel Drancourt used the term when speaking of Europe.[53] Individuals, enterprises, associations and governments, are in the process of developing the vast institutional network of interdependence, but they each choose their restaurants, make up their menus, and fix the constraints that they impose. In return, habits are formed, mentalities are created, solidarities are established, and a fabric is woven. A fabric which is sometimes torn by the tensions of multipolarity, but which is then restored differently, based on new relationships and different supports.

One more step towards globality, and what do we find? The two great military pacts of the East and West – the North Atlantic Treaty and the Warsaw Pact – whose vitality depends on the strength of their federators, and fluctuates according to Soviet-American tensions... The continental mini-United Nations (the Organisation for African Unity, the Organisation of American States) that are trying – usually in vain – to solve within them regional problems that are subject to much wider range of forces; economic organisations like the OECD for developed countries, or the 77 Group for the Third World. However little control these two last structures may exercise, they present at least one danger: that of ossifying the international economic system by reducing negociations to arrangements between set groups of countries. Were this to happen, (anticipating our future vocabulary) the social oligopoly would be transferred from the national to the international level.[54] With equally disastrous results: the growing rigidity of membership, the globalisation of protest platforms, the substitution of great abstract issues for concrete problems, the impossibility of taking advantage of the complementarities characteristic of sub-groups of countries... The West would gradually turn into an economic ghetto of rich countries, while the new industrial countries would find themselves turned irresistibly into leaders of the proletariat of poor nations. A decisive reason why international life as a whole should not be based on the United Nations system.

And system is precisely the right word. Although we should point out the independent organisations to which Eastern bloc countries do not belong (the World Bank, the International Monetary Fund, and GATT), and the group of UN planets that revolve round the 'Sun' of the General Assembly.

The former (with the OECD) have been instrumental in regulating world economy from the days of the American 'imperium.' This origin has passed on to them some less important internal conflicts and an unquestionable efficiency. Their future will be the choices that Western governments make concerning their mutual relations, and their relations with the Third Worlds. Depending on the degree of collegial structure that will emerge, the OECD will either become a lively organisation, or will confine itself to being a relatively ineffectual think tank. Depending on the development of the monetary system, the IMF will either become a keystone or a mere back-up element. Depending on the strength of protectionist trends, GATT will either manage to channel them, or be swept away by them... The Third World for its part, would gladly take over the whole lot – except the OECD – through the UN. This would be the worst possible solution. We must choose openness by extending the number of countries taking part while preserving independence, which is the guaranty of efficiency.

And finally we come to the planets and the sun: a prospective assessment of their destiny only makes sense in relation to their functions. Specialised actions (for instance the saving of historical sites by UNESCO, and the fight against disease by the WHO) deserve admiration. Let us also congratulate the work of gathering and processing statistics, the effort to disseminate knowledge of social and economic problems throughout the world. This is where total agreement ends: certainly, United Nations teams are sources of suggestions for the development of the international system, but the context within which they operate often leads to passivity or a lack of realism; certainly, the organisation could be a framework for negociation, but its formalism and unwieldliness do not lend themselves to the diplomatic resolution of delicate problems. As for the decisions of the General Assembly, they are such in name only, for they are binding on hardly anyone. We should not be at all surprised: in the multipolar world that we live in, this parliament of states can have only technical powers. The same will hold true for the future. Until the day when, perhaps, a federator arrives that will give the whole ant hill a tremendous kick, or will retain only the façade of structures. A federator which, paradoxically, will base its power on the awareness of human unity that the UN will have popularised.

Furthermore, between now and the end of the century, the institutions of interdependence should give the impression of exhuberant growth, more than that of an organised structure. All the better. Disorder is creative.

# The challenges of the international system

Multipolarity and interdependence. These two themes have been developed in turn like the opening phrases of a duet. A long preparation so that, now, they may answer each other, and their dialogue may form the outlines of what I have called (for lack of a better expression) the third control deficiency. Whether we like it or not, the past has bequeathed to us a world divided into states with precise frontiers whose sovereign governments theoretically have no other limits to their power than those that are the result of the functioning of their national system. It is obvious that interdependence between these states has never been so intense or so complex. What have we observed in fact? A world that is in the throes of a cultural explosion, in which the network of nascent Utopias does not yet have a federating power; a dangerous world in which military power is spreading; a world in which each one needs the oil, grain, or machines of others, but in exchange would like to have one's textiles and cars accepted; a world in which the idea of a common heritage is beginning to gain ground; a world with a fragile monetary system in which a good many countries would like to pass on the grimalkin of their balance of payment deficits; a world that wavers between liberalism and protectionism; finally, a world in which a rich variety of international institutions thrives. But is it possible to give an intelligible structure to the various dimensions of this interdependence?

To a certain extent, yes.

The analysis that has just been outlined confirms the dichotomy mentioned at the beginning of this section: on one hand there are the forms of interdependence that may be understood by looking at every national society as a whole, and on the other hand there are those which imply a distinction between the actors within these same societies.

Among the former we find not only some old acquaintances such as the threat of the use of force, intergovernmental institutions, international rules, and trade flows, but also more subtle relations: the existence of 'public goods' that are common to the whole of humanity and the presence of externalities (please forgive the economist jargon) that a country projects onto others unconsciously, pollution of their territorial waters or free access to their scientific work...

As for the second type of interdependences (i.e. between agents), they are becoming more intense at a time when governments are themselves trying to strengthen their hold on their own societies: military subversion and terrorism, private international organisations, contracts between private persons, trade between economic agents, externalities peculiar to social groups (such as oil pollution for the Bretons) public goods that have no value except to certain communities (such as language for an ethnic group that is split between several states).

Consequently, the same visible phenomenon often covers radically different forms of interdependence. An example? Human migrations: the simple transfer of manpower when the Algerian workers were given permission to enter France by both governments, a peaceful invasion when Mexicans cross the American border illegally; in the case of welcoming political refugees, they express the recognition by national societies of an item of public goods, human life, to which people do not always have the same attitude as their governments.

Master interdependence, certainly. But the issue does not make any sense in the abstract, for its true content depends on the political structure of the international system, on its type of polarity, as the experts of political science would say.

The first of the possible types is the Empire, that political equivalent of the economists' monopoly. A hierarchical system with a central government or quite simply a dominant government that ensures the regulation of the basic interdependences, less by managing the flows themselves, however, than by seeing to it that the rules of the game are respected. Our contemporaries have an example under their noses: the Soviet Union. They remember another example, the American Empire; in fact they know that at the end of the Second World War, despite its great political rivalry with the Soviet Union, the United States found itself in the position of being an uncontested, dominant, economic force. It had a power to determine the rules of the game that the assent of its European allies sanctioned *ipso facto*. Furthermore, the principles promoted by the United States (non-discrimination, reciprocity, the lowering of customs barriers) were not formally questioned by anyone, and the US deliberately refrained from giving priority to its interests alone. Thus it was possible to set up a system of rules which facilitated the efficient reallocation of the factors of production on an international scale. Some have called this an International Economic Order.

After the Empire comes the bipolar system, a political form of economic duopoly. Unstable by nature, it can nonetheless experience the kinds of balance that Soviet-American relations over the past quarter century have illustrated: the Cold War that dodges interdependence by reducing the volume of trade to almost nothing, the condominium that is expressed by a common management of interdependence and of crises; cases that involve the maintenance of a fragile strategic balance, and the fact that it is impossible for either adversary to eliminate the other.

A third type of international system is, curiously, known only to economists: the so-called perfect competition. Its political counterpart may be described thus: no national society could, by itself, change its environment or influence the environment of others; it would have no choice but to adapt itself! No doubt such political decentralisation would manage admirably the interdependences of flows that are open to market prices, but would be helpless when confronted with public goods and externalities. Why does this system hold so little interest for political scientists? Because, in reality, there are always relations between geographic neighbours or inequalities in the distribution of resources that give some national societies a certain power over their environment. Besides, the conditions for perfect political competition are never fulfilled.

There remains one last system: the multipolar system, the political transcription of the oligopoly. Here the balances are complex and unstable, very vulnerable to coalitions or to the development of the strength of players. Interdependence is hard to master: it increases each one's vulnerability to others, and often plunges nations into an unpredictable environment. It is a particularly dangerous system when the actors are inspired by heterogeneous ways of reasoning. As time passes, nothing demonstrates this better than Henry Kissinger's experiment in the White House, an experiment that (in the West) is one of the most coherent attempts at foreign policy of the last twenty years, and which took place at the very moment when Soviet-American bipolarity, while being close to strategic balance, was beginning to crumble; one in which the first outlines of a multipolar world were sketched. Everything is there: the difficulty of cooperation within the Western Alliance with

Americans who continue to act like leaders without having the means, and Europeans or Japanese who show themselves to be incapable of developing policies that measure up to their economic strength; the need for 'linkage,' that bond established in negociations between the various dimensions of interdependence; the interference within American democracy between foreign policy and fluctuations of public opinion that may be instantaneous or take place over a number of years; the clash between Soviet logic which is constantly seeking to exploit the weaknesses of the enemy and erratic and pragmatic American logic which would be happy with the status quo; the obliviousness of Western actors in the face of the imminence of Third World revolutionary logic, logic that comes from the dark areas of the soul, and which great prophets will embody... For the multipolarity that we shall experience will not be a resurrection of the multipolarity of 1750 or 1840 very wisely organised around Great Britain, Austria, Prussia, Russia and France... Tomorrow's multipolarity will embrace the aging duopoly of the United States and the Soviet Empire, and the enormous revolutionary potential of the Third World.

As in modern music, this dialectic of multipolarity and interdependence allows the instrumentalist to choose between several scores. Utopianism? Reflection on the survival of the West? The search for possible policies? Paths that are more complementary than competitive.

Utopias flourish. In all the non-pejorative senses of the word. And they all strive to overcome the challenges of the international system. Let us listen to them. The first advocates a world government that would take on the responsibility of the major interdependences, but has nothing to say on the conditions that would make such a government possible. The spread of the Soviet or Chinese empire over the whole world? The gradual emergence of a supranational power based on the United Nations parliament? One path conjures up the spectre of nuclear holocaust; the second presupposes the solution of the problem. Then comes the divided family of Utopians who seek to destroy interdependence. Some would like to make basic communities quasi-independent, each a kind of modern-day village using all the resources of technology to produce its energy and feed itself; others see autarky on a national level as a means of protecting them from the adverse effects of dominant economies (in the case of the Third World), and safeguarding a privileged standard of living (in the case of the West); a third group, aware of the exorbitant cost of national autarkies, divides the world into blocs; it imagines a Latin American common market, a united black Africa and a reinforced Arab League both maintaining privileged links with Western

Europe, then a Southern Asia and a sphere of Japanese co-prosperity... but finds it difficult to trace the limits of these zones on the map and feels helpless in the face of military imbalances and local hatreds; another group is content to cut the globe up into three, adding a great North-South division to the Northern fault separating East and West; and *voilà*, the South is at last protected from the economic and moral pollution of the West! But within this, how then does one solve the new dominations, by Brazil or the oil-producing Arab countries? A mystery... And a final group of Utopians rally round the flags of cooperation. The red flag of cooperation between peoples, that flag of the masses who cannot be wrong and who, in their innate sense of the welfare of the species, will impose good policies on their governments; the white flag of cooperation between elites, of the scientists' Internationale or governement advisers... In both cases these flags also disguise traitors. Cold realists for whom cooperation is only one of the means of preparing for the future Empire, or the pragmatic means of managing interdependence by creating an evolutive core of countries capable of mastering the changes of the international system.

When these traitors are Westerners, they think (as Général de Gaulle did) in terms of the survival of their civilisation, as all the great political leaders of all times have done. Conscious both of the inevitable flexibility of day to day tactics and the permanent need for strategies devised to ward off long-term danger. For this Western world (in which, for the first time in history, despite inequalities, inflation and unemployment, the level of incomes allows each person to seek quality of life and to be the centre of a personal questioning of the meaning of his existence), is doubly threatened from outside. Just like all the great civilisations that have preceded it.

Threatened by the Soviet Union, that ossified country with its moribund ideology, and uncreative economy, which has concentrated all the vitality of its bureaucratic planning on the methodical construction of peerless military might.

Menaced in the long term by the innumerable external proletariat of the Third World which will eventually demand different distributions of power, and will be the bearer of other religions, other morals, other ideologies.

Two heterogeneous threats: one precise and almost immediate, the other diffuse, enveloping, progressive; one which may well be settled between now and the end of the century, and the other which will only be in full bloom then – if there is still a West. Combatting one while forgetting the other is illusive: arming fragile Pakistan to contain the

Soviet advance to the Afghan border, yet begging for the Soviet contribution to help the Third World.

But the response to this double threat – the Soviet threat and the
threat of the Third World – presupposes one condition: that the West
master its own internal challenges, challenges on the national level that
are analysed in the next section of this book, and challenges of trilateral
cooperation. How? By strengthening the weakest side of the triangle, the
one that joins Europe and Japan. Through Europeans and Japanese
becoming aware of their responsibilities. Through a reexamination of
their behaviour by Americans as a whole... Built on renewed cooperation
between the three great poles that compose it (the United States, Japan,
and the European Community), a Western strategy presupposes policies
(coordinated policies) relating to the Soviet Union and relating to the
Third World.

*Vis à vis* the Soviet Union, the necessary mixture of firmness and
cooperation will evaporate if it is not based on worldwide military
balance and on the ability of Europe and Japan to defend themselves
independently.

What idiocy! With 15% of world income, Eastern bloc countries make
the West and China (who hold more than 70% of this same income)
tremble. As for the EEC, whose overall income is much greater than that
of Warsaw Pact countries, it would not hold out against Soviet agression
for more than three days. We need relative military security in order for a
reasoned cooperation to develop, one that takes into account all
worldwide geopolitical relations and all forms of interdependence. Our
revenue, and our technological ability make it possible for us – if we have
the will to survive.

But Moscow should not make us forget Mexico, Kinshasa, Teheran,
and New Delhi. With regard to the Third World, we need a strategy that
is more than pompous formulas on the New International Economic
Order or a vague feeling of sympathy fed by guilt and Christian charity.
A strategy that rests on the reality of the differentiation of the Third
World. A strategy that masters the development of the international
system.

"Get rich and we will accept you as one of us," we have said to Third
World countries as Guizot said to the masses. It is now up to us to honour
our promise, for it is in the interest of the West to accept the new
industrial countries (that middle class of world economy) on an equal
footing. The clubs of the rich such as the OECD will lose their *raison d'être*
if they become closed clubs for a decadent aristocracy. Let us accept the
new blood of the new bourgeoisie. Let us accept that the essential thing

for these developing countries is a regular increase in their exports, a diversification of their economy, easy access to foreign capital, and participation in the running of world economy. In exchange let us ask them not to inflict too sudden industrial adjustments, not to put up barriers to our exports without reason, and to adopt reliable policies in relation to our investments.

Let us stop seeing oil producing countries as upstarts and let us consider them in the reality of their uncertain tomorrows. They have incredible luck, but it is their only joker. They must extract secure and growing resources from their soil and ensure the success of their development plans for moving smoothly into the post-oil era. It is up to us to adopt vigourous energy policies. It is up to us to make the effort to adapt our exports to programs of development that are realistic for them.

Then come the intermediary countries, the ones for which it is essential to combine aid for the development of subsistence farming, the perfection of modern, adapted industrial techniques, aid for the development of national energy and mineral resources, better management of the markets for basic products, and large, long-term loans.

Then come the poor countries, black Africa and Southern Asia. Countries with gloomy prospects, but the future balance of the world also depends on them. The vital issue? To come up with policies that ensure their populations a certain dignity, even with their anticipated low per capita income. Balkanised as it is in countries that are just barely surviving, the case of black Africa is particularly urgent. These two regions still (and will for a long time) need regional aid plans. It is up to the government of developed countries to understand this.

Finally there is China: it will need the West and the West will need it for several decades, for as it becomes an independent military power, it will become a factor of stability.

But these varied strategies should be answered by a will to channel interdependence. If we would avoid the explosion of an international economic system that is incapable of adapting to the evolution of power relations, let us discard empty words like 'New International Economic Order' – as if one fine day, a world conference were going to create, through a few legal rules, an order for which the conditions, according to all the analyses, have not yet been fulfilled! Let the UN intellectuals wear out their grey matter, and let us be pragmatic. Acting rather than dragging our feet. Rekindling once more the political inspiration which prompted the great American post-war constructions, and which drags governments and people after the cold decisions of administratiions. Everything revolves around five main ideas:

• Helping the non-oil-producing developing countries to reduce their energy dependence by encouraging them to invest in this area with the help of a system of long-term financing, while at the same time making it easier for OPEC countries to enter the post-oil era. This is the number one priority.

• Improving the functioning of the markets for primary products by stabilising export earnings, by reducing import barriers in developed countries, by bearing in mind the impact that the fixing of the prices of agricultural products on the markets of developed countries has on developing countries, and by stepping up food aid.

• Formulating positive policies for structural adjustment in industry. Trying to further a gradual, general lowering of mutual barriers in relations with these countries. Avoiding measures that encourage over-capitalistic forms of industrialisation in the Third World. Setting up active policies dealing with scientific cooperation, the perfection and use of adapted technologies, and education.

• Stepping up food aid. Sharing it differently by geographical zone. Making it a part of a general policy towards the country or group concerned. Orienting it towards satisfying basic needs. Seeking institutional methods that complement the present methods of distributing aid.

• Promoting simultaneously world-wide negociations and multilateral or bilateral negociations on the level of groups of countries. Inventing new forms of regional cooperation. Attaching importance to all forms of non-government co-operation.

This list reveals a basic truth: there is no one correct answer to an interdependent relationship. In the context of today, limiting its energy consumption does not only reduce the vulnerability of a country. It lowers possible future tension within the international system, averts the danger of a breakdown, and increases stability. In a word, a lowering of the level of this first form of interdependence is desirable. A counter-example? Refusing industrial imports from Third World industrial countries slows down growth and may well accentuate the fragmentation of the world into a bourgeoisie and a proletariat... In other words, it is dangerous for the international system to eliminate this second form of interdependence. Desirable policies should be modified according to the degree of interdependence of each field and of each country, but each government should know that by not being aware of the influence of its policies on others, it contributes to the spread of non-cooperative solutions that endanger the functioning of the international system.

For it is eventually the third control deficiency that poses the greatest threat to humanity. The fact that it condemns decadent civilisations is just about acceptable, although we may not agree that this applies to ours; but it can destroy civilisation itself by reproducing on a world scale what happened on Easter Island, or by creating hunger and chaos for a long time. These dangers will probably not be averted until political integration gives birth to a hierarchical de facto or de jure organisation of the world system. By cooperation or by imperial rule. Meanwhile, we must try to learn to manage interdependence in a multipolar world. Aware that only national communities which are sufficiently strong will keep their independence, while those which refuse to open themselves will condemn themselves to decline. Governments' chances to arrive at a balance between external pressures and internal demands will depend on their cohesion and their creative ability.

# DEVELOPED SOCIETIES:
# CONTESTATIONS AND OSSIFICATIONS

"No other civilisation to date has had such power, none has been so alien to its own values. Why conquer the moon if it is to commit suicide there?"

André Malraux
*Le Miroir des limbes.*

# Governments between the devil and the deep blue sea

The international environment of developed societies may change, but basically the daily lives of the citizens within their borders is not interrrupted. Reread the programs and public declarations of the great 1978 legislative battle in France: the world does not exist. The majority speak of nothing but social justice and freedom to act: the socialists talk of nationalisation and reducing inequalities, the communists about cutting out waste and strict planning. In the midst of the oil crisis and one year away from Afghanistan! And the situation was to be practically identical at the time of the presidential elections in 1981. Follow the policy of British trade unions over these last years. What does it matter if Britain goes under as long as the trade unions hold on to their privileges? Think of the American election campaigns: the fact that the candidates are less familiar with the names of other countries than a middle school pupil of twenty years ago is of little consequence compared with promises of savings in the federal budget.

In the aftermath of the Second World War, the men and women of industrial countries were motovated by a double conviction: they believed in their hard-won freedom from Fascism that was constantly threatened by Stalinism; they believed in growth, less as a means of escaping poverty than of regaining their dignity. But once the nightmare of the conflict was driven away, they learned to live without external threats. Détente made them forget the proximity of the Soviet Union, decolonisation, and the dire poverty of the Third World. Peace, freedom, economic prosperity, a different job structure, and the change of educational methods in the family and school have given almost everyone the strength and means to fulfil themselves. To be a source of creativity and trouble for society; and a tremendous cause of satisfaction, aspirations and *Angst* for themselves. Post-war faith has been followed by a crisis of values which has, in turn, renewed questions about society.

However, 1945 was not only the point of departure of many an individual journey. It was also the origin (in Western Europe and Japan above all) of a social regeneration built on the institutional ruins left behind by the conflict. Social groups were equipped with new superstructures; political parties were born; other unions came into being. Then, as time passed, this creative fever cooled; it left the firmly entrenched elements of a social oligopoly (armed for negociating between themselves and with the government) facing each other. Powerful enough to check the redistribution of the factors of production within the economy. Too weak to extend their interests to the whole of society.

There is also evidence of gradual ossification in the development of the institutions that were the pillars of the economy of the *Thirty Glorious Years* (1945–1975) so dear to Jean Fourastié: the market, the Welfare State, and macroeconomic policy.

The *Renaissance of the Market*. That could be the title of another book on that period. A market (already ossified by the sequels of the Great Depression, and which the War finished oligopolising, except in North America) that was to smash monopolies, stir up people, facilitate innovation and make adventure possible. Helped in some OECD countries by state aid for development. But gradually, governments, businesses, and unions were to take control of the institution once more and fit it into a network of rules, while questions about it were to reappear, and many more or less legal forms of informal economy were to blossom on the fringes of the official market.

As for the Welfare State, it has been the counterbalance of the market – and also its guarantee. Bringing security and greater equality where the market aimed only at efficiency. Partially redistributing the goods and services that its confederate had created. Equal opportunity through education. Equality in the face of illness or accident through Social Security. Relative equality through pensions and guaranteed minimum salaries. But it is also passing through a period of crisis: weighed down by the lack of connections between the behaviour of citizens and resulting expenses, handicapped by the complexity of its organisation, badly regulated because of budgetary constraints, threatened by the polymorphous wave of the claims of social groups seeking loans through taxes or special levies...

Finally, macroeconomic policy. Its prescription may be summed up in a few phrases: give a new impetus to the economy through a budget deficit or easing credit when an economic low brought on unemployment; apply the brakes when expansion came close to full employment or when the appearance of a foreign deficit and the rate of inflation got dangerously high. A single type of unemployment caused by insufficient demand; a single type of inflation caused by an excessive demand in relation to production capacity. However the spell was to break starting in the early seventies when types of unemployment emerged which the economic climate could not explain. Types of inflation were to come into being which were not created by the full use of production capacities. What caused them both? Undoubtedly the social inflexibility that has slowly matured throughout the period of growth.

Seething values, the emergence of a social oligopoly, the crisis of economic institutions – developments that are as legitimate as interdependence and multipolarity. Nothing would be more ridiculous than wishing to make the future of industrial societies depend on their international environment alone. Moreover, these domestic phenomena are two-sided: though on one hand they bear the mark of ossification inherited from the past, on the other, they are harbingers of the future. Thanks to them, new relations with nature, things, and other people are maturing. Thanks to them, social innovations are emerging which are made possible by the state of science, technical possibilities, educational levels, volumes of production, and the diversity of economic activities. Hence, an entirely new approach to the problem of democracy. But in the coming decades the national political systems of developed democratic societies will be confronted with such contradictory and volatile demands, and will be subject to such multifarious (and partly ephemeral) group pressures, that they could well become ungovernable.

Thus the program for understanding the national control deficiency is all mapped out: after questioning values, after analysing the social oligopoly, an examination of the future of institutions such as the market, Welfare State, and state macroeconomic policy, ending with a sketch of the future of democracy will be apposite.

Then the new conditions of interaction between the international system and national political systems will take shape. At the main junction, between the devil and the deep blue sea, governments will be compelled to perform the heavy task of somehow mastering multipolarity and interdependence while trying to maintain a balance between the aspirations of their citizens and realistic possibilities. And *voilà*, the game of the second and third control deficiencies will appear.

But, inspite of their similarities, developed countries remain profoundly stamped with their individual histories. Japan bears the traces of its
Buddhist and Shinto traditions; America holds on to the memory of its
great Nineteenth Century adventure; Western Europe cannot escape the
complexities of its long history. And one might have wished to study
seperately the contestations qnd ossifications of each of the three poles of
the North. But in order to avoid repetition, I have chosen not to do this –
a decision that nonetheless creates a major difficulty, in that it stresses
the European bias and is sometimes rather over-inclined to project the
problems of the Old World onto the developed world as a whole.

# Values: continuity or change?

If the value system, that secret mover of human actions, is in the process of being changed in industrial societies, what a tremendous harbinger of the future! Who does not immediately understand its immeasurable significance! Moreover, the many essayists who proclaim it insist on the importance of their theses. But making a statement is one thing. Understanding and providing proof, another. There is no other field in which reality is so hard to grasp, or concepts so hazy, or where schools of thought clash in the dark more... Hence, before devoting myself to prospective analysis, I shall propose a conceptual model. A three-block system: the individual, the influences that he absorbs from his social environment, and the relationhips of social groups to society as a whole. Each person is free to determine his position vis a vis this model.

In order to analyse the individual we shall need four concepts: *values*, *demands*, *behaviour*, and *abilities*. But let us be careful about the use of words.

I use *values* here to mean the underlying preferences that exist in an individual after the formation of his personality in a given society. They rise in tiers on several interdependent levels, and express in depth a more or less conscious conception of the existential meaning of human life and of relationships between the individual and society; on a more superficial level they find expression in arbitrages between dimensions such as power, prestige, security, comfort, escape, the desire for action...

On the other hand, *demands* are made up of the whole of the individual's aspirations in response to the interaction of his values and all possible environments. It is the old idea found in elementary political economy textbooks, but greatly enriched, because:

1. Demands are obviously not confined to the pursuit of an income in exchange for labour, or to obtaining goods and services in exchange for currency, not only because individuals expect other satisfactions from their work apart from an income (contacts with other people, the use of their intellectual ability, the exercise of a power), not only because even a simple purchase is not merely a question of exchanging a cheque for an object, but also because many demands lie completely outside the financial sphere.

2. Demands do not only come from the environment, but also depend on the individual's perception of this environment, because any adman knows very well that the qualities of Evian water or a political program do not match those projected in their images.

3. From the train ticket that gives one the right to a means of transport to the human contact with parents that this transport makes possible, the chain of demands that only make sense in relation to a deeper demand is very long; from demands for goods and services provided by the market or the welfare state to the final demands that are the object of preferences.

4. Finally, the environment is not limited to the price system and the limitations of income. It must incorporate all the messages that come from outside. It must include all the constraints that hem in the individual: regulations, technical constraints, the constraints of time...

There remains *behaviour*: it will pose fewer problems, since this is simply the actions that allow the individual to satisfy his demands in a given concrete situation, whether he accepts the situation (for example when he buys something), or rejects it (as in fraud, petty crime or strike action). Observing behaviour will be easy. But it will have to be understood in the widest sense: invention and creation, the search for information, the choice of roles in society, decision based on the roles played. Along with the environment, they will determine the level of satisfaction of aspirations and, eventually, the level of preferences.

One last idea for this first block: that of individual ability. It will be understood of itself and the usefulness of introducing it will become evident, for, these abilities (neither totally innate nor totally acquired) will contribute to the formation of the individual's demands; they will extend the range of his behaviour patterns and will condition his efficiency. Why this complicated (and yet so brief) structure? It has only one aim in view: to begin to unravel the thread of the complex influences that an individual absorbs from the social environment, and thus tackle the second block.

The first and most direct influence is very simple: an individual's behaviour changes when his environment changes, because his options change. Double my income and I will flee noisy areas and dark apartments. Divide transport costs by three and I will spend my holidays in Bangkok or Tahiti... There is absolutely no need to invoke changing values!

Next comes the influence of the environment on the perception that the individual has of it: this is the road favoured by admen, when they create images of sturdy or elegant cars and politicians that are wise administrators or good family men. This is the manipulation that is dear to the hearts of Leftists, but on the most superficial level.

Let us go down one step to deeper preferences: the environment can modify the way in which consuming this or that thing satisfies fundamental motivations such as comfort, prestige, power, and adventure. What a tremendous feeling of power it is to drive a Beetle in a civilisation of hackney carriages! How embarassing to have only a Beetle when all the neigbours drive Mercedes, or at least a Volvo! Ah, the secret joy of displaying your lack of interest in an item of goods as common as the car if you can show off your battered VW at the door of the historic manor that you use as a second home... Let us not deceive ourselves: this kind of manipulation is not at all within the range of advertising; you need even more powerful messages coming from the whole of society. How? And can we speak of changing values? In my opinion, not yet. However there is nothing to prevent the satisfaction of new demands from reacting in turn on underlying values to the point of making these demands indispensible in a changed environment. It is the well known ratchet effect: a person whose income has permitted him to enjoy travelling in a certain style will find it difficult to give this up if his income falls from that level.

One more step and we come to the crunch; because the issue is now the respective significance of profound motives, the structure of the individual's relationship with his fellowman and with society. How? One thing is certain: the advertising messages of the consumer society are not sufficient, neither are hymns to the Cultural Revolution nor the incantations glorifying the national socialist superman. Changes in a person are no more wrought by decree than changes in society. A path to explore? That of sociopsychoanalysis. During the crucial childhood years, the psychoanalytical personality of each person (based on parents who have themselves been moulded by their parents and their past) is built up, the personality that will be remodelled at the time of the adolescent crisis when the Oedipus conflict resurfaces and Society in its turn is identified with the Father or Mother. Thus, the continuity in a culture of a single basic personality which underlies the range of individual diversity, may be explained. Thus when you have a large number of parents moulded in new sub-cultures, changes will be possible. Hence the ambiguity of the word 'values' which at once indicates individual preferences as a whole, the social norms that the individual interiorises as preferences in his super-ego, and the norms that appear in communication between individuals.

To end, suffice it to introduce one more relationship – the influence of the environment on the moulding of each individual's abilities, and, as a result, on his options, his perceptions, and the associations he makes between motivations and 'consumptions.'

Now to the third block. "And only just in time," the sociologists protest. And justly so, for all these individual evolutions do not float like clouds in the social sky. Certainly, the behaviour of all determines the social environment of each person, but there are propinquities, and similar situations that reinforce influences, facilitate interactions, structure languages and thus give birth to social groups within which the same norms are partly recognised and ways of behaving are more homogeneous than in society as a whole. Consequently, there are always certain innovative groups, while on the other hand, others will be guardians of obsolescent values, demands and behaviour.

Let us end by making a common-sense observation of the past, rather than an idealised reconstruction of it. Developed societies have not emerged from a period of value monolithism. Although between 1950 and 1975 there was a quasi consensus of the aspirations of their citizens on economic growth, deep rifts between the different social groups (inherited from the great social struggles of the beginning of the century), have survived. Isn't France at the beginning of the Fifth Republic a beautiful example? The difference between the aspirations of the conservative peasant from the west of the country, the communist Renault worker, and the liberal executive of an industrial group cannot be reduced simply to differences in votes.

There you have the conceptual framework: whatever the imperfections of our model, it shows that changes in individual behaviour can emerge on levels of varying depth, and that the innovative groups that carry such changes depend on these very levels.

Now the way is clear for us to return to prospective analysis and formulate the questions that must be asked about the future of values, demands and behaviour. What will the probable changes involve? How deep and permanent will these changes be? How much diversity may we expect on the level of individuals, groups and countries?

Some people summarise the content of emerging aspirations by saying that the search for quality of life tends to take preeminence over material well being. The proposition is a little simplistic. What do the few available facts suggest?[55] Changes that revolve round two basic poles: liberation, and the search for roots. But certainly with differences between Europe and the United States, and within Europe, and more than slight variations between one country and another. However, these differences and variations do not mean that one cannot sketch a common picture.

Since 1955 the affirmation of individuality through small differences in behaviour has emerged in innovative groups. At the same time, the notion of duty has tended to fade and the gratification of desires to be seen as not only justifiable, but necessary to the equilibrium of the personality. Sexual liberation has been one manifestation of this. On another level, the primacy of economic security has declined, and over the years, the proportion of individuals that feel the need to be creative in their daily and professional lives and leisure has increased. Power to the imagination! It has become important, consciously or unconsciously, for a person to affirm his individuality, to develop and fulfil it. It is up to each person to influence it. Through psychoanalysis, through yoga... The days of models handed down from above, from the powers that be, from the old, from parents, from those who delight in a status sanctioned by custom or convention are over. Pyramidal structures, whether they be fashion or great institutions, are crumbling. More individuals are looking for their models beneath or near them. Among the young, in the street, in little-esteemed social groups. People are becoming more sensitive to social constraints. There are many who are becoming aware of the conditioning that society imposes on them, and are taking more care to detect it and free themselves. There is a growing fear of being manipulated. Big and powerful organisations that could take advantage of their power, messages that do not ring true, and novelties whose real value is not apparent, all provoke distrust and defensive reactions... Isn't it obvious that all these manifestations are the expression of a formidable need for freedom that spills over the narrow framework of political and entrepreneurial freedom. and which is revealed in all the social roles that an individual plays, whether it is the sexual role, the family role, or professional roles... But perhaps some groups have already reached the final stage of liberation. Surveys over the last few years show that an increasing number of people are bored, lack motivation, no longer aim at surpassing themselves through their jobs and work, seek stimulation, sensations, and the accumulation of different experiences to fill the void. Some, attracted by the irrational, turn away from logic and science to delve in the mysterious and unexplainable.

On one hand a thirst for freedom, on the other a need for roots. But the days of identifying with huge, abstract social groups of the past (the working class or the international proletariat) are over! The search for personal dialogue expunges social conscience. Everything takes place on the primary and concrete levels where personal relationships are dominant: groups of friends who work in the same workshop or office, small geographic communities, associations with specific aims, religious sects, political cliques, linguistic or ethnic communities. Whereas turning inwards on the nuclear family was once prevalent, an openness to others is developing. The need to dialogue and communicate betrays a fear of loneliness. But dialogue is pervaded by an atmosphere of understanding in which each person avoids judging, imposing himself, and condemning. The other person's desire for freedom is acknowledged and accepted and as a result, differentiation between the sexes is becoming more an individual characteristic than a social one. What is the counterpart of this profound experience of direct democracy and the psychology of small groups? A lack of interest in the functioning of society as a whole. Little liking for order. Indifference to the responsibility of the individual towards nation, church, or party. A loss of understanding of the mechanisms that ensure the upkeep of the standard of living.

The two tendencies just mentioned often reinforce each other, but they sometimes oppose each other. Together they take the edge off the attraction of a high status (which is no longer being strengthened except in the most underprivileged groups). They lead to the desire for a simpler life and rejection of complicated products technologies, services, regulations and life styles. They change attitudes to nature and the framework of life. For the individual who is asserting himself, the physical environment becomes the opportunity for manifold exchanges that are not limited to conventions or formalism; for the individual who is becoming established, this environment is a part of his human space. So it is hardly surprising that the artificial and the chemical, industrial products and bureaucracy arouse growing hostility. They are experienced as an aggression against what is an extension of the individual himself.

However, liberation and the need for roots do not always go together: being free means making all the decisions that concern one by oneself; participating means sharing in all the decisions that influence one's environment; and thus interfering with the decisions of others. And that is one of the greatest problems of the new aspirations. Will the dictatorship of the small group not take the place of overall social constraints designed to limit individual liberty?

Let us beware of naïvely interpreting these innovative attitudes described by surveys, as a deepening of personal and collective ethics. They would not be at all authentic if they were not ambiguous, capable of being lived in diversity. Communion with nature can be narrowed down to a bucolic and selfish return to the land, the rejection of everything chemical, and old-maidish finicalness. The desire for freedom can be narrowed down to a rejection of all personal discipline, and identification with a limited group and a sectarianism that can lead to violence. Nonetheless the adventure also involves the conquest of freedom, learning to look at our fellow-man differently, and an awareness of the relationship between humanity and the ecosphere...

If we look at the criteria for the success of human societies from the outside, six dimensions (which are no more than the components of a more global optimisation) can be distinguished: efficiency, security, equality, freedom, participation, and adaptability. Industrial societies have experienced efficiency, security, and in some cases, freedom. Could it be that the ascendent values are now freedom and participation, while equality may be experienced more in day-to-day life than sought through rules?

But if the contents of the new trends seem clear enough, what about the groups that carry them? When it replies "The youth," the popular voice is only stating a truism. It is obvious that a person is most open to new values in the formative years, and that it is when one generation replaces another that the values that permeate the younger age groups become tangible. Nevertheless, young people are not at all the monolithic bloc that some people believe them to be. The following observation is more interesting: if you take the socioprofessional group of the person surveyed (or that of his or her father), or their educational level, it becomes evident that the percentage of 'post-materialists' increases as you rise in the social hierarchy. You would notice in particular that in the early Seventies, it was only among students and university graduates of between 16 and 44 years of age that 'materialistic' values seemed to be really the preoccupation of a minority. It is true that the changes in attitude concerning the notion of country, sexual relations, religion, work, money... extend well beyond campuses (as Daniel Yankelovich's regular surveys have demonstrated in the case of the United States). However, the 'silent revolution' that has taken place in the scale of values of advanced industrial societies is focused particularly on the middle classes, a remarkable phenomenon if you reflect on the fact that, in the past, these classes have always upheld traditional values.

Middle class youth, granted. But let us go further. The innovators are drawn from groups with very distinct characteristics. Firstly, they are expanding rapidly, and see themselves as the skeleton of the post-industrial or hyper-industrial society of tomorrow; young men or women graduates of institutions of higher learning who fill the universities, research centres, research consultant firms, firms that deal with commu-nication and information, the manifold service industries... Young men and women who are drifting in the nebula of these environments... Then, their consumer needs are broadly satisfied, or at least they think that they will be covered automatically at the very time that they are being offered new possibilities, the extreme case being that of women, who, in a few decades, have seen their life span extend, the number of months spent in pregnancies reduced, and the level of their education rise, while learning to master their own bodies and control the number of their pregnancies. Finally, these young men and women have a presentiment that in terms of prestige, power, and relative income, society will not offer them the same opportunities as their elders. This is the result of a higher level of education and drop in the economic rewards of education: if a Frenchman is the only one to speak English, his salary in the market will be high; if he is the only one not to speak it, he will get the same pay as anyone else. In the preceding generations, most graduates became executives, invested with authority by the leaders. Over blue- and white-collar workers. Over the white collar workers. But in a research centre or research consultancy, the graduate will have authority over himself only. He will only be one among many colleagues. As for his work, its effect will be lost in the complex social decision-making networks. Hence a frustration among some professionals paralleling that of the workers of yesteryear, manifesting itself differently according to people's temperaments: seeking areas in which the professional initiative of the individual will survive, moving the major focuses of interest away from work, trying to have an intense experience of the workshop or office community. A personal experience: how amazed I was a few years ago to observe, among the professionals of research firms, reciprocal links between aspirations and consulting activities. The management consul-tants were conservative. They gave leaders advice in restoring order to their affairs, identified with them, and took a bit of their power. At the other extreme, in research into town planning and regional development one finds the leftist innovators! Hoping to change society, but choosing an area in which the least endeavor required years to come to fruition (that is if it did not get lost along the way) and in which the resulting frustration reinforced their desire to identify with the inhabitants of the working class districts and new urban areas. Between these two groups come the marketing specialists, pleased to influence the consumer, but sometimes feeling guilty about doing it, and the scientific computer consultants for whom their work as skilled craftsmen offered no hope of strength and power, but who dreamed of small groups in which rises in salary would be equal, while at the same time showing themselves to be disinclined to play that game when confronted with others who simply wanted to make a career.

No doubt an isolated observation, but it confirms the fact that the groups which carry new aspirations do not spring up at random in advanced industrial societies, but in the environment of middle class young people who see themselves as representatives of a future society in which there will be exchanges of information and knowledge, who have many of their motivations satisfied, but who also perceive that it is impossible for them to assert themselves in the same ways that their elders did. The pursuit of freedom, roots, and symbiosis with nature are thus a response that takes the place of the accumulation of goods, the acquisition of prestige, the quest for self-assertion through competition with others... As for the young women, they often waver between two revolts: whereas some of them dream only of liberation and want to experience for themselves the adventure of the men of the preceding generation, others would wish, by readjusting the balance of sex roles, to lessen the influence of male values (which, like the pursuit of power or prestige, are a thin disguise for agressivity) and permeate society with values (such as openness, cooperation, and a respect for everyday things) that they think are profoundly feminine.

The time has come to ask the basic question – concerning the depth of these changes. But we must put it back into its context, for the emergence of different priorities in the value systems is still far from assuming the significance that student agitation in the Sixties and pro- and anti-contestation have given it in the eyes of the public at large. By limiting ourselves to complete swings, the proportion of 'post-materialists' revealed by the surveys carried out in 1972–1973 (and therefore, before the eruption of the 'crisis') oscillates between a minimum of 5% for Japan and a maximum of 14% for Belgium (USA 12%, France 12%, West Germany and Britain 8%)... In the early Eighties, the landscape had changed very little; the post-materialists were largely in the minority, but the aging 1968 veterans had spread it through all age groups.

What will become of it in the future? Won't slower economic growth and more conflict in inter-state relations undo, at least partially, what the peace and prosperity of the Sixties had built up? The answer depends on the explanation. It would seem that many new behaviour patterns are simply the product of changes in the possible options and in their probable consequences. Other basic factors also intervene: the higher standard of individual education and sharp rise in the percentage of graduates; then, at a deeper level, the change in meaning of consumption in terms of motivation, the strengthening of the motivations least well satisfied (and most easily satisfied) by the environment. Is that all? Probably not, because the weakening of authority suggests the crumbling of the Father image, the fusion with nature, and the maintenance of archaic relations with the Mother. The sons and daughters of 1968 were perhaps the vanguard of people with a new psychoanalytical history... If that is so, it would really be a 'Silent Revolution' that is in the air in so far as the values of the innovative groups would tend to become dominant.

However, let us be wary of a linear extrapolation of the evolution of values and aspirations. Other trends parallel to, or in competition with the aforementioned may come into play. Do we not now already detect increased hostility to the spreading of these values by violence? And in the conflict between liberation and establishment, will not the small group one day be the source of a new authority over the bored individual? It is noteworthy that the new values are synonymous with diversity, and also with incoherence. On the level of the individual who finds it difficult to reconcile an improvement of the environment with a rise in income; the rejection of nuclear power with an increased use of energy; leisure time increased with consumption held steady; the wish for protection with the desire for autonomy... On the level of social groups, of which some very small ones express their demands for liberation and establishment in very extreme ways, while others only experience moderate versions.

The extreme forms range from vehement eloquence to terrorism, from partial combat over a precise area to a total rejection that demands freesom from the centre of all groups perceived as marginal, whether it is a question of capital-province, dominant language-dialect, colony-imperialism, child-parent, man-woman, or natural environment-technology relations. A total rejection that proposes the organisation of groups liberated in this manner into autonomous communities maintaining only minimal links with the outside world...

On the other hand, the moderate versions involve a majority centre which, according to surveys, would represent 40 to 60% of the population. This majority centre (in some ways, not very homogeneous) is characterised by the fact that its members reject any extreme allegiance... Having benefitted from the upward social movement allowed by economic growth, they are clearly more sensitive to development in terms of the absolute value of their standard of living compared with the past, than to their relative position compared with better off social groups. For all that, they are not closed to all the post-materialist 'values' which they accept in a more subdued and heterogenous manner by more or less bringing about a synthesis with the more traditional values. For example, it is conceivable that travelling abroad and owning a house (two aspirations that are very strong among the Europeans of today) are for them a way of fitting into everyday life the double motivation of freedom and establishment which others express through ecological militancy or the back-to-earth movement. But the majority centre distances itself from the extreme forms of post-materialism on one particular point: it rejects violence as a method of political action.

Nonetheless, extreme forms and moderate versions produce a common result: the birth in advanced industrial societies (whether within the majority centre or on its fringes) of many minorities making a variety of demands in different directions. Thus, belonging to the majority centre does not in any way preclude a great variety of life styles and a wide range of wild claims on varying issues: the planning of a motorway, the opening of certain jobs to women, the conditions of abortion legalisation, the use of Basque or Corsican language... Consequently, winning people over quickly to the 'new values' does not in any way guarantee the return of advanced societies to a new form of consensus. What is most likely to happen? The continued existence for several decades of societies that are fragmented with regard to the values, aspirations and behaviour of their members, this fragmentation being no more than the reflection of the slow pursuit of a synthesis of the cohesion vital to society and the individual's pursuit of his liberation and establishment. This fragmentation will perhaps be reinforced by the reappearance (due to the crisis) of conservative groups avid for physical and material security, eager for economic growth and the redistribution of wealth, hostile to immigrants and nationalists. This is the trend within a section of the working class in many countries.

The diversity and incoherence of these aspirations it will finally emerge once more on the level of the industrial nations, for subtle differences of balance between social groups can be enough to provoke a great variety of responses. With a United States transformed into coalitions of minorities, a Japan that will retain its cohesion (because in that country awareness of dependence on the outside world will check the swing), an exploded Western Europe in which Britain, owing to its decline, will see the rebirth of the class struggle and the struggle of the believers in the New Growth, in which Germany will mourn its consensus buried by the blossoming of a new Left, in which Italy will settle into the chaos of seething confusion, Belgium will resolve its linguistic struggles with difficulty, and France will finally flounder about caught between security and freedom.

This diagnosis of the crisis of values retains some ambiguity, an ambiguity that is not solely created by the mist surrounding the future, but which is also a result of the understanding of complexity that should distinguish prospective analysis from utopianism. However, despite this ambiguity, the analysis stresses a key impulse of advanced industrial societies, an impulse that will challenge almost all of their institutions once more.

• We begin with the family, the family of the industrial age, which, if we believe the forecast of Pierre Chaunu and Georges Suffert in *La Peste Blanche*, is limited to the couple and children, never shaken by non-marital cohabitation, and which could be increasingly reduced to a single parent family, or dissolve into communities of adults and children. The differentiation of the economic and sexual roles of the sexes will become more and more blurred, while the gradual and multiform reduction of working hours should make other family equilibria possible at the end of the century. However, during a whole transition period of one to two decades, women's conflict between career and motherhood or between freedom and motherhood, may well continue, conflicts which, because of continuing time budgetting restrictions, may only be resolved by limiting the number of children. Western societies would thus experience a fourth family model: in our grandparents' time, the model of a marital institution aimed at ensuring the survival of the household through precise and strict norms; later, after the war, came the model of the alliance marriage that postulated a pre-established harmony between duty and happiness, and because of this, tolerated the failures of divorce; later, in the near past, the model of the fusion marriage that made the couple and children into a self-sufficient emotional space; all of which would herald the association marriage of Scandinavian countries that questions the institution itself since "here, the de facto union and marriage are reduced to a reasonable arrangement in which each of the partners finds the most foreseeable satisfactions, on a more or less long-term basis."[56]

• Work and time bring us to the heart of the connections between individual demands and economic and social life. Apart from a few collective festivals, agrarian societies in which subsistence farming was predominant did not know the clearcut division between leisure and work time. It was industry that demanded time-keeping and a working day with fixed hours. But there is a revolution underway: aspirations concerning time are developing. Already, according to a survey carried out by the CREDOC at the beginning of 1979, two-thirds of French salaried workers prefer more free time with the same salary to more pay for the same working hours.[57] How would they be spending their time in the year 2000? According to André Danzin, out of an average life span of 72 years, 31 would be devoted to basic physiological time (food, sleep, hygiene), 8 to childhood and education, 6 to transport, 8 to work, and 19 to adult free time. How far away our children will be from our forebears of 1800 who, of their average life span of 45 years had no more than 5 years of free time in their adult life![58] But whoever speaks of a reduction of working hours is also speaking of a broadening of options (part time work, flexible working hours, wide individual variations), and above all, a revolution of the meaning of free time. Will not this free time (with its deceptive name) support economic and social activities which themselves are equivalent to a job, but a job that is either unsalaried or not highly paid? Will work be rejected? Doubtless not, but it will no longer have a moral significance. New expectations will emerge, because work will be seen as an opportunity to fulfil oneself and as a source of satisfying relationships... So another possibility seems likely: the widening of the range of behaviour patterns. At the end of the century, at the extremes of the confusion of timetables, a new type of 'persons of independant means' who limit their paid work to the strict acquisition of a minimal monetary income and who do not involve themselves in it either morally or emotionally, will coexist with stakhanovists of the market economy who find their *raison d'être* in their work.

● But the revolution will not stop at the doors of the productive cells: undermined by disaffection with work, the big organisations will try to change their ways of functioning to rely on the needs for decentralisation and participation expressed by their personnel. They will strive to split up into medium-sized establishments, to limit the number of hierarchical levels, and to make work more stimulating... resigning themselves, if they fail, to live on a hard core of committed staff dragging a nebula of indifferent employees behind them. In their own way, they will have reconciled bureaucracy and self-management. All sorts of small organisations will flourish alongside them, attracting the most active and the most creative, an ever-changing breeding ground. Finally (and we shall have to come back to this subject), a part of economic activity will revolve round adult free time, thus escaping the formal economy that has dominated the industrial era.

• The legitimacy of science and its applications: another sensitive area for developed societies. The questions arise from profound psychoanalytical causes, for science challenges the permanence of our Ego through neuropharmacology, the maintenance of our hereditary patrimony through genetic engineering, the existence of the human race through nuclear energy, and our place in the universe through space technology. In the past, man opposed Science when it shook the foundations of his psychological security: the movement of the earth around the sun, the dissection of corpses, high-speed transport, surgery... And this questioning is no less ethical at a time when Science makes it possible for man to destroy himself. As for the need for establishment in small groups, it reappears in the hostility to 'high technology' fast breeder reactors, transport infrastructures, iron and steel factories, and huge oil tankers, technologies that overturn the framework of the life of local human communities...

• The link between attitudes to technology and attitudes to the environment is obvious. It is not just a question of green spaces and pure air. The man who wants to merge himself with Mother Nature no longer sees himself as a chosen, ruling species, but as one of the many branches of a luxuriant biosphere. He has moved from being a tamer of nature to being its guardian. From master of other species to older brother. From then on the arbitrages become dramatic, because we must find a standard of measurement that is common to antipodal dimensions: to the profitability of a mine and the protection of a natural park; to saving seals and whales, and the redeployment of the activities of human groups... The crisis of values also opens onto a crisis of the use of space: how does one reconcile the desire of small communities to plan their own space with controlling the use of space for the functioning of society as a whole? There is no doubt whatsoever that advanced industrial societies will have to rethink their town planning and national development.

• As for economic growth, its relations with changes in values and demands cannot but assume many forms. Even if the evolution of values muddles along as innovative groups develop, the intensity of growth may well influence this evolution. Some signs already suggest that the recessions of the last decade and the slow growth that followed them have retarded the changes in values, whereas the lively growth of the Sixties had contributed to their genesis... If, however, economic growth were to fall even lower (a situation that would plunge advanced industrial societies into serious difficulties), it is not inconceivable that more abrupt sociocultural changes will take place. A return to the past or acceptance of new values? The question has been asked. Moreover, by challenging the aims of society, the new values demythify growth in terms of gross domestic product. They bring to mind all the conventions that are the principal factor in this particular measure of social production. They dwell on its fragmentary nature, and underline its negative effects. The rate of growth, which was being deified as an aim in itself, finds itself brought back to the position of indicator, and economic growth to the status of an instrument that has no meaning except in relation to the material and spiritual needs of human groups. Finally, the new values will lead to a change in the content of growth. On two levels. By encouraging new investments, by developing the demand for a host of services, and by pushing up the cost of exchanges with the physical environment. That is the economist's interpretation. By forcing productive units to change their organisation, by multiplying their conflicts with watch-dog associations or protest groups, and by adding to the weight of regulations. That is the sociologist's interpretation. This will probably result in a slowing down of growth. Not, as some think, by simple substraction, but by the addition and substraction of many terms... And perhaps we shall be able to replace our traditional GNP by a better indicator, a sort of Net National Happiness, something that the Japanese have already tried to compute, without much sucess...

• The above does not leave us in any doubt as to the pressures that the changes in values and demands will put on the political systems of developed countries. How can a small number of political parties, distributed over the Right-Left axis and on one or two other complementary axes, hope to reconcile demands that come from such a host of minorities? How can they expect to satisfy needs for participation that will not be limited to the desire to drop a card in the ballot box every four or five years? How will cumbersome central administrations respond to 'post-materialist' demands which aim to obtain (for widely varying groups) the recognition of a certain number of rights of access or action that are generally technically impossible to grant or refuse except all together, since by definition, it is a question of collective rules of the game that apply to everyone? How will they be able to meet these 'non-negotiable differences' with the compromise solutions befitting conflicts over the sharing of infinitely divisible resources such as money, solutions which are practised in the normal political life of a democracy?

• The religious institutions themselves will not be protected, for the numerous incarnations of religious renaissances will not, especially in Catholic countries, put up with a centralised hierarchical organisation, and sects could well flourish on the imposing ruins of the Apostolic Roman Catholic Church... But my subject is not religious prospective analysis. The only thing that matters to me here is establishing the fact that no institution of developed countries will be able to escape changes in values, however superficial these might be.

Perhaps the reader will now understand the anxiety underlying this book (an anxiety that is not synonymous with pessimism), and which derives from the two main thoughts that inspire the analysis of values in developed countries.

On one hand, I have a presentiment of what could become of the advanced industrial societies if they follow the trend of their own dynamics, and if outside constraints are toned down. The dialectics between their values and their social structures will give rise to other forms of economic growth, other institutions, and other life styles. Of course, it will not all go smoothly; existing organisations and, above all governments, will be under a great deal of pressure.

On the other hand, I shudder when I think of fitting these societies into the multipolar, interdependent world of which they are a part. Will this Man-Child who brings the new values into the advanced industrial societies, this man who is seeking a new alliance with Knowledge, with Nature, and with his Fellow-man, this man, at once liberated, established, and protected, the precursor of a future humanity, be easy prey to the insurgent man of the Third World or to the regimented man of the Soviet Empire? And if the harsh realities of geopolitics make him lose his naïvety in the short term, is he not in danger of turning in on himself, in a self-centredness that is just as fatal because of his refusal to be adventurous?

# The conflicts of organised groups

If the crisis of values is a seed of the futures of developed societies, the organisation of the social groups is a legacy from the past, but a legacy that will weigh more and more heavily on their destiny. It is a very simple process: competition – whether economic, political, or social – is not stable in the long term, because everyone strives to escape its steel jaws. It maximises national production, but it does so by compelling companies to struggle to cut costs, by forcing workers to change their jobs or region in order to maintain or increase their salaries. It brings political programs closer to the aspirations of the electorate, but it does this by making parties fragile, reducing the barriers to new candidates. It homogenises society through the free circulation of élites, but it does this by redistributing the cards in each generation and within the very lifetime of each person. Its only champions are those who have no fear of competition: the strong. At least, for as long as they remain strong. All the others, the majority, work conscientiously to rip it to shreds...

In 1789 the triumphant French bourgeoisie smashed the trade guilds so as to avoid workers' unions; it will not scorn either customs duties, nor agreements, nor the pursuit of monopoly situations. It will learn to its cost that price competition can be fatal, that it must limit the economic struggle and not try to destroy a competitor under all circumstances. With the lowering of transport costs, mass consumption and economies of scale, many markets will evolve towards oligopolist structures: a few producers confronted with a multitude of buyers. But the members of the oligopoly will not fight to the death. They will manipulate prices prudently; they will prefer to fight by way of advertisement or innovation, nibbling at, or conceding percentages of parts of the markets...

We are all familiar with the response of the Nineteenth Century working world to business concerns that consulted each other over wages, or held a local monopoly of employment: the creation of unions to force the owners of concerns to negociate or to destroy the capitalist economy. "Workers of the world, unite!" It has left its indelible mark on the economic and political structures of developed countries: from the American AFL-CIO to the trade unions and British Labour Party, and the French CGT (*Confédération Générale du Travail* =General Confederation of Labour).

But the mechanism did not stop there; particularly in Europe it has gradually taken in all the other social groups. Firstly, the peasants, who for a long time had very irregular incomes because of the vagaries of climate and the collapse of the market if the harvest was good. Then civil servants, emboldened by the fact that they ran very few risks, and eager to pit union bureaucracy against the bureaucracy of their faceless employer. Then middle-managers, then doctors, then... What name can we give to this concatenation? Since no better word is available, a neologism is called for: so I shall speak of the 'oligopolisation' of social life, using the obvious economic analogy of a market in which the number of business concerns is gradually reduced to a few.

This is a vital phenomenon.

In the first place, social oligopolisation tends to curb growth and slow down adaptation within developed societies. No one has expressed it better than Mançur Olson: "Organisations that supply public goods,[59] are, for very fundamental reasons, very difficult to set up, especially for large groups; none of these organisations will attract a significant percentage of numerous, scattered groups like consumers, taxpayers, or the poor; in such conditions, organisations that devote themselves to promoting the common interests of certain groups can only be created in very favourable circumstances, often long after these interests have come to light; when such organisations appear and have political power or a monopoly, they tend to delay the innovations and reallocations of resources that are at the roots of economic growth; this trend can only be sharply curbed if the producer groups include a large enough proportion of those who will lose out in a deceleration of growth."[60] In other words, it is generally more important for organisations representing social groups to obtain direct advantages for their members than to promote overall economic development.

Whence the second reason for the importance of the phenomenon, one that has to do with negotiation procedures: social oligopolisation tends to transfer the satisfaction of many demands from the economic system to the political system. Nothing can be more different than the functioning of these two 'markets.' In the economic market, every bit of demand adds up, and the seller takes even the smallest buyer into account... On the political 'market' the only profits and losses that matter are the ones that are big enough to impress those concerned... Furthermore, political power satisfies the demands of diverse groups in turn, always neglecting the losses that these measures inflict on the majority, since taken separately, they are small, but on the community level they can sometimes be considerable. But there is worse: each player in this game of oligopoly is supposed to represent all the interests of a social group. It is the fiction of representative organisations well known to Europe. A necessary simplification of the social game, but it obscures widespread demands that are sometimes those of the majority... History supplies us with many an example of societies with a strong social oligopolisation. The French know at least one, the France of the *Ancien Régime* on the eve of the Revolution with its orders and corporations, and its various types of fiscal and administrative areas. The 1787 Assembly of Notables is the mirror image of our contemporary Social and Economic Council.

The conclusion is self-evident: oligopolisation alters the performance of a society. It does not favour efficiency and adaptability, because it reinforces security by dedicating itself primarily to the maintenance and improvement of acquired advantages; in terms of equality, freedom and participation, its effects are ambiguous, because it can also contribute as much to the protection of privileges as to the defence of oppressed groups, as much to the liberation of dominated people as to the multiplication of regulations, as much to the broadening of participation as to its seizure by representative structures.

From the point of view of the social oligopoly, the recent history of advanced industrial countries has been marked by three successive phenomena:

The first was the destruction of the existing oligopoly of countries like Japan, West Germany, France and Italy by the War: the retirement of all Japanese leaders above the age of thirty-five imposed by McArthur, denazification in Germany, the change of political personnel in Italy, and the French purge, have had a direct effect on the circulation of élites. But we must add such diverse facts as the complete renewal of the press of these countries, the dismantling of the Konzerns in Germany and the Zaibatsu in Japan, the flood of refugees from East Germany to the West, and finally the desire of these peoples to break with all organisations associated with the disaster. These societies were to reemerge rejuve-

nated. It was to become possible once more to create and not conceive
the future in the image of the present.

The United States has experienced no such unpheaval since the
American Civil War, but the wave of immigration and the conquest of
the West retarded the process of oligopolisation for a long time, as the
creative people left the East Cost, sweeping the country along in the
whirlpool of the growth in the new territories. As for the United
Kingdom, its oligopolisation continued throughout the whole of the
Nineteenth Century, not in the least interrupted by two victorious wars
which only served to reinforce existing organisations and increase
institutional ossification. Many economists see that as the underlying
cause of the deplorable British rates of growth in the post-war period. A
contrasting example? Sweden. Though Mançur Olson thinks it isn't,
because according to him, interest groups in that country are so broadly
based that they cannot ignore the development of society as a whole.

In most OECD countries, the weakening of the social oligopoly would
thus be at the root of their extraordinary post-war structural adaptability.

But – and this would be the second phenomenon – the progress of
oligopolisation was not slow in recovering. It won over new groups in
passing, while within the great organisations copied from pre-war ones,
a number of sub-groups acquired structures of their own. In times past,
doctors, nurses, air traffic controllers, magistrates, and police escaped
the social oligopoly; now they are part of it. Cauliflower growers, sheep
breeders, and Languedoc viticulturists each have their own specific
organisations within the great agricultural family, as do butchers, or
bakers within the shop-keeping family. Another novelty is the emergence
of organisations that offer to defend the interests of huge heterogenous
categories on specific issues: telephone subscribers, motorcyclists,
motorists, taxpayers, tenants, landlords, consumers, women... The
mechanism is simple: each state regulation gives birth to its own lobby,
and each lobby strives to get a regulation passed. Governments could not
have it easier. There is absolutely no need to ask about participation
procedures. One need only consult the relevant lobby for each coming
measure. It matters little that it is not an accurate expression of
grass-roots aspirations. It is there; its officials speak the same language
as civil servants, they know the layout of the front, the list of words that
will set off their tempers, the fortified position that will be their reasonable objective... The inspiration of the great post-war debates has evapo-
rated from this petty haggling that is only resolved by making the law
more complicated.

As for the third phenomenon, it is no other (and the reader will have
already anticipated it) than the mixture of the new values with oligopoli-

sation. It has a variety of consequences. To begin with, a supplementary influx of small organised groups which further complicate the social oligopoly, groups of ecologists, defence associations, linguistic groups... Then, with the respect of others, it is possible for anyone, as soon as he represents an identifiable group, however tiny it may be, to block the functioning of vast systems in the name of its interests. Everyone remembers the dozen charwomen whose refusal to clean the toilets brought a British factory of thousands of workers to a standstill! Or the thousand or so French air traffic controllers who, every now and then, decide to disturb all the air traffic of Western Europe! But the new values do not only change the functioning of oligopoly; they challenge it: the individual is not interested in union directives geared to social struggles on a national scale; the group to which he is attached has more immediate demands: giving his opinion about his work, adapting its content to his aspirations, using his abilities fully, and having some freedom in the use of his time. Consequently the unions are afraid. For years, they have sought to limit interplay in the firm to an exchange between management and their members, and *voilà*, there is a chance that a third participant is emerging: the grassroots. And if management were to come to some agreement with them, that would be the end of their power. Hence, they stress the part they play in reducing unknown factors, and they also block the introduction of all measures that restore spontaneity to the social game.

It is no exaggeration to say that the future of advanced industrial societies will, to a large extent be controlled by the evolution of their social oligopoly. Protected by growth, this oligopoly has prospered in response to the aspirations of a multiplicity of social groups, increasing the security of each one, but at the price of ossification... A more unstable external environment, stiffer international competition, decelerated growth, plus new values and demands will try it severely.

Already, widespread unemployment in Europe is weakening the power of unions who increasingly see the social dialogue focusing on the company. But, while the great leaders of the social oligopoly are beginning to understand that they will have to pursue the same objectives using different means, the militants and apparatchiks cling to their hard-won gains, even to the detriment of the interests of the social groups they are supposed to represent. Hence, there are not many options open to the large blue-collar unions in particular:

Lock themselves into strict corporatist defence of the interests of the workers belonging to the sectors where they are most firmly established (often heavy industry), trying to pass on the cost of protecting these sectors to the rest of society. In other words, to fall into conservatism.

That used to be the choice of British trade unions, and it is now the temptation of American unions. But it is also the death of the great historical dream of the trade union movement, and a rejection of the future.

Facilitate the economic growth of the whole society and accept the structural changes involved, only ensuring the equal sharing of the fruits of growth. Will this perhaps be, after Sweden, the path taken by German trade unions? But it will not always be easy to get the grassroots to understand this policy.

Adopt the new aspirations. Rely on the groups that are harbingers of the future. Recognise the reality of the international challenge and militate in favour of a creative but egalitarian society capable of surmounting these challenges. That is the path that attracts the French CFDT (*Confédération Française Démocratique du Travail* = French Democratic Confederation of Labour) and a section of Italian trade unionism. It is the most difficult option. The one with the greatest number of possibilities. It is also the most uncertain, because it means managing diversity.

On a smaller scale, similar choices will have to be made by many other structures of organised groups: European peasants' unions faced with changes in the Common Agricultural Policy; doctors' unions faced with the revolution in medicine; teachers' unions faced with changes in education.

One thing is certain, the future of economic institutions in developed countries will continue to be inseparable from that of social oligopolisation.

# Markets and substitutes

The long history of the market reads like a real serialised novel. Practically dead at the height of the Middle Ages in the West, triumphant in the middle of the last century, barely tolerated for the vegetables produced by Kolkhozes in Soviet Russia, partly underground in continental Europe during the Great Wars, and rising once more like a Phoenix in the last twenty years, the market has in fact constantly lived in symbiosis with two other extreme forms of distrubition – practiced by the state and self-sufficient systems. These three are the vertices of a triangle that sanctions many intermediary solutions, from barter between self sufficient producers to the public monopoly that is subject to the demand of a host of buyers, or the market that is more or less state controlled...

I believe that it is hardly necessary to begin with a hymn to the glory of the market, or to acknowledge the essential part it has played in post-war prosperity by destroying fossilised business concerns, forcing others to reform themselves, and allowing innovation, though I am convinced of its usefulness. I find it more interesting to think about its future prospects. Beyond the horizon of current experiences and in terms of the broad trends that are emerging: multipolarity and interdependence, the crisis of values, social oligopolisation... To complete the picture for the four main groups of markets (the goods and services markets, the labour market, the credit market, and the exchange market) we would have to consider up to what point these trends favour or inhibit the development of the traditional disorders of the market: the existence of dominant positions, the underestimation of the future in relation to the present, the excessive quest for security, indifference to external repercussions, malfunctioning caused by high information and transaction costs... A heavy schedule which I shall simplify by limiting myself to the essentials.

With the greater short- and long-term uncertainties that they entail, multipolarity and interdependence will no doubt have an increasing impact on market procedures. Turning states into rather curious arbiters which sometimes negociate the rules with their equals, and at other times enter the arena with their champions to help or dope them if necessary. Prompting the same states to build up emergency reserves and to preserve a core of strategic activities. Pushing them to reject the arbitrage of private enterprise between the near future and the distant future in the name of national security, and, as a result, leading them to finance long-term investments in research, energy, and raw materials... Backing them in their restrictive immigration policies. Forcing them to intervene in the exchange market... An impressive list. I shall stress one point only: the more industrial competition between countries revolves round the high technology sectors, the more the outcome will depend on upstream activities dominated by the state in all countries: education, scientific research and technological research. The conclusion of this initial diagnosis? What we should expect is not so much a reduction of the role of the markets, but rather that their areas of overlap with states will become more and more complex.

Curiously, social oligopolisation should work in the same way. Certainly it will multiply demands in favour of women, young people, the old, farmers, regions... Certainly, it will propose a widening of the scope of nationalisations, sometimes with government support, but at the same time, it will reinforce the desire of governments to avoid taking on the responsibility of new markets by becoming the only direct operator within them. For the lesson of the past is a bitter one: nationalisations do not eliminate strikes; they increase them and force the state to leave its comfortable armchair of arbitrator between employers and unions, and call down the anger of employees and the cold fury of users upon itself. The most powerful trend? It is becoming obvious: regulations, subsidies, preferential loans, taxes, distributions of public orders, information, consultation, and mediation procedures, but, as far as possible, no suppression of markets! The majority of French Socialists are themselves convinced of this, and if their program takes the form of nationalisations, it would be more a sacrifice to the gods of their fathers, or bowing before the faded flag of 1936, than preparing for the future.

So, nothing really original. Although all that is a far cry from leftwing predictions of twenty years ago. But once the analysis begins to question the influence of the evolution of values and demands it becomes much more interesting, because it shows that a whole host of social demands could well be added to the reinforcement of the aforementioned trends.

The yearning for liberation that motivates the active minorities of developed countries should find expression both in a rejection of the widening of the role of the state, and in a desire to create new business concerns. And this is where competition will be strengthened. Not between the big industrial groups or the glass and steel sectors, but between the small units providing the infinite variety of highly developed services and products of tomorrow's society. And whether the state wants it or not, it will not be at all easy to control markets that are as diverse as they are variable.

On the other hand, the need for roots may bring the market hard times, by multiplying the local repercussions that it is blamed for: endangered species, beauty spots monuments, threatened jobs, competing activities... and by seeking to control it, less through general regulations on a national level, than through collective local decisions or varied actions by several associations. The market will emerge from this with its arbitrages decelerated, its creative power winded, and its destructive capacities weakened... Compromises will be difficult because the active minorities will often reject the very existence of a monetary compensation for all kinds of repercussions. They will thrust aside the actualisation that translates future effects into a present sum; they will spurn the calculation of probabilities to determine permissible risks; they will oppose compensation when the damage will, by its very nature, be irreversible... Neither the market, nor the civil service, nor even the government will be acknowledged as having the right to accept risks in the name of the community. Each community will want to be responsible for them itself.

But let us now look at the innovations. They are already around us in embryonic form, and may described in a phrase that comprehends several realities – 'the informal economy.' In other words, the economy that escapes the monetary relations of the market and the Welfare State.

Part one: the return to direct consumption by the producer which had gradually disappeared following the Industrial Revolution. As with all renaissances, it has nothing to do with the reproduction of the past. The mechanism is simple: households can choose between buying their services outside (having the painter in) or supplying them themselves, or acquiring some goods (buying paint and... taking up the brush). In the long term, and as a result of differentials in productivity growths, the price of industrial goods compared with that of services will tend to fall;

meanwhile, there will be more free time, and the abilities of the members of the household will be greater. The conclusion is self-evident: 'Do it yourself.' The new values play hardly any part in this economic commonplace. But they do interfere, because a standardised service is replaced by a work of personal creation, a simple purchase by an emotional adventure in which all the members of the family participate, and time spent outside in unsatisfying work by an activity in the home which brings all the faculties into play, as with the artisan of yesteryear. Business concerns will rush into this new market, proposing an infinite range of (electronic or non-electronic) building games, making it possible to make houses, gardens, furniture, jewelry, books, confectionery, pottery, films, records... with the help of domestic services, a real puzzle for national accountants.

One further step. Why not join forces with other households to pursue such activities? This will be the second part of the informal economy: "You make me some furniture and I'll do your plumbing repairs" or: "We'll work together on building your house three days a week" or "Let us set up a drama group." What is emerging here is more than a revival of barter, but the supply of free services based on unpaid factors of production. Consequently, we have been able to speak of the birth of a third system that is as far removed from the market as it is from the Welfare State, a system that is adapted to the supply of cultural educational, charitable and mutual aid services. But, as may often be the case, if a portion of purchases must be paid for, if the state contributes a modest subsidy, or if the users pay a small contribution, we find ourselves in a grey area between the three systems.

An interesting phenomenon, some will think, but its role will remain marginal in relation to the other two pillars of the temple! But is this true? Let us make a rough calculation of the relative importance, on the level of final production, of the various institutions: four days of paid work, three days off: of the four days of paid work, two go towards covering state expenditure; of the three days off, one is devoted to leisure and shopping, one to the production of DIY goods and services, and one to work in the third system. The result: the market accounts for 33.30% of the distribution of final production, the state 33.30%[61], the third system and direct consumption by the producer 16.60% each... We are no longer on the level of extravagance, even if the method of calculation overlooks other components of added value and dodges the role of the market on the level of all intermediary goods... And straight away it gives rise to a political question: what should be the state's attitude to these two first aspects of the informal economy? Neutrality? Encouragement?

Hostility? It would be easy for the state to be indifferent or favourable if it didn't have to suffer the attacks of all the producers who will believe themselves to be injured by the unfair competition of benevolent organisations that are not licensed, or do not insure their members against work accidents, etc. I leave the task of writing up the complaints book to you.

But already the informal economy includes a third section (the black sheep of the family): all illegal economic activities. Let us pass over drug trafficking, the restaurant racket, the funding of all kinds of terrorists, and the transfer of capital to Switzerland; the main phenomenon has a name – 'moonlighting' – and there is nothing suprising in its spread, because everything in advanced industrial societies contributes to its expansion: the level of fiscal or social contributions (long ago, N. Parkinson proclaimed a 'law'[62] – not the one that made him famous - which stated that when taxes passed a critical threshold, taxable objects went underground); the existence of unemployment benefit and the continuous availability to the unemployed of free state services; the presence of unemployment and the brevity of work; the removal of the state from its pedestal; the competitive pressure of low Third World salaries. Moreover, the dividing line between the third system and moonlighting is so hazy... Helpless, governments (in France and Britain for example) adopt a laisser-faire policy, or even encourage it surreptitiously (as in the case of Italy). Rather than a systematic offensive, we must expect them to exert erratic pressure varying according to fluctuations in employment...

And are you forgetting the temptation of a bureaucratic socialism? Is it not possible that in certain countries of Western Europe, the market could be swallowed up by the great wave of centralised planning supported by a rapid spread of nationalisations? For example, is France not in danger of going the way of Poland with certain unions opposing a centralised and inefficient state machinery? So what lies around the corner?

From within developed societies, nothing. The future Left will be inspired by new values or it will not be. Marxist psalms of the past apart, the dynamics peculiar to state bureuacracy are the only force working for an authoritative planning of resources on the national level. These dynamics may well wrap the market in their coils, but are unlikely to smother it completely.

But let us not be deceived; this survival of the market in certain European countries in no way precludes the pre-eminence, in large sectors, of unwieldly state organisations in which a meddlesome bureaucracy and a self-management that only manages laxity lean on each other like the blind man and the crippled man.

External threats make the forecast less black and white: what influence could the proximity of divisions of the Red Army have on Western Europe one day? How would citizens react to a dismantling of the international economic system that created widespread unemployment and inflation? These two centralised socialisms of crisis are both conceivable; they would find it very difficult not to be either Stalinist or national.

Thus prospective analysis leads to a double diagnosis: under the influence of the American Right and a section of European public opinion the medium-term trend is towards economic liberalism; the policies of deregulation will be pursued, and the market will assert its primacy whatever the development of the informal economy. But look out for shifts in direction in the long term if this liberalism produces unacceptable social inequalities.

# The crisis of the Welfare State

The term 'welfare state' has a familiar ring to British ears, but it may be defined as a developed economy made up of two interacting sub-systems, a commercial sector and a non-commercial sector; all production that is sold at a price covering at least manufacturing costs is assigned to the former sector; all activities that are not sold and which are financed by voluntary or compulsory contributions, to the latter. Within the non-commercial sector, the Welfare State is simply "the body of civil activities that provides services, norms of behaviour and the redistributed of incomes that public power effects with the aim of improving the well-being of the national community or changing its distribution."[63]

This Welfare State has expanded considerably since the end of the Second World War. Some figures? Between 1962 and 1975, government spending as a percentage of potential GDP moved from 29.50 to 34% in the United States, 33.60 to 42% in West Germany, 36.30 to 40.30% in France, and from 19% to 23.40% in Japan. And it has continued to rise. The causes? The emergence of demands that only the the non-commercial part of the economy is capable of satisfying, and, of course, our old friend social oligopolisation.

But a crisis of the Welfare State is coming: a financial crisis due to the difficulty of raising the sums necessary for it to function in a time of slow growth; a crisis of confidence characterised by many indicators: the rejection of the Thirteenth Ammendment in California in 1978, the emergence of anti-state parties in certain countries (the Progress Party in Denmark, the Citizens' Party in West Germany), dissatisfaction in France with the great public services such as the postal service, declining

interest in social programs in the chosen countries of the welfare state –
Sweden, Denmark, and Great Britain. There is no doubt whatsoever
that the slowing down of growth and the development of the aspirations
of some people are at the root of the illness, but, in the area that we are
thinking of, these general causes assume more specific forms – the four
diseases of the welfare state.

The discovery of the first is due to two Oxford economists, R. Bacon
and W. Eltis.[64] The crucial point of their analysis is that the market
product of an economy is exposed to three sets of demands: consumption
by the active people in the commercial sector; net investment and net
exports, which are necessary for balanced growth; the many demands
coming from the non-commercial sector. If the latter two increase, there
are several possibilities. Hypothesis number one: those who are active in
the commercial sector agree to have their private consumption cut.
Hypothesis number two: the proportion of the commercial product
allocated to investment and export drops, whereas the private consumption of those active in the commercial sector remains unchanged.
Hypothesis number three: at first, greater tax pressure reduces the
private consumption of those who are active in the commercial sector,
but they re-establish their position through pay claims, and this intensifies inflationist pressures, slashes profits and curbs investment. Clearly,
only the first hypothesis is compatible with a healthy functioning of the
welfare state.

What has happened in fact in the United Kingdom, Canada, and the
United States, all countries where the non-commercial sector has absorbed a growing proportion of the commercial product over the years? The
British reaction has been to pursue a higher per capita consumption by
active persons at the expense of business profits, so that the weight of
adjustment has been borne by the balance of payments and productive
investment. Resulting in a reduction of the possibilities of growth.
Canada has experienced the third type of development – the "slow and
continuing increase in union power... which... allowed workers to start to
pass the rising costs of the non-market sector on to companies from 1973
onwards but not before."[65] And finally, the American response, which
falls into the first category. But with particular adverse effects. Why? If
we are to believe Bacon and Ellis, it is because two thirds of the increased
tax pressure needed to finance the non-commercial sector has been in the
form of local taxes: "Given the federal structure of the USA, this process
is very unevenly distributed geographically... so that capital and high-
income labour have tended to flee the high tax areas and settle in areas
where the the growth of the non-market sector and resulting increasingly

heavier tax burdens are developing more slowly. This has produced a series of negative effects that are hard to redress, for while the city centres of the great conurbations saw their tax base shrink, the growth of social spending attracted low-income immigrants whose arrival inevitably exacerbated the imbalance."[66]

The lesson may be summarised in one sentence: "Where non-market spending rises faster than the rate a population wishes to finance, there will be countervailing action of various kinds by that population"[67] to get rid of the burden. But we need to go further and put systemic reasoning in the place of economic reasoning. Why is it that the mechanisms which determine the level of the non-commercial sector are able to create a rise that is not really desired by the majority of the population?

Because of a double defect.

Since it has already been analysed, there is no point in expanding on the first of them: the political decisions that create new categories of social spending are often made under pressure from active minorities, because those who have a great deal to gain individually from a measure form a vociferous coalition, whereas those who risk a very small loss per person (one of which they are often unaware) constitute a silent majority.

The second merits more reflection: contrary to a widely held misconception, state budget constraints are infinitely more elastic than those of the market. Thus, in a remarkable analysis, the Hungarian economist and recent president of the Econometric Society, J. Kornai, attributes the permanent poverty of socialist economies to the lack of adequate restraints to government spending. In other words (and J. Fontanet's argument in *Le Social et le Vivant* seems totally justified), the level of social services is not really controlled.[68] When the governments managing them notice deficiencies they naturally tend to try to make up for them by increasing their allowances; those individuals who are associated with the distribution of services (for example, doctors) obviously strive to provide the best service permitted by the current level of knowledge, without paying attention to the resulting costs for the community. As for the recipients, why should they establish a connection between general abstract services and their behaviour as consumers of specific services? It is all as if we were not dealing with resources that are in short supply, resources whose use in one area will mean forgoing them in others.

Where should we look for answers? Perhaps the most effective (though it raises a good number of objections) would be to perfect methods of allowing people to become aware of what their behaviour costs the community. It has also been suggested that people be given tickets that they may use for this or that social service (with the understanding that if they were to wish to consume more, they would have to pay, not in tickets any more, but in money). I understand governments that hesitate to take this road.

The second disease of the Welfare State is less widespread. It is linked to the challenge of the tax system. Economists have known for a long time that there is no such thing as a 'neutral' tax system. The 'fixed' contributions of their theoretical models which do not in any way change the allotment of their famous rare multiple-use resources are very difficult to put into practice. In practice, all contributions have a particular basis and consequently, by their very existence, cause economic agents to change their behaviour.

What have certain countries done for a part of the social spending of the Welfare State? They have changed fixed costs on the national level into expenditure that is proportionate to salaries on the level of the firm. An example: work accidents excluded, the cost of protecting French people against illness does not, at a first glance, depend on the level of activity and work. However, health insurance contributions are added to salaries. In other words, the tax system for social insurance contributions raises the marginal costs of labour above its level for society. The result? When companies make their calculations, examine the profitability of a production which requires additional jobs, or contemplate an investment that cuts down on labour, they underestimate the cost of this labour from the social point of view, and create fewer jobs than would be desirable. For a long time, the adverse effects of this procedure have not been evident because labour costs per unit produced rose slowly. This has not held true since 1968, whereas at the same time, a part of the Third World became capable of producing labour-intensive manufactured goods. Thus, the problem of the basis of assessment for social insurance contributions will probably crop up more and more acutely in the future. A problem that is totally independent of the level of supply of collective services. and which is created by the need to avoid distorting the arbitrage between extra production, extra jobs, and extra investment and productivity. The solution is not a simple one. It certainly does not consist of giving tax relief to labour-intensive industries, or equalising branches. No doubt a way worth exploring would involve the partial replacement of the present basis of assessment with the wider use of VAT, or income and capital tax.

In the case of the third disease, we must question the social efficiency of the Welfare State, "that is to say, the relation between the results being aimed at and the costs involved in achieving them."[69] In fact, the welfare state is no more protected from malfunctioning than the market. Thus, a non-commercial public organisation is in great danger of suffering from one or another of the following shortcomings: allowing a rather wide gap to develop between its official functions which are of general interest and its internal norms of behaviour; tolerating wasteful and rising costs; provoking unforeseen adverse results; giving rise to unfairness in the sharing of powers or revenues... In most countries this is coupled with the extreme complexity of the structures and procedures of the Welfare State to such an extent that only specialists can find their way in the jungle of treasuries, the scrubland of regulations and maze of procedures. Consequently, the apparent cost of redistribution is broadly lower than the real cost, because no one takes into consideration the expansion of the personnel departments of companies in business concerns, the doctors' and pharmacists' time wasted, the many procedures that users must go through... these inefficiencies do not come about by chance: they are mainly caused by the characteristics of non-commercial supply and demand: a final service that is tricky to define (if you are interested in the efficiency of the police, how do you define the security of citizens?), and whose level you evaluate by the volume of intermediary services that have only an indirect link with the real objective (the number of patrols carried out); a quality of service that is difficult to check in spite of Parliamentary Commissions, defence associations, and anti-fraud services; a lack of competition which makes it useless to look for comparisons; the impossibility of drawing up an account of advantages and costs, an impossibility that makes it possible for the 'private' objectives of each agency (such as maximising its budget or adopting the most sophisticated technologies) to be pushed to the fore... a demand that is seldom the direct expression of the aspirations of the users, but which is transmitted by the media and interest groups which take it upon themselves to express it (environmentalists, consumer groups, etc.); a political process that attaches much more importance to adopting the legislative or statutory solutions needed to supply a service, than to its effective implementation...

A sad fact for reformers, but there is no human institution that does not have its share of inefficiencies.

Finally there is the fourth disease, the nature of which is more ambiguous. Like Bernard Cazes, I would call it: the misleading redistributions of the welfare state. Misleading in terms of absolute poverty since, according to several studies, it may be that the reduction of absolute poverty in OECD countries would be due more to the general development of the economy than to the actions of the welfare state. Misleading in terms of relative poverty, since in the United States for example, only a small proportion of extra taxes on high incomes seems to have been actually assigned to the poorer section of the population. The prospects are not at all encouraging, because a significant redistributive effect involves taxes on the middle classes, and it is not certain that these taxes are politically possible.

This diagnosis of the pathology of the Welfare State heralds serious long-term problems for advanced industrial countries. In a context of slowed growth, bitter conflicts are ahead over the stake that the percentage of the national revenue devoted to public spending represents for different social groups. Conflicts that will be exacerbated by the spread of new aspirations.

Let us try to identify the main trends of the development of public spending common to OECD countries:

Naturally, social spending accounts for the greater part of this expenditure: education, health, transfers of income, etc. absorbed 46% of the total spending of states around 1975, against 37% around 1950. There are many reasons for this increase: the gradual growth of the population concerned (whether it is a question of higher education, health, pensions, or unemployment benefit); the relative rise in the the cost of public services compared with the costs of other goods and services; the influence of demography, especially on transfers (changes in the age structure explain 40% of the increase for pensions). In the future, the first reason will disappear, but the same cannot be said for the third... And certain demands in the area of health or transfers will continue to increase at the very time when new demands will be emerging. In Europe in particular, the rise of health spending will reduce, and could even make negative the growth of the income that households will have free use of.

A few years ago, the OECD constructed two scenarios for 1985: the first led to an increase in public social spending of 2 % of the GDP compared with 1975. It presupposed unchanged policies, but took into account demographic factors, the rise in the cost of public services, and an increase in allowances that adjusted itself to the per capita income; the second meant a rise of 6.5%. It assumed conformity with the best levels of services achieved by OECD countries, the introduction of new programs and a major expansion of allowances. For the leading countries, reality will fall somewhere between these two figures. There is absolutely no doubt about the conclusion. In the long term, the proportion of the national income assigned to social spending will increase, but, undoubtedly, more slowly than in the past, due to pressure from taxpayers. In order for the percentage of overall public spending to remain constant, the other items must be gradually reduced.

What will happen to another item – public financial aid to agriculture and industry? In recent years these have accounted for about 2.5% of the national income. The erratic and slow growth of these last years has brought about a sharp rise in direct and indirect subsidies to industry. In the future, the greater the difficulties of structural adaptation, the more governments will be under pressure to set up new programs aimed at fighting unemployment or helping industry.

What more is there? Spending on defence, infrastructure, general administration and national debt repayment. In the case of defence, the answer is already well known: an upward trend. The current development of policies of regulation does not favour an appreciable reduction of the cost of general administration. As for national debt repayment its short-term increase is written into the budget deficits of recent years... The only reduction possible is that of spending in urban and housing aid, taking demography into account. And even that is not certain.

The conclusion is inevitable: there will be heavy pressure on industrial societies to devote a higher proportion of the national income to public spending at the very time when a deceleration of growth will strengthen resistance to new taxes. Fine headaches ahead for Finance Ministers!

But the confrontation will be particularly aggravated by the new aspirations, and doubly so, because these aspirations undermine support of the welfare state by a growing proportion of the population while at the same time suggesting new functions that could well prove to be a mixed blessing.

In France, for example, A. de Vulpian notes "a major, but latent antagonism that is growing between socioculturally advanced Frenchmen who are motivated by a trend towards independence and spontaneity (they are particularly numerous among the youth, students, white collar workers and executives) on one hand, and on the other, the great unions and state bureaucracy that depend on those Frenchmen who are ruled by a quest for security (they are particularly numerous among people over 50 and among blue collar workers)[70]. Michel Crozier speaks of "the profound crisis of the models of administration, management and government in the face of growing complexity and the explosion of human freedom."[71] Any expansion of the cost of the welfare state therefore may well come up against the overt or covert opposition of large social groups.

But do not the new values constitute a 'new frontier,' and new opportunities for the Welfare State? Doubtless. As long as it resolves a tremendous difficulty, because it is no longer a question of providing identical services to individuals or families with fixed socioeconomic characteristics. Multiple demands from diverse minorities with hazy and variable outlines must be satisfied... A whole intellectual tradition must be changed, new institutions conceived and new laws invented.

Faced with this crisis, will advanced industrial societies give up whole sections of the Welfare State? A ridiculous solution. More than ever, slower growth will demand that there be none excluded from growth. It is also an unlikely solution, bearing in mind the powerful interests vested in the existing institutions. The only way open? Adaptation... probably a painful one. How?

First of all by viewing social policy as a whole, and not an aggregate of successive isolated measures. By being very aware of its overall impact on the various social groups. This integrated approach should expose flagrant injustices, unnecessary advantages, unjustified unearned incomes and inadequate protection, and prompt a concentration of effort on groups with a mass of handicaps.

Next, by seeing the Welfare State as a system in which interdependent social and economic agents interact. Not an isolated system, but one which influences the whole of the economic system, and which is in turn influenced by it. From then on, seeking to eliminate involuntary adverse effects that are the result of the modalities of its functioning.

And finally by accepting redistributions of tasks: between the welfare state and the market, between the welfare state and the 'third system' that seems to be on the horizon.

A tough job for future reformers.

# Unemployment and inflation at a time of inflexibility

For sixteen years, from 1952 to 1968, from the end of the Korean War to the student explosion, the Keynesian approach seemed to be a definitive recipe for hemming in the economy between full employment and moderate unemployment, between the indicator of inflation and a quasi-stagnation of prices, between the harbinger of a foreign trade deficit and a balance of trade. Then, a few years before 1974, the machine began to malfunction, unemployment became more sustained, inflation keener, and the burden of foreign trade balances became heavier. What is more, phenomena (such as the coexistence of unemployment and inflation) that the theory excluded, began to appear; and it was in this period that the waves of the two oil crises hit twice within a few years.

The iconoclasts hastened to cry, "The Keynesian theory has had its day; the time has come to throw it out!." "Absolutely not," replied the conservatives led by Paul McCracken, economic advisor to President Nixon: 1975 was no more than just another cyclical crisis, only aggravated by an independent political event – the Yom Kippur War and the rise in oil prices that it occasioned[72].

It is too early, at this stage in the book, to try to reconcile the contending forces. Because the comprehensive interpretation that goes beyond, and includes their point of view, combines the analysis of the international system and national economic systems. On the other hand, it is urgent that starting now, thought be given to transformations within advanced industrial countries that have, particularly in Europe, changed the genesis of unemployment and inflation.

Keynesian unemployment is caused by insufficient world demand. Companies do not take on more staff because they do not have any outlets. The prescription? Income distribution. Possibly in the form of wage rises. These incomes will generate spending, and, (if capacities are not fully utilised), rises in production, and thus increased employment.

Before 1974, other forms of unemployment began to emerge in OECD countries. Observing the development of the rates of residual unemployment from the period of boom (the unemployment rate during the time of full employment, so to speak) is enough to convince us: in the United States it moved from 3.6% in 1966 to 4.7% in 1973; in France it rose from 1.1% in 1964 to 1.6 in 1969, and 2.4% in 1973; in the Netherlands it climbed from 0.8% in 1965 to 1.4% in 1969, and 2.4% in 1973. What happened? We witnessed the simultaneous rise of classic unemployment and an unemployment of adjustment.

Why the term 'classic?' Quite simply, because this type of unemployment was identified by Nineteenth Century economists. It comes about when companies stop taking on more workers because they consider that the production they might get out of an extra worker would not cover the extra cost. The answer is to cut labour costs. New productions would become profitable and new workers would be taken to ensure them. Why is it then that in many advanced industrial societies, the cost of an extra unit of work has become both high and rigid? At least in the eyes of the employer. There are four related causes: the rapid rise of real wages even above increases in productivity; considerably heavier social contributions based on wages, at least in some countries; higher reversibility costs (it being thought that there is a greater risk of a future fall in demand, as well as higher monetary and legal costs of laying off workers); the soaring rise of the psychological and administrative costs of managing personnel under the double pressure of new aspirations and union demands. And the rigidities take many forms: agreements that fix relative wages by categories or regions, automatic promotion by seniority, regulations governing working hours and overtime, the right of worker representation... There is no doubt that these rigidities are socially desirable, but the hard fact remains: in many advanced industrial countries, there is such a firm expectation that labour costs will go up that industrialists – and even the government – will not take on more workers except as a last resort. They prefer to replace work with capital through investments in productivity. And if they still needed to take on workers? They would use temporary labour or create subsidiaries so as not to increase the number of workers with privileged status. Thus the working of the social oligopoly and the crisis

of the welfare state are dimly outlined. It is because these two phenomena are more markedly evident in Western Europe that classic
unemployment is so rampant there. One figure demonstrates this very
plainly: in the past ten years, European economies have not created a
single job; in contrast, the American economy, thanks to its greater
flexibility, has employed millions of extra people.

Keynesian unemployment has its victims: workers in sectors affected
by the deceleration of growth. And so does classic unemployment: young
people, easily taken on and even more easily laid off; women who often
do not have adequate technical training; and finally those unfortunate
people with several handicaps who could well find themselves gradually
excluded from the economic system.

But added to Keynesian and classic unemployement we have
adjustment unemployment which is created by a more or less accurate
balance between the supply and demand of jobs by professional category, sex, age, and employment area. The extent of the structural
adjustment of the economy, and the speed with which jobs are created
and destroyed directly affect the level of adjustment unemployment.
Even more so because industrial jobs are being destroyed and service
jobs are being created. Changes of behaviour on the part of people
looking for a job are also important: the generations now entering the
active population are much better educated than their predecessors.
They aspire to different jobs, but can we be sure that the structure of
supply is able to change so quickly? Furthermore, with changing values,
the rise in the standard of living, and unemployment benefit, the people
looking for jobs attach greater importance to the maintenance of their
social environment, the preservation of the quality of their private life,
and the content of their work, and as a result accept (should unemployment arise) a longer searching period so as to better satisfy many
aspirations. Let us not cry "Shame!" Unemployment in such a context is
also social progress... And finally reduced geographical mobility comes
in, because of the higher number of households with more than one
bread-winner, because of house and apartment ownership (in countries
where the tax systems and the functioning of the real estate market make
buying and selling onerous), because of the nature of the education
system in countries where decentralisation makes curricula so heterogeneous that moving from one region (or school) to another poses
difficult problems with regard to continuing the education of children.

"Keynesian unemployment, classic unemployment, and unemployment of adjustment, but what do you make of technical progress?
Where then do you place technological unemployment?" some readers

will be thinking. "Don't microprocessors cut out as many jobs as did the weaving machines of yesteryear?" My answer is clear and very close to the one given by Alfred Sauvy:[73] technical progress only generates temporary unemployment. It is one of the forces that creates the unemployment of adjustment.

Evaluating the extent of these three forms of unemployment is no easy task. Furthermore, there can be no question of pointing to someone and saying "You are an unemployed person of the Keynesian or classic type." However, certain studies suggest rough estimates:[74] in France in 1978, adjustment unemployment would have represented around 30% of the total, classic unemployment around 40%, and Keynesian unemployment only 30%. Ah, Slower Growth! What a good excuse you are!

Thus the causes of unemployment are deeply rooted in the functioning of developed societies. Should we therefore expect a vigorous shake-up on their part to eliminate said causes? We may well doubt it. The heads of companies think: "that's no concern of ours. Governments have other interests to defend." Trade unions are divided: ready to fight to preserve jobs in desperate rear-guard struggles, they are loath to start off along the road to making the labour market more flexible, to making a U-turn on decades of struggle, a path that is not in the least tempting to their members who are in secure jobs. Scattered and isolated, the unemployed themselves do not manage to form pressure groups. Unless they identify themselves with an ethnic minority (the blacks in certain American cities, for example), or are concentrated in a single regional industry (the iron and steel industry in Lorraine, for instance). Then and only then do governments become alarmed and take vigorous action.

However, what is at stake is important. For one thing, unemployment wastes a precious resource. What is worse, it may well render it useless for the future. By eroding people's abilities. By ruining their attitudes. By creating social outcasts. And then, if that is not enough, it costs the public treasury dear.

The labour market has not stopped tormenting the governments of developed countries with its two aspects. Is it not, on one hand, the distributor of incomes and purveyor of basic individual satisfactions, and on the other, the distributor of labour services, a distributor that knows how to take into account the infinite variety of human abilities and aspirations, individual flexibility, the malleability of organisations and jobs, and possible interchanges between labour and equipment? Whence a major political problem: how does one find forms of intervention that make social aims compatible with the way the working of the market affects employment? The problem is all the more difficult since the the present concepts to which developed societies refer implicitly could well lead them to one of two extreme situations:

Either the combination of a labour market that is very flexible, very competitive (and consequently very worrying for those seeking jobs) with specific protection of deprived social and economic categories, or a gradual ossification of the labour market with a narrowing of the range of net remunerations, strong protectionism and measures which ensure an artificial level of employment without preventing a section of the population from being excluded from the economic system because of the cost of employing them. The result is a serious weakening of the ability to adapt.

As for inflation, having run rampant for more than ten years, since 1983 it has resumed modest levels in the greatest industrial countries. But it would not be sensible to forget that their economies remain very vulnerable to this disease, and that improvement on the price front has only been achieved by bringing about the worst recession in 50 years.

We know that for the most part, the inflationary sequences have external causes such as the mechanisms that create international liquidities and the rise in the price of oil. But it is just as useful to be aware of domestic developments that generate inflation.

Obviously, a domestic explanation of inflation in Keynesian or monetarist terms is not enough: it is easy to understand that an excessive total demand which comes up against fully employed production capacity sets off an inflationary tendancy, but under such conditions why should inflation persist in a period of economic decline? Because of a cost-based inflation. I am convinced (naturally following the line of the analyses of the preceding chapters, but strongly reinforced by the research of Jean-Pascal Benassy, Robert Boyer and Rosa-Maria Gelpi[75]) that this cost-based inflation is the result of a gradual modification of the method of regulating capitalist economies, especially in Western Europe. These economies have moved from a competitive method of regulation (which operated in the first half of the Twentieth Century) to an oligopolistic mode of regulation (in the second half of the Twentieth Century) with the inter-war years being the roughest period of the transition.

Now, "competitive control is based on three sets of basic characteristics: a very precise codifiction of wages which, owing to the individual nature of the work contract and its time limit, makes the use and remuneration of the work force subject to the play of the market; a certain type of competition between capitalists that basically depends on prices even if the structure of production is not 'atomistic;' and finally intervention on the part of the state or monetary authorities which interfere very little – though not negligibly – with the spontaneous play of the market. It is therefore characterised by features which basically bring *price flexibility* into play. And according to the classic schema, prices react to demand being greater than supply, thus tending to bring about the balance of these two.

In oligopolistic control on the other hand, new institutional mechanisms (with financial concentration and centralisation replacing the old competition with a competition of the oligopolistic kind, the extension and codification of collective negociations gradually changing the individual character of the work contract) mean fresh procedures for making up prices and wages: prices are 'managed;' wages (their evolution is more and more parallel in all sectors, whatever the evaluation) include the rises in the cost of living and secondly rises in productivity. This relative lack of relationship between prices and the imbalances of the market presupposes the existence of social procedures to validate production and income: cyclical policies governing public spending, the extension of the indirect salary of unemployment benefits, and the quasi-guarantee by central banks of the solvency of the banking system help to stabilise fluctuations in demand, while the fact that wages increase in line with productivity makes consumption demand grow in proportion to potential production. These new procedures imply a relaxation of monetary constraint which allows the institution of forced currency and which, on the contrary, would have blocked the search for mechanisms linked with the gold standard."[76]

In terms of prices, the new control system has some major effects: it increases sensitivity to inflation, does not eliminate its adverse effects, and reinforces resistance to deflation.

Sensitivity to inflation inevitably follows these complementary propositions: (1) the members of the social oligopoly are constantly struggling to improve, or at least hold on to, their share of the national income; (2) the more an economy experiences high and lasting inflation, the more it learns immediately to adapt its expectations to the rise, and the more it strives to institute indexation; (3) through the acceleration or deceleration of prices, a country with rapid indexation amplifies all the exogenous shocks that affect costs. Until recently, in many countries of Western Europe, *de facto* indexation of incomes and prices had become a reality: thus the smallest price increase tended to spread and intensify.

Moreover, this indexation takes various forms. In the case of France, didn't Raymond Barre mention in his declaration to the Social and Economic Council in 1980 three other causes of inflation apart from indexation in the strict sense of the word (the way that agricultural prices are being set, the absence of competition in the commercial sector, and a fiscal system that relies mostly upon indirect taxation)? J. Delors repeated the same analysis, in different words, when in 1982 he began battling with the social oligopoly to reduce inflation.

"What does it matter?" some will say: "Indexation may increase the risk of fire, but it also diminishes its effects." Wrong. They forget the negative effects of inflation. Effects that are the result of the great uncertainty about its future rates and its lack of neutrality, for indexation has made few inroads into whole sections of the economy: the domestic operations of borrowing and lending, since it has been well established many times that real interest rates fall when the inflation rate rises; transactions with other countries, since it has been proven that in the medium term, variations in exchange rates only partly compensate for the differentials in rates of inflation from one country to another; bookkeeping entries and the paying of taxes, since the regulations only recognise nominal prices; and finally the hoarding of currency, since deposits on demand in the banks give very low returns.

Here are a few examples of some of the consequences.

Capacity investments are discouraged in favour of investments in productivity because companies are afraid of long-term commitments. Is it not true that as soon as inflation slows down the real burden of loans becomes unbearable?

Households are penalised by inflation. They are constantly sold short. In France, in 1978, the decreased purchasing power of the franc made a large hole in the liquid assets of households to the tune of more than 90 billion francs, or 7.7% of their disposable net income, 55% of the annual increase of this income, and 32% of their savings... The beneficiaries have been the borrowers, i.e. the companies which, due to the situation, have seen their added value go up by 5%, or 39% of their gross savings! The protection of incomes does not extend to legacies.

As for companies, they no longer have any gauge of their results, and there is no connection betweeen the taxes they pay and their real profits.

Deflation is therefore desirable. Unfortunately, the process of seeking it comes up against tough resistance in most European societies. Heavily penalised by the drop in inflation, households and companies in debt react strongly. The former demanding wage rises; the latter curbing the deceleration of prices, cutting down their investment, and even their current activity. Inflation has hardly been dealt a blow before recession sets in. Isn't this the message we get from 1981 and 1982? No deflation without a sharp drop in economic activity.

What is left then of the policy of macroeconomic control? Today's Minister of Finance enviously contemplates the portrait on the wall of his predessor standing in front of the levers of his instrument panel. By modifying exchange rates, controlling the amount of money in circulation, adjusting the size of the budget deficit, this predecessor could, if he combined his actions prudently, ensure full employment, price stability, and the foreign balance all at the same time. The instrument panel is indeed still there, but the first lever (the one that acts on the exchange rate) is either in the hands of the market, or produces such dubious results that the minister hardly dares to touch it any more. And as for the other two, he handles them with extreme caution, because braking too hard barely affects inflation while pushing up unemployment, and an over-vigorous boost accelerates inflation even before creating jobs. "Levers! Levers! I need some new levers!" cries the minister in desperation, like the English king who howled one evening after losing a battle: "My kingdom for a horse!"

What levers? We shall return to the subject.

# Democracy on trial

Prospective analysis of the future development of economic institutions must be used as a guide and not as a screen. A guide to the analysis of the core of developed societies, their political systems, serving as the last stage of this reflection on the contestations and ossifications. What is the question that we should be asking? Simply put: what would become of these systems under the sole pressure of the internal dynamics of the societies which produce them if external constraints did not interfere? Or, in other words, how would the control deficiency of national systems evolve in the absence of international pressures?

The clew: Western democracies are (with significant differences on both sides of the Atlantic) a mixture of three democracies. A formal democracy that legitimates the legislative and executive on which the state apparatus depends through the ballot box. A corporatist democracy that brings together the government and the other members of the social oligopoly. A spontaneous democracy that flourishes here and there at the initiative of many groups of citizens.

The interaction of these three democracies is constant, complex, and often jarring. A wildcat strike (spontaneous democracy)? Employers and unions try to end it by means of negociations (corporatist democracy) or ask the government to make an edict or pass a law (formal democracy). Parliament prepares to discuss a text (formal democracy)? Pressure groups are mobilised to influence representatives and pour their members out onto the streets (corporatist democracy); the masses follow or they don't (spontaneous democracy). What are the challenges that these democracies will have to face in the decades ahead? What political systems are likely to emerge from the evolution of their relationships? To answer these questions is to answer the initial question itself.

Honour to whom honour is due: let us begin with formal democracy whose weak points have contributed to the development of the other democracies. Where are these weak points? On the level of the legislative and its relations with the executive; on the level of the control of the civil service, on the level of the links between the political system and the electorate, on the level of regional organisation.

The legislative system of practically all Western democracies is ailing. Ossified by the underlying structure of parties, it shows itself to be ill-suited to interpret the varied demands of an increasingly mixed society... Worse still: when it is not firmly controlled, it engenders (through the interaction of parties or factions) impotence and instability. Present-day Italy is reminiscent of France at the time of the Fourth Republic, and following Watergate, the Americans have discovered the dangers of a dominant Congress... We cannot be sure that the legislative system will in the future be able to avoid the terrible dilemma of becomimg either a rubber stamp office or the source of political inco- herence... Its function is important: much less as a counterbalance to the executive (corporatist and spontaneous democracy now undertake this) than as the protector of those who are not well defended by the social oligopoly, or who do not dare express themselves except in the silence of the polling booth.

The control of government agencies is one of the Achilles' heels of modern democracy. The diagnosis is well known. The ambiguity of relations between the executive and administration. While the former does not make good use of the abilities of the latter, the latter largely escapes the authority of the former, as much in its daily functioning as in the dynamics of its development; furthermore, it exhausts the executive's energy in a maze of technical discussions and turns every broad strategy into a disparate collection of miscellaneous detailed measures... The response of the administrative system to an increasingly complex but mobile society, is a collection of compartmentalised rules, admittedly adapted to particular needs, but inclined to generate ossification. In many developed countries the tragedy of government is inadequate communication. Horizontal communication essential for formulating comprehensive policies that have nothing to do with the regional division of administrative fortresses. Vertical communication that chan- nels information like tree sap and passes on political will to all levels... I shall hazard a prediction: the situation will become so critical in the next twenty years that many Western countries, (led by the United States) will try to make general reforms. Drawing their inspiration from the

Japanese government (yes, you heard me right!), hoping to achieve a more fluid circulation of information, a wider contribution to the preparation of synthetic policies, and much speedier implementation... These reforms will prove to be only half successful, but they will curb the spread of the explosion of government.

The third weakness of formal democracy? It may well rot its own roots, because it questions communication between the political system and citizens as a whole. Whether it is the legislative, the executive or the administrative, the quality of information received is often inadequate. As for the control of individuals over the administrative system, it is virtually ineffectual. Moreover, as at the time of the decline of the Roman Empire, governments set about financing mediators to protect citizens against their own administration. Privileged connections have taken on the form of a confrontation between the head of government and public opinion, two adversaries who look each other straight in the eye armed with opinion polls and television broadcasts. The head of government is ever questioning his popularity. Should his rating fall, he becomes agitated; public opinion, for its part, focuses its criticisms, hopes, respect and hatred on him personally. Reacting against the influence of an anonymous political system, formal democracy is embodied in a face. But this confrontation has a kill-joy, a third actor, perhaps the most powerful of the three: the journalist. Robed in the dignity of his authority which he places above Justice itself, ever in search of buyers, this wholesaler or retailer of information, strives to create the event, predict a catastrophe, declare that there will be no such thing, uncover scandals, disseminate secret documents, simplify, cut, amplify, and caricature. Much more dangerous than data processing, he will not stop until private lives, military programs, public debate, and business negociations are brought out into the open, whatever the consequences for the society to which he belongs. It matters little to him that the State Department in Washington is no longer able to keep a secret, that US presidents are practically forced to go out into a garden to discuss serious business. This Saint George will not stop until he has laid democratic societies bare. Turn the clock back? Out of the question. Information cannot be bottled up because it is the blood that circulates in the veins of democracy. And the need for freedom that motivates those individuals who are the leaven of democracy, forces them to push freedom of information to the limit, until new ethics that everyone will feel the need for, emerge.

The final weakness of formal democracies: their territorial organisation. This will be a growing source of concern for the governments of developed countries. Whether one is speaking of parish, region, state,

*Land*, province or republic, whatever the different names and realities, it is always a system subject, and attached to, the hierarchical control of the national system. How do we evaluate this system? It is a vital element of freedom; an agent that creates certain inequalities while at the same time correcting others; a weapon of participation par excellence; a source of efficiency if geographic boundaries and the delegation of decisions are adequate; a factor of adaptability when decentralisation is moderate, and a source of weakness in tough international competition if decentralisation is extreme; it is always in conflict with the state, with which it only arrives at short-term balances, the long-term trend being towards imbalance, only controlled by the national ideology and the threat of other states. Thus we may aver that territorial organisation will continue to be one of the favoured and fragile links between formal democracy and spontaneous democracy, and that the problem will be reconciling social change with unchanging rules without which decentralisation does not make sense.

Such are the problems of formal democracy; but they may only be fully appreciated in relation to the other two democracies.

There is no point in going over the internal mechanisms of corporatist democracy: they become identified with the interplay within the social oligopoly but here we must underline the constant efforts put forth by corporatist democracy to acquire institutions recognised by formal democracy: that is the true framework for interpreting French labour laws, with, for example the recognition in the company of the union sector and the unions' privilege of being the only ones allowed to present candidates for elections of employee representatives. Nonetheless, the traditions of advanced industrial societies differ on one point (and everything would seem to indicate that this will continue into the future): the nature of the connections between formal democracy and corporatist democracy. It is particularly intense in the United Kingdom where the link is made within the Labour Party, relatively close in Italy and France, and minimal in West Germany and the United States, where it only retains its basic component: pressure on the Congress and dialogue with the executive. That does not prevent political parties and oligopolistic structures from trying constantly to woo each other: with votes and regulations up against each other.

But for some years now, corporatist democracy has been fearful at the sight of its foundations being undermined by spontaneous democracy. The erosion is hitting it in its most vulnerable area – the system of nominating leaders. A system which depends more on cooption or the centralism dear to the Communist Party than on electoral democracy.

So corporatist democracy is trying to adapt, and is making its procedures more flexible so as to avoid a rash of organisations as well as disobedience among the rank and file that would rob contacts between social partners of all value. Because what corporatist democracy wants to do is to redesign society in such a way that capitalism is locked into an economy that is sufficiently planned so that the distribution of the national income and the factors of production in the economy are the result of negociations between the various members of the social oligopoly. It is up to each individual to decide whether such a scheme is revolutionary or if it is not rather the conservative result of a kind of social ossification.

Just as corporatist democracy has got into the habit of dining with formal democracy since the beginning of the century, so spontaneous democracy, the third member of our trinity, has turned up to supper with the other two without so much as an invitation card. It is the most elusive of the three diners. One day here. Another day there. Inventing, creating, upsetting, disappearing, and rising from its ashes. A source of creativity, but also a source of violence. The immediate violence of groups of protesters; the calculated violence of organised terrorism. This spontaneous democracy splinters into a host of minorities whose adherents have the same demands; it tries to live like a fish in the water of a benign majority; it strives to infiltrate the government, political parties and superstructures of the social oligopoly. It shares the tragedy common to all spontaneous movements: continued action implies institutions, and all institutions brings about differences in the participation of members! However, it must get itself recognised by formal and corporatist democracy. Legal or clandestine association, legal action or violent attack: these are the means of taking advantage of formal democracy or forcing it to make compromises that it will not acknowledge. Wildcat strikes, the demand for freedom of expression within the company; this is the way to get corporatist democracy going, or to short-circuit it. But by standing for elections and creating new unions, spontaneous democracy constantly runs the risk of seeing its most active batallions incorporated into the other two democracies.

What synthesis can the dialectics between these three sub-systems lead to?

First conjecture: contrary to a widely held opinion, they can coexist within the same organisation. Proof of this? The French National Centre for Scientific Research: here bureaucracy reigns supreme and defines the least use of funds in detail. As far as it is concerned, a researcher's time is worthless, because it is a fixed expense. The only things that count are train tickets, hotel and telephone bills... Corporatist democracy is satisfied: it has supreme control over the status of personnel, over the rules governing promotion, and parity with other civil servants... Spontaneous democracy gets something out of it: efforts from above to orient research are wasted – researchers do what they like... Tomorrow the same mixture may be found elsewhere: in the management methods of central government, methods that will come to terms with the disappearance of the duty of civil servants not to divulge secrets and not to oppose the government publicly, in nationalised business concerns that adopt simpler systems of management in order to be compatible with the indiscipline of personnel; in methods of resolving social conflicts that tolerate the chaos of spontaneous democracy while all the time leaning on corporatist democracy.

But (second conjecture) each of these sub-systems could also bloom in favoured and favourable areas. the influence of spontaneous democracy could become stronger in the local development of rural and urban space, in small service businesses, on the organisational level of workshops, in production units of the 'third system.' On the national level, it would manifest itself through events that sharply reveal new aspirations as yet unknown to the other democracies, or through social innovations capable of being extended over the whole of society. Corporatist democracy would take root in the large public and private organisations; it would make itself the guardian of security and equality through contracts and codes. Finally, the responsibility of nominating the executive, seeking a minimum of national coherence, and controlling relations with other states will fall to formal democracy.

Which leads us to one last question: do not advanced industrial societies (with their complexity born of creativity and ossification) run the risk of becoming ungovernable? Of forever living in the shambles of a semi-anarchy made possible by their incredible output? And why not? Why should a society need to be governed, when it would seem that hyper-complex systems are uncontrollable, that they have a constant need of 'noise,' of disorder, in order to adapt? That answer would be enough if developed societies were turned in on themselves or were ready to merge with a vast world society... This eventuality is not a part of the possible histories of the decades ahead. During this period, advanced industrial societies (the United States included) will have to confront external threats, and excessive ossification is just as likely to kill them as excessive creative disorder. Moreover, the second control inadequacy (the one that is concerned with the great national systems and takes the form of a kind of impotence when it comes to controlling these systems, and a kind of inadequacy *vis à vis* methods of formulating their objectives) will become more important. The range of the futures of advanced industrial societies? It lies totally in the interference between national and international control inadequacies, in the conflict between the multipolar interdependent world, and the internal dynamics of societies torn between contestations and ossification.

.

# DEVELOPED SOCIETIES AT THE CROSSROADS OF PRESSURES

"He who strives too hard to save his life shall lose it."

Gustave Thibon
*L'Echelle de Jacob*

# Sea winds and land breezes

The winds that blow from the four corners of the earth and those that come off our mountains hold developed societies in a vice like two enormous jaws, kneading, flattening, pounding their structures, while at the same time generating creative volcanic eruptions. The time has come to stand at the confluence of these pressures and finally leave analysis for synthesis.

A synthesis that develops through two stages. If it falls to the latter of the two, spreading the wings of scenarios to try to describe the range of possible worlds, the task of asking how the merging of contrary winds will shape the relief of industrial societies is left to the former.

Firstly, what should one say about the growth prospects of such societies? About the growth of the (monetary and summary, desired and decried) national income which, despite changing values will continue to be a great hope of their citizens and a basic aim of their governments?

And then, how does one characterise the likely transformations of their economic, social and political structures based on the inventory of internal and external pressures that will weigh on these structures, and the list of rigidities that will tend to oppose them? How do we outline the future of these structures? With their significant economic activities, their driving economic agents, their representative social groups and their principal political organs?

But do not be misled by the occasional use of the future tense. The likely and the unforeseeable are the two inseparable sides of the coin of our futures. The descriptions outlined will only take on their full significance within the framework of comprehensive scenarios, when they are put back into the wider context of the major uncertainties.

Before embarking on this programme, there remains one more preliminary that must be dealt with. An important preliminary which might well have figured at the beginning of this book: the study of that vital component of our futures – technical progress. "At last!" exclaim some readers, annoyed, irritated, mystified or disappointed by the scant references made to it so far. And the line that I have taken calls for an explanation. No one can deny that for a very long time – over half a century – scientific and technical discoveries have been among the principal causes of the widening of the range of possibilities of human history. On such a horizon, the systemic description of the relationship between society and science should therefore be one of the clews of thought. I am not convinced that the same will hold true for a few decades. The scientific discoveries likely to be exploited are well known, and it is possible to foresee the outcome of the great technical adventures. Was it not possible to foretell the use of nuclear power to produce electricity, the calculator explosion and the dawn of genetic engineering since 1945–1950? Prospective analysis that gives greater importance to the decades ahead must therefore train its projector on those sequences that may well provoke crises. On geopolitical changes and social mutations that create a framework for the interpretation of current developments. This is the reason that has informed choice.

However, this must not lead to confusion on two points. In no way does it mean that the impact of technical progress on the various national societies is negligible. Neither does it imply an exogenous technical progress whose implementation would be independent of the economic and political system. As we stop for a moment to look at the marvellous film of the great technological adventures of tomorrow, we must not forget that this film only makes sense in relation to a a wider vision of the future of industrial societies.

# New technological frontiers

Technical progress is running out of steam; Technical progress is dying... As in all periods of slow growth, voices were raised some years ago blaming sluggish economic development on the exhaustion of this *deus ex machina*. Without telling us whether they were concerned with cutbacks in research resources, a reduced capacity for making new discoveries or greater resistance to the utilisation of results. Consequently, they did not differentiate between the dynamics of technical research itself and the dynamics of its interaction with society.

Nevertheless, it is absolutely essential that this distinction be made. Let us adopt it. After that, according to the almost unanimous opinion of the experts, the conclusion is inevitable: the dynamics of technical research itself have lost none of their vigour. Four of the greatest adventures of all time are unfolding before our very eyes, while at the same time a host of less important adventures are taking place. We have already encountered these jewels in the crown: the rise of the electronic complex, the explosion of biology and bioagronomy, the conquest of the ocean and space, changes in the methods of producing and consuming energy.

Why use the term 'electronics complex' when we already have Nora and Minc's apt neologism – *telematics*[77] because, in my opinion, the marriage of data processing and telecommunications is only one of the components of a much wider whole which also includes all the applications of electronics to industrial automation (robotics), the performance of service tasks (office computing), the making of traditional or new products with a high electronics content. Like a rising tide, this whole development is in the process of spreading to all areas of industrial society, changing profoundly the whole structure of its technical system.

One thing is certain: "In the next twenty years, we shall see appearing on the market new intelligent systems made up not only of microprocessors, but also of new types of sensors, pick-ups, and actuators, as well as glass fibres and lasers, all of this coordinated by sophisticated software."[78] The basis of this revolution (the word is not too strong, because we are dealing with a decisive qualitative leap) has been a drastic drop in the size of components: in twenty years, as much due to rapid access memories based on conductors as to large capacity magnetic memories, the amount of data that can be stocked on a square centimetre of medium has been multiplied by 10,000. And the evidence would seem to indicate that this rate of progress will continue up to the year 2000. Moreover, the cost of a computerised operation should continue to fall by 20% each year. Regarding the logical circuits of computers, densification – and consequently increased power – comes up against the need to use up the thermal energy given out, but new technologies, based on the use of liquid helium, should soon be available. However, between now and the end of the century, they will only affect large computers[79].

As a result of the advances made in components, data processing will come into more general use. Microprocessors will make it possible to equip terminals and data acquisition units with a capacity that they lack at the moment. Gone will be the days of the hierarchy of the central computer directing limited peripherals! Data bases will multiply, because the cost of memory will have become negligible, and owing to the use of parallel search microprocessors, access time will be reduced. As for the arsenal of input-output devices, it will be enlarged with laser, ink jet or electric printers, devices for synthesising and recognising the human voice, and scanner systems that make it possible to read images.

These are the wedding gifts brought by the bride's family. What about the groom's marriage settlement? It includes the new transmission technologies such as satellites and optic fibres, progress in commutator technology and the widespresad use of electronic commutation, the linking of computer networks and data banks, the use of a wide range of input-output devices: teleprinters, telecopiers...

Gradually the electronic revolution will reach every factory, office, hospital, school and home.

Right now, factories are becoming more and more automated each day. Whether it is a question of regulating, by means of calculators, continuous processes such as oil refining, or producing sequences of discontinous operations such as the manufacture of cars or gear-boxes (with the help of robots). A tour of the office will feature accounting machines, file storage, devices for typesetting and transmitting texts and teleconference installations. The electronic transfer of money will radically simplify banking systems. The computer will become indispensable in hospitals, not only for management, but also for the examination of analyses, the continuous monitoring of the condition of patients, and as a diagnostic aid. Gradually, the teaching machine will take its place in schools where children will be introduced to the computer from a very young age. As for households, they will send their letters by telefax, check their bank balance or a price list long-distance, subscribe to special television services, ensure their security by means of electronic locking devices, drive a car with its carburation or the contents of its exhaust fumes regulated by a microprocessor, and will even be able to work at home tapping away at their terminals.

We have seen this film a dozen times. In technicolor and cinemascope. It has fascinated some and pained others. What does it really mean for our futures?

1. First, an observation: the emission, transmission and processing of the most varied data will be the hub of the economic and social activities of our societies. So many of our dreams will come true: from the tyre that says to the driver "I need air" to the dial in the car that indicates the least crowded route from Heathrow Airport to Hampstead, from the robot that replaces interpreters in international conferences to checking all the prices of the shops in the area from the comfort of your home. But let us not get carried away. The fact that an electronic application is technically feasible does not automatically mean that it will be introduced. The cost of the hardware will indeed be negligible, but the same cannot be said of the time it takes to develop the software, to collect and update data, and for systems to be used by individuals. Scarcities will change, because a computerised society will be a society where a close check on the use of time and grey matter will predominate.

2. Next, a question: will not the triumph of electronics generate higher unemployment in developed countries? Listen to what the economist has to say on this difficult subject: there is no reason why this should be so in the long term. Even if computers were to prove themselves better than people in every job possible (an extreme hypothesis) the mere fact that their relative superiority varies from one kind of job to another will be enough to guarantee the full use of people. Why? The parable of the executive who knew how to type is a good enough illustration. He was a better manager and better typist, but (and this is perhaps a heroic hypothesis) his *relative* superiority in management was greater. When

asked, an economist used a rough calculation to demonstrate that efficiency demanded that the secretary be used to type and the director to manage... Now, none of us would argue that a calculator is relatively much better at doing additions than at giving a charming welcome to the participants of a congress... This long-term conclusion about employment does not in any way exclude the possibility that improved living standards will lead individuals to apply different arbitrages to the organisation of their time, but this no longer has anything to do with unemployment. It will create new jobs. In industry, banking, insurance... In new services especially, and (for those countries that are capable of securing a large share of international markets) in the electronics industry itself. But there is no guarantee that there will always be a balance between destruction and creation. On the other hand there is no doubt that it will cause an upheaval of the structure of jobs: a reduction of repetitive jobs, monitoring posts multiplied, more jobs in data transcription or in intellectual investments... Less laborious work but more nervous tension or boredom, less physical exertion but more mental activity.

3. Finally, another question: is this combination of telecommunications and computing a threat to freedom? The question is badly put, because it will not impose a distribution of power in society; it will only modify the technical context within which choices will be made. Choices about centralisation and decentralisation, choices about participation and life styles. It will facilitate the monopoly of information by the holders of the big data banks or increase the risk of crucial computerised files intruding in people's private lives, as much as it will make it possible for everyone to select the data that they receive, work out themselves what to entrust to others, and enrich their contacts with the outside world. On a more prosaic level, the electronic complex will only reinforce an old tendancy of democratic industrial societies: a gradual widening of individual possibilities at the price of openness towards others.

If the microprocessor is our steam engine, and gives coherence to the nascent technical system of the next twenty years, its successor – or accomplice – is already on the horizon: it is the living cell, instrument and symbol of a new revolution, for biology could well have as great an impact on our societies in the Twenty-first Century as chemistry and physics in the Twentieth.

In the past forty years, biological engineering has advanced so much in the knowledge of genetic material, the reproductive processes of species, and the biochemical foundations of cell metabolism that it is now flowing into the high seas of applications.

An initial direction: the domestication of strains of microbes, and with it the possibility of "isolating strains of mutant bacteria that have the ability to secrete very interesting metabolites wuch as lysin, a basic component of the food intake of animals; of using the enzymatic metabolism of bacteria to biodegrade waste produced by urban and social activity; of establishing a veritable discipline of biometallurgy thanks to sulphate-reducing bacteria; of using bacteria to detect the carcinogenic effects of a product through the bacterial mutations it creates; of replacing present-day non-degradable chemical insecticides (whose long-term effects are unknown) with toxins derived from the metabolisms of bacteria..."[80]

The second family of new applications "is concerned with bioconversions, beginning with the production of natural (wood, plants) or artificial biomasses (cultures of yeast on hydrocarbons to produce proteins). Cultures on sewage that make it possible both to purify them and to reconstitute a food biomass for animals. Real chemical factories become possible through suitable biological cultures: the production of methanol from cellulose, gas from animal dejecta, acrylic or lactic acids."[81] There is only one obstacle: productivity is as yet too low for the method to be commercially viable.

Finally there is the royal road of genetic engineering: it consists of putting a foreign gene into a bacterium. Cultivate the infected bacterium and hey presto! You have a factory that produces the protein made by the gene. This obviously heralds a revolution in pharmocology, with the emergence of new generations of medicines, as well as in agriculture, with for instance, the possibility of cultivating plant cells without manure!

Apart from genetic engineering, we may expect considerable repercussions from transformations in immunology: the application of the technique of hybridomisation to obtain highly purifed antibodies with diagnostic and therapeutic uses; the multiplication of vaccines against tropical diseases; the artificial modification of an individual's immune responses in order to fight cancers or infectious diseases; the selective suppression of transplant rejection while maintaining responses to other foreign invaders.

In neurobiology? The experts agree that the chemical transmitters of the central nervous system will soon be indexed and their receptors better known. Moreover, a whole range of mental illnesses will become treatable with drugs.

No area will feel the impact of the biological revolution as much as agriculture. Listen to Jacques Poly's synthesis: "Twenty-first Century

agriculture will avoid all waste; it will be more sparing in its use of
industrial, and especially energy products, by creating plants capable of
fixing nitrogen from the air without fertilisers; it will use waste
intensively to produce energy, animal feed or chemicals: thanks to
specially adapted plant species it will be possible to cultivate presently
neglected land. After the industrial revolution that has completely
changed agriculture in our century, will come the biological revolution
which, thanks to sophisticated techniques of selecting new species, will
make it possible to improve reproductive processes, and create micro-
organisms that will replace pesticides in the fight against agressive
agents: the bioconversion of waste products will develop rapidly..."[82]

Time to catch our breath. And to reflect.

On time lags: confidence in the future of the bioeconomy does not
preclude some caution with respect to the speed of its diffusion. If we are
in the middle of the electronic revolution, then the biological revolution
is only just beginning. No doubt it will mature for one or two decades
before exploding. But those who want places must take them starting
now. On the level of laboratories for basic research.

On the effect it will have on economic structures: the biological
microfactory looks very much like a laboratory. No workers. Minimum
consumptions of energy. An output that is measured in grams or kilos. A
far cry from late Nineteenth century factories with their heavy
machinery!

On moral questions: having become the driving force of evolution,
man works at creating species; he gives himself the power to reproduce
himself. A power that is much greater than his ability to destroy himself
with a nuclear blast. What will justify the use of this power? What
regulations will limit the risk of it getting out of control? There is no
ready answer. The *praxis* of ethics is also a progressive creation.

The film continues. The third adventure takes us from the infinitely
small to the infinitely large. From the cell to the ocean and to space.
From man's power over his natural environment to the expansion of the
frontiers of this environment. But we must keep our heads firmly screwed
on: the stakes here are of a different dimension altogether.

The sea? We know that thanks to advances in the techniques of
submarine intervention (divers, manned submarines and robots), it will
be possible to exploit oil in wells 9 to 12,000 feet deep by the end of the
century. We have all heard of metallic nodules of manganese, nickel,
copper and cobalt lying at a depth of 15,000 feet; it is conceivable that
they may be exploitable towards the end of the century. The laying of
pipelines at 6000 feet, the operation of floating factories, aquaculture: all

examples of the colonisation of the sea. But aquaculture is a difficult art, and we should not expect revolutions. According to the FAO, the production of marine farming (molluscs included) should add 25 million tonnes to the 70 million tonnes of traditional fishing by the end of the century. Current studies cover fish whose price justifies the cost of research: thunnidae, salmonidae, bass, doradoes, turbots and sole.

As for space, its exploration will revolutionise astronomy, but apart from military uses, direct application will continue to be insignificant: certainly "the installation of weightless production units in space, or solar captors that would transmit energy to earth by means of laser beams is conceivable, but between now and the end of the century we cannot expect satellites to be used for any purpose other than observation and the relaying of transmissions. Satellites are primarily a means of observing the earth. Beyond military uses and teledetection, we must mention applications to geophysics, cartography, mine prospecting, and following the evolution of vegetation. With regard to metereology, geostationary satellites or satellites in polar orbit are absolutely necessary for collecting various three-dimensional measurements on the state of the atmosphere which are necessary for integrating the thermohydrodynamic equations that govern its evolution, and for making both better weather forecasting and a better understanding of climates possible."[83] All this is very important, but not essential.

Let us now come to the last of the great adventures – energy. Here we find a tremendous technical effort. Its aims? Better exploration of the earth's deeper strata through geology and geophysics; deep, controlled drilling ; assisted recovery of oil; submarine pipelines laid at great depths: the distillation of coal *in situ*; transportion of mixtures of water and coal through pipelines; the production of synthetic gas; development of breeder reactors; the domestication of nuclear fusion; solar-powered heating for buildings; the production of industrial temperatures of between 100 and 500 degrees from solar energy; the production of electricity by means of solar-powered stations with fields of parabolic mirrors (heliostats); the production of electricity from photovoltaic batteries; the transportation of energy in the form of liquid hydrogen; the use of biomass and geothermics; the storage of secondary energy, either underground or through chemical bodies capable of creating endothermic reactions; energy-saving industrial techniques, such as induction heating, as opposed to flame-based processes. About when should we look for these areas of research? Either in the next decade (breeder reactors), or in the second quarter of the next century (nuclear fusion, liquid hydrogen)... But there is an obvious paradox. Although the availability of energy will determine the growth of world economy (the way a leash defines a dog's sphere of action), none of the upheavals that are currently taking place in the field of energy will have an effect on everyday life comparable with that of electronics or biology. Basically, the consumer of the year 2050 will (like us) use the electric switch, the gas valve and the petrol pump. He will be able to forget the tremendous changes taking place in the basic stages of the production process.

Reducing advances on the technological front as a whole to four major battles may have the advantage of clarity, but it also has the disadvantage of neglecting a multitude of areas: climatology; the control and protection of the environment with the development of 'clean' technologies; the perfection of new materials that correspond with characteristics defined a priori; the mastery of phenomena that cause breakage, corrosion and wear, to cite but a few examples. In the technological war against the unknown, the armoured divisions should not cause us to forget the infantry.

But as soon as "The End" appears on the screen, someone must stand up to protest. On behalf of the two technological adventures that the film has passed over, despite the fact that they are in no way less important than those mentioned so far:

• The adventure of adapted technologies which rallies part of the huge technical effort of the Third World round its flag. From the improvement of the traditional techniques of artisans to the transposition of Northern industrial techniques. From the perfection of new methods of education or health protection to research on the specific problems of tropical areas.

• The adventure of social innovation which regroups all the advances of praxis and methodology in such widely varying areas as national development, town planning, community life, the management of business concerns and civil services, worker management, communication, training... This innovation has two roots. On one hand, there are the advances inspired by the humanities, from psychology to economy, and from sociology to political science. The fact that one may (as in the case of technical progress) dispute the value of such knowledge to the well-being of society detracts nothing from its magnitude. On the other hand, there are the spontaneous initiatives of small creative groups that grow and die or gradually spread through the whole society.

In another period, a chapter on the future of technology would probably have restricted itself to this overview of the vistas opened by the state of research. Nothing would be more alien to a book such as this one which professes to be inspired by a systemic approach. The technical system of a society does not only have its own dynamics. It maintains close and complex links with science, economics, politics and culture.

It is continually fed by science, and is the most extraordinary example of a self-organised system propelled by that tremendous internal energy – the thirst for knowledge, the unquenchable curiosity of scientists, and their desire to gain the prestige of recognition from their colleagues.

That is where the long-term future of our societies is being elaborated. That is where our future power over the ecosphere originates. That is where tomorrow's economic and military competition begins to take shape. That is where you find the roots of future contestations. For, without giving objectives, science is now thinking of the way in which these objectives are framed. And scientific thought is only just beginning to shake human societies.

The economy restricts the technical system at both ends. Upstream, through the volume of investments that the economic agents (including the state) agree to devote to scientific and technical research. Downstream, through the applications that it decides to use. When the rate of growth falls, the struggle over the distribution of the national income jeopardises research funds or concentrates them only on projects that give short-term results. When the future prospects of growth look bleak and uncertain, the only innovations to see the light of day will be those that bring immediate profit. Now this is one of the real problems of our societies, and not an alleged dullness of the technical system itself... Do we need to remind ourselves of the fact (since it has already been mentioned and will be taken up again later) that the technical system in turn models the economic system, as much in the evolution of its structure as in its growth potential?

As for politics, its impact on the technical system often merges with that of the economy, except for some objectives: it makes an autonomous military effort possible, ensures a place in the first division of scientific football, reinforces the competitive capacity of the economy beyond the horizon of short-term profitability, and prevents a revolt on the part of researchers. Consequently, one does not need to be a first-class prospective analyst to aver that, in advanced industrial societies, clashes over the setting of the level and volume of public funds dedicated to research will become more and more violent. Torn between the constraints of slow growth and the pursuit of ever more pressing objectives, governments will find themselves faced with difficult decisions from year to year. In the opposite direction, in an international, multipolar,

interdependent system, the level of the technical system of a country will
to a large extent determine the future options of its government.

But, perhaps the most important interaction will take place between
the technical and cultural systems. Ever since the Industrial Revolution,
the social value of technical progress has only been challenged by a few
people on the fringes. As Alvin Toffler puts it: "Throughout the whole
Second Wave civilisation, three *idées forces* (the war against nature, the
paramountcy of development and the principle of progress) have been
grist to the mill of the agents of industrialism who sought to explain and
justify it."[84] Now the questioning of values is inseparable from a
questioning of the technical system. On several levels. In the depths of
our subconscious it is the fear of transgression, the dread of castration for
having robbed the Father of the power of destroying or manipulating his
work – creation; and that is why the deaths at Hiroshima weigh on us
more heavily than those at Dresden or the victims of traffic accidents.

On another level, awareness of the first control inadequacy emerges.
Though it never appears in this book, it remains omnipresent, and gives
its dramatic dimension to the growing imbalance between man's power
and the ancestral motivations inscribed in the phylogenesis of his
nervous system. Thus, it is "unlikely that culture will ever return to the
naïve, linear, and blissfully optimistic positivism that characterised and
inspired the Second Wave."[85] With its course checked, and its direction
partly reoriented, the torrent of technical progress will lose none of its
creative impetus. Prometheus will perhaps be hobbled, but not fettered.

# What growth?

Before the gloomy resignation provoked by the second oil crisis, the elites of industrial countries shared the most simplistic attitudes to a lasting recovery of vigorous growth. Such attitudes were the result of a double dichotomy: to believe or not to believe in it; to want it to be different or the same as before. And four discourses were often heard:

"Long live growth," the first would say, "the good old growth of yesteryear! Happily, it will soon be back if governments do not misma- nage the economy in the short term."

"I wish for your growth with all my heart," the second would reply, "but you don't understand anything about recent events. Gone are the conditions for a vigorous growth. And for a long time too!"

"So much the better," the third would reply. "Your growth is an illusion! In what way does it increase human happiness? Besides, it is a sin against the Earth which we are despoiling, and against the other people whom we exploit. And it has destroyed its own foundations. The only hope? The only possibility? A moderate, gentle growth."

And a more quiet, fourth voice would comment: "Growth may well pick up again. Aren't you making every effort to that end? But the real issue lies elsewhere. It relates to the finalities of society. The battle that must be won revolves round changing them."

Let us leave the debate on social ethics aside for the moment and concentrate on a single problem: are there lasting restraints on vigorous, traditional growth in developed countries? Growth as measured by gross domestic product?

Two initial stumbling blocks, two common arguments, encumber our path: the impossibility of long-term growth would be the inevitable consequence of the exhaustion of natural resources and the drying up of scientific discoveries. Let us not be taken in by this film set. These are cardboard blocks: as far as natural resources are concerned, the only problem (and it has to do with energy only) is temporary and geo-economic; for the foreseeable future, the slowing down of technical progress could only result from the rate of implementation, thus of investments, and therefore of economic growth itself.

So let us continue on our way, limiting ourselves to the next quarter century. This time there are real obstacles ahead of us. Both national and international. We need only skim through the earlier chapters of this book.

The name of the first international obstacle is well known: oil. Whenever an industrial country with few energy resources increases its rate of growth by 1%, the volume of its oil imports goes up by 0.4 to 0.7%. And it must export more if it is to maintain the equilibrium of its balance of payments. The higher the price of crude oil, the bigger the extra bill, the more it will strive to push up exports or reconquer the domestic market (and this will be intensified by the fact that practically all industrial countries will be doing the same thing). If the rise in the price of crude oil is slow and regular, all well and good; the economy then has time to adjust. But intermittent and abrupt rises creates recessions that are rather prejudicial to growth. Even if this obstacle is not in our immediate path, it could, as we have witnessed, appear in ten years.

Thus this obstacle hides another: the constraint of the balance of payments (except in the case of the United States). Let us examine it more closely. In theory it would not be necessary to analyse external restraint in a world of flexible exchange rates since their automatic adjustments should eliminate chronic surpluses or deficits. But, as in many other areas of economics the delays and imperfections of the methods of adjustment are at the heart of the difficulties. Where do they come from?

First of all, capital flows are not subject to the same dynamics as the exchange of goods and services; the fact that agents are able to convert considerable holdings from one currency to another at any moment must inevitably constitute a source of instability.

Then, exhange rates are sensitive to prices, to domestic costs and to their anticipated value, but their pact on imports and exports takes time and is less clear than that of the rate of growth or that of the structure of production. If the national production of a country goes up too fast, the fall of its currency will not be enough to curb the rise of imports.

Finally, market pressures are not in the least symmetrical: even if national policies for fighting inflation are inadequate, the whole order of international financial institutions enjoins the need for action to eliminate balance of payment deficits, while the pressures to reduce a surplus are less immediate and less direct.

The result? A fundamentally asymmetrical system with limited capacities for returning to an equilibrium. As a result, each country is strongly inclined to see its growth prospects as being directly limited by balance of payments considerations, and to take the view that, since it is uncertain as to the expansion of others (and hence, of its own possibilities with exports), it prefers to reduce its own rate of growth so as to limit imports. A splendid game of non-cooperation which has the effect of placing each competitor in a worse situation! Thus growth is reduced by the inability of the big industrial countries to coordinate their cyclical policies.

This second obstacle is produced by a third, and even more formidable one: for a long time the multipolarity and interdependence of the international system has made it a source of unpredictability. It also makes governments and business concerns cautious. Governments, because any policy that brings about economic recovery increases energy dependence, pushes up imports, upsets the balance of payments, and jeopardises the exchange rate. Businesses because higher international risks (the price of energy, fluctuating exchange rates, conditions of competition) reduce the expected return on their investments, and hence the volume of these investments. Governments and business concerns, because they help to implement protectionist policies that keep alive out-dated productive structures and obstruct adjustments that are both indispensable for more vigorous growth, and difficult to accept at a time of slow growth.

But it is too easy to lay all the crimes against growth at the door of the international system, because it has accomplices: the sociopolitical systems of industrial countries.

The top accusation: the evolution of national systems is in danger of making the measurement of growth more and more meaningless. In two ways: (1) Everyone knows it is generally accepted that in national accounting, the value of non-market services is equal to their cost. There are no profits in such activities! If their weight in the domestic product goes up, growth automatically tends to slow down. This is self-evident since this is what happens in an industrial country when per capita income goes up. (2) All the goods and services produced within the framework of the informal economy escape the net of national accounting. In some cases through fraud, in others, through the strict application of the rules of national accountancy. If the emergence of new values, the intensification of competition, and a heavier tax burden bring about an expansion of the informal economy, it is 'official' growth that will automaticaly suffer...

After these artifacts come some more serious charges: when minorities within industrial countries challenge the legitimacy of growth, they help to erode the kinds of performance that would have made this growth possible. They urge wage-earners to question the sense of higher productivity, and encourage leaders to be doubly cautious in their calculation of future demands; they exert pressure on high officials to multiply regulations. This sapping is added to the direct demand for a massive reduction of working hours. The point here is not passing judgment, but making a prognosis. By stating simply that the emergence of new aspirations in industrial countries may, in the future, prove to be one of the causes of the deceleration of their growth.

As for social oligopolisation, by freezing the appropriation of resources, pushing for a proliferation of regulations, limiting the margin of play of participants and multiplying appeals to tribunals, it usually produces the same effect. Isn't America itself (the land of free enterprise, whose law once channeled creative energy) in the process of being more securely bound by its jurists than Gulliver by the Lilliputians? The aura of the jurists is growing at the very time that the star of entrepreneurs, engineers, and even scientists, is fading. Jurists - the infantry of all societies that are becoming rigid... The economist perceives these underlying trends through employment and investment:

An employment that is reduced by classic unemployment, that is to say, by the refusal to increase growth through the replacement of scarce resources with the available labour of the unemployed.

An investment that is threatened by the drop in profit levels, and by the perception of the risks associated with changes in the rules, new regulations, and tax and duty systems. An investment which, in the majority of developed countries, is subject to the double limitation of external and internal constraints to such an extent that the levels of investment involved in vigorous growth may prove impossible without sustained political action, and may even be simply unattainable.

In a word, national and international obstacles combine to create a final constraint that weighs on the growth rates of developed economies – the constraint of inflation.

Naturally, we are not dealing here with the type of inflation that is engendered by the full utilisation of production capacities. The forms of inflation that come into play are of another type. With their *primary causes and mechanisms of perpetuation.*

The price of energy and raw materials is at the top of the list of *primary causes*; but it is the sudden rises triggered by shortages, rather than the long-term trend of real prices that are a threat to monetary stability.

A second risk arises from depreciations of nominal exchange rates, depreciations that we know arise easily in an uncertain world where short-term flows of capital constitute a considerable component of the balance of payments. The higher the share of imports in the national income, the greater their impact on domestic prices.

The third risk – the way in which international monetary liquidities are created and interfere with national money supplies – is of a more specifically monetary origin.

However, the main problem lies in the mechanisms of perpetuation. No doubt they are more sensitive and harder to reverse in many developed countries. The speed with which forestalment adjusts to the least acceleration of a rise, and on the other hand, the sluggishness displayed by such forestalments when it slows down, are often an expression of greater awareness of the central problem of the distribution of added value. Social oligopolisation makes it possible for the various social groups to find the means of protecting themselves more quickly against the consequences of inflation; contractual clauses that automatically compensate for the effect of inflation tend to multiply... These mechanisms of perpetuation are characterised by the speed with which they amplify price rises as soon as growth tends to accelerate, regardless of the rates of utilisation of production capacities. In the other direction, any slowing down of price rises costs dear but this does not mean that a very slow rate of growth does not intensify the struggle over the distribution of added value and stimulate inflationary tendancies!

The list of checks to growth is impressive. It explains why the slowing down of growth since 1973 is not an accident, and why this slowed growth could persist to the end of the decade. However, the prerequisites of greater growth are on the horizon: a less critical energy situation, attitudes more favourable to growth, a rediscovery of adaptability by the American economy, the beginnings of a return to flexibility in Europe, new opportunities for investment created by technical progress, a spectacular drop in the rate of inflation, and the hope of mastering Third World debt.

The future could be marked by the progressive movement from moderate growth to considerable growth between now and the end of the century.

But there is more than one kind of moderate growth. Other models oppose one that is no more than the unintentional result of macroeconomic constraints and structural rigidities: in Europe for example, the type of growth proposed by French socialists in 1981, based on the reconquest of the domestic market and the development of the collective services, or new growth built on a broad social consensus based on new aspirations.

The first of these three types of growth has its roots in the fragmentation of values and social oligopolisation. Its low rate makes it all the more unstable because it involves domestic conflicts, the dissatisfaction of social groups, and lasting unemployment... However, this rate, like the volume of unemployment, can be influenced by governments. And pushing growth back up by one point, or reducing unemployment by a third would greatly reduce individual anxieties and social tensions.

The second type of growth presupposes the use of restraint. The centralist state depends "on the social forces preoccupied with full employment within the framework of a planned economy, and those that are above all anxious to preserve the country's independence in relation to the world market" to force economic agents to refocus growth on domestic demand with the "protection of domestic activities that face competition from imports, and redirecting national demand towards goods and services with a low import content and high labour factor."[86] The development of collective services and shorter working hours completes the purview. There is a considerable risk of failure: the stagnation of export industries, the rejection of solidarity by social groups, and the collapse of efficiency. The French experiment (1981–1984) has been conclusive on this score.

Finally we come to new growth. Unlike the type last mentioned, it is not brought about by decree. There is no point in hoping for it without a rapid change of values throughout the vast majority of the population. A change of values that would reduce the importance attached to monetary income and recommend a different organisation of time, while at the same time recognising the need for economic efficiency in order to satisfy demands for material goods that continue to be potentially strong. Is this a likely hypothesis? We may well doubt it in the short and medium term. But the longer-term judgement is more mixed.

Obviously, these three types of growth are only archetypes, and there are many conceivable combinations: a growth of the first type seasoned with a slight protectionism or spiced with some new growth; an awkward marriage of planning and worker-managed new growth; a new growth that degenerates into chaos and sinks into inefficiency... However, one thing is sure: the rhythm and content of growth will depend on the transformation of structures; gone are the days when economic growth could be understood in purely macroeconomic terms, and only on the basis of investment, employment and technical progress.

# Structural adaptation: from creation to destruction

At this stage of our reflection, it is obvious that what is at stake is not a simple rate of growth, but the way in which industral societies get over the conflict between the opposing pressures that are brought to bear on them. What is at stake is their flexibility, or in other words, their ability to respond to the challenges that threaten them with structural transformations. These transformations are not limited to passive adaptations. They will generate creation and destruction.

But if we are to ask ourselves effective questions about these developments, we must, in a few pages, remind ourselves of the play of forces that will condition the dynamics of these structures, a play made up of internal and external pressures, and rigidities.

Three types of external pressures have appeared in this book: the shifting of competitive positions, the impact of technological adventures, and the rise in the cost of exchanges with the physical environment (whether it is a question of extracting resources, fighting pollution, or limiting damage to the natural surroundings).

For instance, the cost of energy does not only curb growth, but it is also a lever that distorts, deforms, massages and pounds productive structures by increasing the relative cost of transport, necessitating the insulation of buildings and heating cuts, encouraging companies to substitute coal and electricity for fuel oil, to replace energy with equipment, labour or computers. By giving heat pumps a chance, along with solar houses, and distribution networks of hot water from electric power stations or geothermic sites; by increasing the profitability of an economical, aerodynamic vehicle, lightened by the use of new materials, its carburation regulated by a micro-processor; and by handicapping sectors that use a lot of energy to the advantage of those that consume little.

The analysis for industrial raw materials is practically identical, but the problems of pollution and damage to natural surroundings are obviously more complex, because the aims of the policies set up to resolve them are manifold: complements that are essential to a market that is blind to damage inflicted on the environment, the limitation of certain risks, protection of the interests of future generations, encouraging the perfection of clean technologies, an acknowledgement of things aesthetic..., and arbitrages will continue to be particularly delicate. As for impacts on productive structures, they are easy to describe, but much more difficult to quantify: bringing forward the dates for closing down old factories that are almost always condemned for other reasons, accelerating of the decline of certain sectors in industrial countries, contributing to the emergence of new activities or relaunching old activities (such as the treatment of water and the purification of waste water), distorting trade relations between countries with different standards, transfering activities from developed countries to countries that attach less importance to their environment... A conjecture? Although the management of the environment has become an integral part of the nervous system of countries with a high standard of living, within the context of slow growth, it will undoubtedly have to suffer the constant attacks of those who will try to push it to the fringes in the name of economic priorities. Vigilance will perhaps be necessary to protect the long term.

The rise in the cost of exchanges with the physical environment may be (relatively) new[87] to Western man, but he has been familiar with the impact of technical progress for generations. A familiarity which does not rule out fear, and all the more so because the long-term qualitative consequences are easier to predict than the quantitative dynamics themselves. Thus, with the automation of continuous, semi-continuous or sequential processes, machine tools with digital control, computer-assisted design, office computing, the electronic transfer of money, data banks, and consumer goods equipped with micro-computers, electronics will, at the same time, reduce the number of jobs for a given output, bring about market expansions by reducing costs, make the conception of new products and services possible, and give pioneers bigger export markets. But above all, it will change the relative scarcity (and consequently the powers) of the different categories of employees: a higher proportion of executives and foremen, an increase in the number of maintenance staff, the replacing worker know-how with operating system software, the disappearance of certain jobs (reelers, milling machine operators, fitters...), the appearance of new repetitive jobs (perforation, coding, checking), the use of very highly qualified personnel – often from outside the company – for system design, the possibilities of internal promotion restricted to young graduates. Altogether, the number of jobs requiring little skill in industry, insurance and banking will decline, but the same will not be true of many of the services from catering to gardening. The improvement of the average lot of man does not mean that there will not be winners and losers. Losers who will make the bitter discovery that what they believed to be their personal abilities were not an intrinsic characteristic of their manual skill, knowledge or intelligence, but the result of overall social scarcities that technical progress is continually destroying and recreating.

As for the impact of changes in their competitive positions on the productive structures of developed countries, it is not much different from that of technical progress.

First, let us suppose that prices in each country are flexible and reflect the relative scarcities of the factors of production. Then the imports of this or that developed country would only be an indirect way of importing factors of production that are more expensive within it. As long as this involves iron ore or coal, everyone will applaud... But when it comes to labour... End of consensus! Because even if the nation as a whole wins, the human groups which compose it will see their relative income rise or fall in relation to their relative scarcity *in the world* and not *in their country*. Europe's unskilled worker no longer has a few hundred million competitors in countries with comparable organisations, which are trying to ensure a minimum income for all, but billions of people throughout the world who are trying to survive. At the other extreme, the highly specialised technician no longer offers his services to industrial countries alone, but to all humanity. The former loses and the latter gains. Never will the dual role of salary be more dramatically revealed: it being the price paid for a service like any other as well as the main source of income for the vast majority.

But the hypothesis of flexible prices is only a very rough one... Rigid prices, and prices that are the result of taxes and subsidies abound in the economy... Leading to artificial competition, shortages and under-employment. The cost of capital is a flagrant example that we have already encountered in this book; although it is often very low in companies in those countries that have privileged access to credit granted by OECD governments...

Thus, through some of their policies, developed countries needlessly help to reinforce external pressures on their economies.

Let us open the next file – that of internal pressures. Its contents may be summed up in one sentence: a demographic evolution distinguished by the aging of the population and alterations in the structure of the active population, changes in final demand under the combined influence of demography, values, income levels, price structures, and the size of the important social groups.

From Japan, through Europe and on to the United States, the aging of developed societies recurs in literature like a leitmotiv. All the same we must not make a mistake regarding its extent or rhythms, or even underestimate the influence of the age chosen to set the boundary between maturity and old age: within the OECD, the percentage of people over 65 years of age in 1950 was 7.6%, in 1975 it was 10.50%, and by the year 2000 this figure should reach 12.40% assuming reasonably favourable birth rates. But what is more significant is the proportion of the old that are very elderly: by the end of the century, 38.50% of old people in developed countries as a whole will be over 75, as opposed to 34.50% twenty-five years earlier. And there lies the real problem. We must give a more detailed description of the effects of demography on the structures of developed countries: the most important result is the need to create new economic and social roles for the growing proportion of men and women whose age falls between that (generally decreasing) of the ending of an active role in society and that (generally increasing) of death. Another perceptible effect is the obligation to face the increased consumption of medical and social services (in the USA for example, an individual between the ages of 17 and 44 'consumes' 4.6 visits to the doctor each year, as opposed to 6.7 for the individual who is over seventy years old). On the other hand, we usually overestimate both the sectorial impact due to changes in the structure of the demand for consumer goods, and financial repercussions: in France, for example, assuming a long-term low birth rate, the burden of pensions should not become appreciably heavier until the period 2000–2020.[88]

After the total population comes the active population. With the two principal factors that will characterise its evolution: the probable growth (at least until 1990) of the rate of female activity,[89] and the gradual deceleration of the growth of the total active population. But the situation will vary considerably from one country to another: whereas the active population of the United States will still go up by 1.1% between 1975 and 1990, and by 0.7% between 1990 and the year 2000, the figures for Japan are 0.8% and 0.4%, and for France 0.6% and 0.4%.

In the case of West Germany (excluding immigrant workers), the reflux has already begun – 0.2% over the next decade, and −0.8% in the following one. Apart from the country last mentioned, the dilemma of all the others is practically identical: how are we to reduce the gap between the supply and demand of jobs in the next ten years without restricting growth and without creating irreversibilities that will limit the active population over the next ten years when there will perhaps be a shortage of labour?

Thus, like the road rollers of yesteryear, demographic forces move slowly and powerfully! On this issue, the end of this century is a horizon for the short-sighted. It is twenty years after that time that the consequences of present trends could become dramatic; however, if we hope to alter them, we must act within the next ten years.

We now come to the final pressure on the economic structure of industrial countries: the evolution of final demand. Its components are well known to the greenest of economists: investment, household consumption, government consumption, exports... A very complex subject that we shall give a rough sketch of. Revealing the more reliable conjectures and major questions pell-mell.

*First conjecture*: For a given rate of growth, the proportion of investment in the gross domestic product should go up in advanced industrial societies as a whole for a number of reasons: a general rise in the volume of equipment marginally necessary to increase production; modification of the domestic product to the advantage of more capital-intensive activities; acceleration of the economic and technical obsolescence of equipment.

*First question*: What will be the eventual effect of the new values, since their influence will go well beyond the structure of consumption alone? It will question the content of personal life, the allocation of time, use of space, and professional activities. In fragmented societies, the various groups will be able to hope for different arbitrages between work and leisure, market and non-market consumption... Some possible trends? A reduction of conspicuous consumption, more informative advertisement, an increase in the lifetime of durable goods, a development of collective non-market services on the level of different communities.

*Second conjecture*: Added to the effects of demography (on medical spending, on the standard and composition of housing demand, and on the use of certain equipment) will be the almost mechanical impact of the variations of real incomes and modifications of relative prices on household budgets: producing a drop in the share of food and clothing, and a rise in the share of culture and leisure, of hygiene and health...

*Third conjecture*: the gradual saturation of the markets for new durable goods such as cars and traditional household appliances, while in the future, new generations of durable goods in areas such as computing, culture, telecommunications, education, health, security, etc. will appear.

*Second question*: How will households divide their private consumption between goods and services? This is a problem that those who shout "Services, Services!" all day hardly perceive. Because they insist (and rightly so) that households will reallocate their expenditure to the advantage of sectors (such as leisure and transport) with a high service content, and they forget that new goods will be developed that will incorporate services or make it possible to receive them (video cassettes, terminals...). And above all they forget that shorter working hours and higher labour costs will encourage households to buy goods in order to turn them into services themselves. All things considered, the share of services to households in private consumption should increase more slowly than some may think.

*A final question*: On the division of final consumption between public and private consumption. Unless there is a swing in values, it will certainly be the subject of conflicts – whether connected with the crisis of the Welfare State or the emergence of the informal economy. With strong resistance on the part of certain social groups to increased public services.

*And finally, the last conjecture*: the structure of exports should be characterised by an increase in the share of industrial services and hard goods, and a reduction of that of intermediary or semi-finished products.

All told (and even if our intellectual categories that separate goods and services, industrial activities and service activities belong to post-industrial societies with their archaic distinctions), nothing would seem to indicate that in the future, changes in final demand will, by themselves, constitute greater pressures on the structures of industrial societies than they have in the past.

The real challenge arises less from a single cause than from an accumulation of causes.

Faced with growing pressures, will industrial societies (and Europe in particular) be able to show the adaptability necessary for it to invent the future? Or, will they, incapable of manoeuvering, turn in on themselves in a static and probably hopeless defence? Everything will depend on the extent of their rigidity. A rigidity that is both the conscious realisation of legitimate social objectives, and the unintentional accumulation of institutions, procedures and rules that are by nature partly irreversible and which are a source of inefficiency. Inefficiency in the pursuit of the aims of the community, and to a large extent, due to indirect negative effects.

Since we are familiar with these sources of rigidity, we need only give them a brief inspection. Most of them bear the stamp of social oligopolisation:

The aging of the population with the risk of a reorientation of values (including the new ones) towards a more conservative direction,[90] a persistent suspicion of the young societies of the Third World, a restriction of geographical and professional mobility, and a lack of imagination in the implementation of new solutions.

The functioning of the labour market with fixed or semi-fixed labour costs; hierarchies of salaries that do not vary from one sector, or from one socio-professional category, to another; systems of social protection, which are indeed legitimate, but whose modalities burden the marginal cost of labour; a tax system which, in certain countries helps to reduce mobility and weaken the entrepreneurial spirit at the very time when the level of income, education, and new aspirations are changing people's behaviour vis a vis work, at the very time that the swing of the labour supply towards the services reveals new job seekers and makes the relocation of industrial workers more difficult.

State interference with the conflicts surrounding higher public spending, with new forms of government participation in industrial activities, with action to protect traditional sectors which, although justified in the short term, become definitive and ossifying measures, with a multiplication of regulative policies, and a lengthening of their train of difficulties: the choice between price control and inelasticity, the inclusion of the participation of citizens in the formulation and execution of policies and the dilemma between centralisation and decentralisation...

The danger of creating a new protectionism that is both the expression of existing rigidities and the point of departure of new rigidities; a new protectionism that is less concerned with reducing an overal deficit than with defending specific industries; that depends less on customs duties and quotas than on bilateral agreements or non-tariff barriers; that is to be found less at frontiers than in the maze of domestic aid. With the possibility of a chain reaction on the international level; a possibility that is too obvious to merit any comment. Risking a chain reaction on the national level, in which the introduction of measures in favour of one sector would legitimise the claims of others. With the threat of a concentration of economic power in the hands of central government officials.

Gripped in this vice of pressures and rigidities, but shaped by the creative power of their actors, how will the productive structures of industrial societies evolve? What margins of play remain open?

The best thing is to start with a simple accounting balance: the rate of growth of an economy is equal to the sum of the rate of growth of the active population and the rate of growth of productivity per hour worked, less the rate of growth of unemployment and the rate of reduction of working hours. Thus, if an economy like that of France increases its GNP by 2.5% each year in the course of the next decade, the rate of growth of annual productivity per person will not be more than 1.8%, assuming that unemployment remains constant, since the active population will grow by 0.7% per year. A ridiculously low figure! As for productivity per hour, working hours would have to fall by 1% per year (a 36 hour working week, with annual holidays remaining the same by 1990) for it to reach 2.8%! If this rate were to go up to 3.8%, then, all other things being equal, unemployment will rise by 1% per year, or a little over 200,000 people. There is no more dramatic illustration of the difficulty of clearing an acceptable path by combining a stimulation of growth with a deceleration of the rise in the cost of labour and a reduction of working hours.

The path is narrow. What can we do to widen it?

Some people who have forgotten the preceding chapter will say, "Acclerate growth." Indeed, but first we must free ourselves speedily from the constraint of energy.

"Slow down the rise in productivity," others will reply. Absolutely. But we need to fight classic unemployment by altering the relative cost of labour and equipment, and not by forcing businesses (or governments) to keep on people to do nothing, because the collapse of competitiveness would reduce the ability to export and to hold on to the domestic market and at the end of the day, slow down future growth.

"Reduce the increase in the active population," a third group will suggest. "Send the immigrants back where they came from, and put women back in the home!" This reactionary solution scorns the aspirations of generations of women and the problems of other countries.

"Cut working hours." Yes. But conditions would have to be Draconian for a slowing down of growth to be avoided: if we want to face Japanese competition, buildings must be occupied and machines run for at least the same number of hours per year; the cost of labour per hour must not go up faster, and that may mean a cut in annual pay; rare specialists who are temporarily indispensable, must continue to work as before; and finally, the form this reduction takes must encourage firms to take on workers and not to close for annual holidays twice a year instead of once.

But there is more: in the future, each person's disposable income may well rise more slowly than the per capita GNP. Owing to soaring contributions allocated to health costs. Owing to the relative rise in the retail price index compared with the GNP price index. An example? Let us suppose that the income of a European over twenty years moves up from 100 to 120. Does that mean that he will have 20% more money to spend? No. Because he will have 17 instead of 10 francs deducted from his salary for the National Health, and he will have to pay 8 francs rather than five for his energy. Thus he will be left with 95 rather than 85 francs, and the rise in his real disposable income will be no more than 11%. As a result, new values or no, there will always be individuals who will defend every cent of their monetary income and will fight against any reduction of working hours. Even here, there is some latitude, especially around the total amount of obligatory deductions, but it is limited.

At the same time, in Western countries, technical progress and international competition will challenge the relative scarcity of the various professional skills, pushing some towards falling job demands and limited pay, and others to widening possibilities and improved pay prospects. Too many unskilled workers, too many architects, too many doctors, too many psychologists, not enough computer experts, technicians and agronomists. And all this in a society fragmented by the diversity of values and individual aspirations. A diversity that cannot but engender a wide range of behaviour patterns.

Whence a new risk – that of seeing people split up into the adapted, the protected and the rejected. Adapted people will be the spear-heads of competitive firms. Protected people will ensconce themselves in the many refuges offered by the non-market services. The rejected will rub along on the fringes of the formal economy or try to make it in the informal economy. The age of a dual society will have arrived. Some even see it as an answer to the challenges of the future of certain European countries. Let us listen to them:[91]

"Rather than forcing society as a whole to an adjustment to the world market that is laden with constraints and uncertainties, or, on the other hand, to slip towards decline and withdrawal," why not accept "a heterogeneisation of lifestyles and attitudes in the face of change, so as to soften the transition and prolong the period of adjustment, instead of making society as a whole confront the challenge of rapid change, and thus run the risk of having it split into rival groups!"

"This is how we should interpret the concept of dual socio-economy: that of a society deliberately divided into two great sub-groups of activities and of complementary and different individuals.

On the one hand, a sub-group adapted to the new technologies, an integral part of the world scene, led by managers equipped to handle the most advanced data processing as well as foreign languages. But also made up of workers and employees of which some (those with the highest performance) would be paid accordingly, while others would probably be relegated to precarious, low-paid jobs.

On the other hand, a sub-group 'embodying the heritage of our cultural traditions, composed of bodies isolated from international competition, less preoccupied with productivity and technological progress, and of persons less given to work and market consumption.'

On one side the pioneers of the post-industrial society, the hippies and apostles of the back-to-the-earth philosophy meet up with the new generations that prefer to live in the country rather than submit to the constraints of the world market. On the other, 'the pressures of competition will increasingly force firms to use a kind of homogeneous man..., the selection and motivation of those individuals with the highest performance leading to the exclusion of those elements less adapted to industrial competition from its centre, pushing them out towards its perimeter (the growth of sub-contracting) and the protected sectors. The consensus on competitiveness will bring together the salary earners and leaders of industrial firms, the dichotomy being between citizens working in the high-performance sectors and those who, lacking aptitude, or above all, motivation, will prefer activity in protected, aided, or pioneering institutions (collective services, the informal economy...).'

Those who desire the advantages of a high income and market consumption will have to accept the rules of the keenest competition... Those who reject these disciplines, or who are unable to adapt to them, must resign themselves to an obviously much lower income and market consumption."

The facts show that such a development is possible; its desirability is not quite so obvious. Would the equilibrium between those who make up the dual society remain intact in spite of the evolution of attitudes and relative positions? Wouldn't this mixture of those forcibly excluded and those voluntarily excluded be an explosive one? We can therefore understand the apostles of another kind of dual society,[92] this time one in which the split would pass through each of its members: shorter paid working hours for all, a slower growth of monetary income, a blossoming of independent activities, each one free from the other. New growth by another name. "In order for such a trend to lead to a new social and economic equilibrium, it must obviously be seen in broad sections of the population. And particularly in those categories that presently enjoy satisfactory incomes as a reward for the constraints of productivity that they are subject to... The greater flexibility of the chronological distribution of paid professional activity would no longer be aimed simply at a shorter working day or week. It would take in the whole life cycle following compulsory schooling, tending towards the encouragement of widespread voluntary part-time employment in the three phases of life:

The period devoted to studies would be more systematically combined with paid employment than it has been in the past.

The period corresponding to what is today known as 'active life' would be divided equally between work, study, and free time.

The concept of retirement would be perceptibly modified, insofar as each person will have the option of working part-time for as long as he or she might like, without any obligatory age limit, of course."[93]

The conclusion relating to the second dual society is the reverse of the one relating to the first: it is obvious that this development is desirable; whether it is likely is doubtful... Nonetheless, let us leave the door open...

I have just shown three possible – though limited – margins of play: the link between growth and employment, the relationship between national income and the real disposable income of households, and the nature and extent of the phenomena of duality. But the future of the structures of industrial societies cannot be reduced to these major questions. The nature of activities, the distribution of jobs, and the size of the significant social groups will also have some importance.

Take France for instance. In 1975 it employed about 22 million people: 2 million in agriculture, 6.3 million in industry, 1.9 million in construction and public works, and 11.6 million in the tertiary or service industries.

What landscapes can we envisage for the end of the century? One phenomenon will override all others: the explosion of jobs in the tertiary sector. By the year 2000, 3 to 4 million more people should be working in this sector, and the service industries would then account for 60 to 64% of total employment. The trend has already begun, for between 1978 and 1985, the number of jobs in the service industries has probably risen by 1 million. The main jobs? Commerce, services to firms owing to the expansion of temporary work and the use of sub-contracting for the study and development of projects, data processing, accounting, law, and fiscal consultancy services to private persons, particularly in the area of health; non-market government services.

On the other hand, employment in agriculture will fall (to between 1.2 and 1.9 million by the end of the century), employment in construction and public works will decrease, and employment in industry will see its share drop (from 29 to 24–25%), though it is not possible to state its absolute level. One Frenchman out of four still working in the factories! A huge figure, you will say. A delusion! Because the distribution of jobs by activity does not coincide with its classification by occupation. For the purposes of the above statistics, the accountant working for Renault has an industrial job, and the garage mechanic, a service job... In the next twenty years, industrial activities will increasingly incorporate service occupations; the secondary sector will continue to be tertiarised, and the tertiary sector to be industrialised. Moreover, by the year 2000, the vast majority of Westerners will only contribute indirectly to the production of goods... That will be the end of industry, some will think, victims as they are of the erroneous reasoning that confuses the production line with the industrial process, because so many researchers in their laboratories, commercial advisors in their embassies, and data processing specialists around their computers will simply be threads of complex warps of which industry will be the woof.

There remain some possible variations within these powerful trends especially in Europe: rigid, protected national societies would maintain a greater proportion of unskilled workers in declining activities. An over-bureaucratic socialism would increase the number of secretaries in public offices who type with one finger...

Be that as it may, the impact on social structures will be considerable: increasingly reduced to a skeletal level, agricultural groups will have difficulty in preserving a power that is greater than their real size. As for professionals, they will be everywhere and nowhere. One third of all Europeans will come to define themselves as such. A situation that will be all the more ludicrous as they will often only be supervising themselves or other professionals, but they will include a jumble of company directors, senior technicians, researchers, teachers, doctors... Often with a hazy dividing line separating them from office workers, that socio-professional group whose volume should increase... And what about the workers, the symbolic proletariat, those archetypes of exploitation in whose name so many speeches are made? Their share will slowly shrink, and they will cease to be the main point of reference around which union analyses are made.

However, this transposition of present socio-professional categories may well miss the vital point: the appearance of new social cleavages around the three axes: technicality, institutional integration, and attitudes to paid work.

Rallying round the first pole would be those who have heavily besieged paid work and are endowed with a technical competence that makes it possible for them always to adapt. Within this group status will be defined by the scarcity of their skill, and integration into small or large, public or private organisations.

Around the second pole will gravitate all those who stress paid work without being able to make this aspiration serve solid skills. Except for civil servants, the situation of those who belong to this group would be infinitely more fragile, and would not preclude rough journeys across the wilderness.

The absence of technical skills and lack of interest in paid work would not leave many options open to a third group: admission to national or local public office, relegation to the fringes of the large public organisations, or manoeuvering at the edges of the informal economy. These last sub-groups will often have a tough time.

And finally there is the (probably small) group of those who will combine solid technical skills with a limited interest in paid work. They will go for certain professions, fit into certain gaps in public offices, make themselves indispensable to the functioning of big companies. Taking full advantage of the margins of play allowed by their abilities. But woe betide them if their technical skill loses its edge or if the rate of growth falls off excessively!

A limited typology, admittedly, but it has a double advantage. It forces us to look at our society the way we look at Soviet society when we see, not classes, but social groups and privileges. And it suggests to us that in the next twenty years, Western societies may well emerge as a complex conglomerate in which the old social classes would begin to dissolve, while new social rearrangements would flourish.

Their three democracies would suffer the repercussions directly:

Political democracy, because the parties will at one and the same time have to continue to express the demands of the traditional social groups and reflect the diversity of the values of the various members of society, the sudden hardening of attitudes on the part of the outcasts, the aspirations of those who have adapted to a new liberalism, and the wish of those protected not to face the consequences of protection.

Corporatist democracy, because it will have to take into account the infinite variety of work situations and the proliferation of service occupations that do not lend themselves to big national negotiations.

Spontaneous democracy, because it will be faced with a permanent dilemma: whether it should use its imaginativeness and its capacity for contestation to protect the existing situation or to invent the future.

Thus, industrial societies, societies which had believed themselves to have historically arrived (having emerged from the torrent of growth and entered the calm waters of the great lake of prosperity), will have to test their adaptability. Adapting means wanting to create, but it also means accepting the need to destroy. The margins of play are limited, but they may be enough to make the difference between long-term, prosperity and decadence, social peace and chaos, servitude and liberty within interdependence. However the chances of success will be all the greater provided that the world will once more become intelligible to the actors of industrial societies.

The object of the task ahead of us (the construction of scenarios) is precisely that of introducing clarity by describing the possible futures suggested by the conjunction of elemental forces on a world scale.

# PATHS OF RUPTURE AND CONTINUITY

"There is nothing more suited to recalling phi-
losophers and statesmen to the paths of modesty
than the history of our Revolution; for never
before had there been greater events, of more
remote origin, better prepared and less
anticipated."

Alexis de TOCQUEVILLE
*L'Ancien Régime et la Révolution*

# In the jungle of our futures

A film scenario is the telling of a story with a beginning and an end. A prospective analysis scenario is quite different: it too professes to be a story, but this story is an arbitrary slice of the future: on one hand the final image, on the other, the process that leads to that image, and it is this pair that presents itself as a possible future. A restricted and impoverished future.

Restricted, because for the author it is no more than the most likely future within the framework of the hypotheses that he has made.

Impoverished, because out of an over-rich reality, he retains only that which has meaning for him.

Under such conditions, why do we need scenarios? Are these fragile constructions anything more than an expression of the futility of prospective analysts?

I think not. Even if reflection on the future cannot be reduced (as this book has shown, incidentally) to a collection of scenarios spread out on the table like the cards of a game. Without scenarios, without the coherence of their figures, how can we reveal the consequences of interactions? Between economic growth and the consumption of energy, between the consumption of energy and financial flows, between the trade of manufactured goods and the structure of jobs? Moreover, scenarios have other virtues: owing to the tensions or contradictions that arise out of processes or subsist in their final images, certain hypotheses show themselves to be much less realistic than they had seemed *a priori*. Owing to the difficulties encountered when choosing relations and the elaboration of figures, the gaps in our knowledge are brought more clearly into focus, and further research suggested.

However useful it may be, the art of constructing scenarios is not, for all that, made less difficult, and the monsters to which certain futurologist works have given birth would be enough to fill a museum of horrors and another of twaddle. Perhaps one day we shall visit these museums. But since my present subject is not epistemology, I shall limit myself at this point to a few introductory reflections that I believe to be absolutely vital for the pursuit of a thoughtful consideration of our futures.

The future cannot be reduced to a combination of chance and necessity. It is not just something to be put up with; it is also willed. A person who constructs scenarios is not adding a number of pictures to a collection; rather, he make tools for action, for these scenarios should serve to evaluate the power we have over our futures. They should allow us to calculate our chances of directing the system towards the desirable goal. They should stimulate imaginative efforts to invent new policies if the range of possible futures seems too narrow.

We hear it said every day that our tomorrows have become so uncertain that it is useless to try to describe the future, even if one limits it with *a priori* hypotheses. If a new prophet were to arise in the wilderness, or a US president die, the face of the world would be changed. So what is the point of passing over the short term and formulating scenarios that are as ephemeral as the day-fly? My answer to that is: in order to control the probable and manage better the unforeseeable.

To control the probable, because in the universe that surrounds us, we delude ourselves if we hope to deviate strong trends – demographic development or the relationship between the consumption of energy and national income, to cite but two examples – without taking determined and continued action over one or more decades.

To manage the unforeseeable better, for by detecting the sources of uncertainty and the types of risk that they create, it is possible to reduce vulnerability by preventive action, or to improve the efficiency of our response to an event by means of a *Kriegspiel*.

Even though each scenario reflects wills, trends and uncertainties all at once, the assumptions on which it rests may stress gradual distortion, or, on the other hand, lay emphasis on changes that commit us to new paths. Continuities on one side, and ruptures on the other. These are vivid words, though not devoid of ambiguity.

Continuity is not the reproduction of the past without changes; it is characteristic of every evolution during which a system retains its identity, like couples in which husband and wife slowly learn to grow old together. Who would claim that the world as it stood in 1972 was simply a carbon copy of the world in 1955? Nonetheless, the one has engendered the other without a major catastrophe, by means of successive modifications that have preserved the structure of certain fundamental relationships.

Rupture, on the other hand, destroys and rends. It replaces the preceding system with one or more new ones. A glass bottle that is broken in two ceases to be a bottle; a couple torn apart by divorce is no longer a couple. The world to which the Treaty of Versailles gave birth died on the 1st of September 1939 when German tanks crossed the Polish border.

The distinction is simple when we are dealing with glass; it is less simple when we are dealing with an international system or a nation. Between 1955 and 1972, there was no year that did not have its share of local ruptures (Algerian independence, the Cultural Revolution in China, the devaluation of the dollar). Why then speak of continuity? In a complex system, when does continuity end and rupture begin? The answer is not simple, because everything depends on the core of relations that the observer uses to define the identity of the system.

Instead of ruptures, I could have spoken of crises; but in the common parlance the word 'crisis' designates too widely varying situations: sometimes an event lasting a few days without important future repercussions (the Cuban crisis between Kennedy and Khrushchev), sometimes a fluctuation that takes place over several years (the business cycle crisis of economists), sometimes a period in which the instability of power relations precludes the implicit acceptance of the rules of the game (the Thirty Years War), sometimes an enduring change that gradually alters the underlying logic of a system (the Industrial Revolution in Eighteenth Century England). From this latter point of view, all the conceivable scenarios for the coming decades are scenarios of crisis. The foregoing analysis has shown this. But they are not necessarily scenarios of rupture.

Rupture. Continuity. However imperfect the concepts may be, they have the merit of facilitating the scanning of futures that cannot be reduced either to the discovery of the Promised Land, or to visions of the Apocalypse, or to the permanence of the past.

# In search of ruptures

Combustion that starts at a point. A chain reaction that spreads through the mass. Whether it is the explosion of a powder keg, the triumph of a revolution, or the triggering of a world war, the mechanism is identical: it involves both detonation and diffusion. And the world of the decades ahead will not be protected from either of these things. It will be full of operating areas inclined to produce the very first spark, and it will have in its power many concatenations capable of turning this spark into a blaze. Hence the variety of possible ruptures. Depending on the choice of the initial hot spot and, on the dominant propagation process. It would therefore seem natural to attempt a double typology. But is it not more convincing to begin with stories, stories of which, as with music and myths, there may be many versions?

And here they are. Seven altogether.

The first one begins in Ryad around 1995, a period in which dependence on Middle East oil has increased once more, a few months after the assassination in Cairo of the Egyptian president (a man of great wisdom and integrity) at a time when Turkey, Iran and Syria are passing through a new spell of trouble all at the same time. Embittered by the ostentatious wealth of some, and by the corrupt practices of the leading feudality, humiliated by the state of the Arab nation and the intransigence of Israel, a group of young Saudi officers, supported by the Lybians, the Palestinians, and a number of princes, assassinates the royal family, seizes the cities, wins over the army and gets the support of the religious leaders. After gaining power, this group decides that Saudi Arabia will not export any more oil, except to cover its immediate import needs, and demands that Israel evacuate all occupied territory.

What does the West do?

*Hypothesis number one*: It does nothing. The various governments cannot agree on any policy. Then in industrial countries, the explosion of the price of oil, plummeting of international incomes and galloping inflation generate either high unemployment, or the setting up of a centralised management of the economy as in war time. In both cases, the international trade system collapses, the economic and military solidarity of the West explodes, and the Third World turns to the Middle East colonels for its oil. And if the recession is not controlled in Europe or Japan, it could conceivably give rise to social disorder and political upheavals which in some countries would wreck the present forms of democracy.

*Hypothesis number two*: OECD governments set up an international agency for rationing oil, including (or not) all or part of the Third World. Immediately after this they find themselves forced to organise the trade of industrial and agricultural products, because under such conditions, a number of countries refuse to play the game of international competition. The chances of political revolution in some Western countries? They do not disappear but they diminish, and a new international system is born. A plausible hypothesis do you think? No doubt, but far from certain. Imagine the atmosphere of the haggling over the choice of rules for rationing.

"You have nuclear power. Be satisfied with less oil."

"Nuclear power? My country owes it to the courage of its leaders and its past energy policy. Since you backed up those who rejected the connection between energy consumption and national income, you must now accept the consequences..."

"If you don't increase my oil quota, I shall put an embargo on my coal exports..."

I leave you to imagine the rest.

*Hypothesis number three*: The United States intervenes militarily, with or without the help of Europe, with or without consulting Israel. Combined forces seize the oil wells, check pipes and pumping stations, occupy the ports and the Straits of Ormuz. Assuming that the operation is successful, it sets off a tidal wave in the Middle East. Moderate regimes are swept away, Western embassies burnt, and rivalries between Arab countries are forgotten for a while... Voices are raised between the United States and the Soviet Union as the latter seeks to exploit the situation to its own advantage. Shevardnadze or his successor proposes a new Yalta. With Afghanistan, Iran, Irak and Syria in Moscow's zone of influence, and Turkey neutralised. As for Arab terrorism, it flourishes everywhere, attacking oil wells, civil aircraft and the odd pro-Westen

Arab personality, spreading insecurity in occupied towns and fear in European capitals.

The outcome is unforeseeable. A return to order owing to the temporary failure of the revolution in the Middle East? Acceptance by the West of tough conditions in exchange for the renewal of oil supplies? Compromise with the Soviet Union? Military escalation? No one knows.

*Hypothesis number four*: The United States uses the food weapon to force radical Arab leaders to change their policies, but even supposing that it is respected, the embargo only has an effect in the long term. In the meantime, it does not slow down the collapse of economic activity in industrial countries. And day after day, Middle East television shows pictures of children with sunken eyes, swollen stomachs, and atrophying limbs. Pictures of a slow death more unbearable than death in a real war.

Within the context of the oil catastrophes, this story, even with its variations, obviously does not exhaust all the possibilities. But though banal, it nonetheless illustrates a major fact: as long as consumer countries do not reduce their dependence on oil, as long as their inability to cooperate prevents them from recovering a certain moral authority, as long as a lasting and balanced peace is not established in the Middle East, this zone will continue to be a source of tremors that may move rapidly from the local to the global level.

The second story will be shorter. At the outset, a very unlikely event: following an accident (or an act of sabotage), an American nuclear power station seriously contaminates some tens of thousands of people. It is expected that several thousand people will die. Less in the whole of nuclear history than in a year on the roads of an average-sized country. Less per unit of energy produced than in coal mining. But what does it matter? Man has the right to have preferences regarding the way he dies... Media campaigns, violent demonstrations, and stands taken by political parties force Western governments to halt the building of nuclear plants and stop the working of existing power stations. The whole West rushes after the least drop of oil, the least tonne of coal, the least cubic meter of gas. And there we are right back at square one (that of hypothesis one or hypothesis two) as if we were playing a game of Snakes and Ladders.

The monetary or financial system will be the subject of the third story, but, as is the case with tales, there are several versions.

One version begins in Brazil: a left-wing government comes to power in the wake of political disorder and violent strikes. Having inherited a devastated economy, it decides to suspend repayment of the country's debts. Panic in the banking system. Even before governments have the chance to consult each other, several international banks suspend payments. In seeking secure refuges for their short-term capital, oil-producing countries set off a series of bankruptcies. Stock Exchange prices collapse... There is only one solution: forbid the export of capital, end the convertibility of currencies, and bury free trade. All the more so because the shock does not remain simply a financial one: while OPEC countries close the oil tap so as to avoid the formation of any extra financial surplus, consumer countries try desperately to increase their stocks. Prices rocket on the open market of Rotterdam. Old and new industrial countries founder on inflation, recession and unemployment. But the Brazilian petard could have been no more than a wet one. For a *happy ending* version of the same story, it would have been enough for the governments of the five greatest countries to give their guarantee to the banking system, thus nipping the spread of the explosion in the bud. Besides, did we not experience a Mexican transposition of the story a few years ago? With a happy ending, because the government of the United States was afraid of having a tragedy in its backyard. And I would aver that such a rupture seems less likely to me than if the shock came from the international banks, as in the second version.

Frightened at the extent of loans to developing countries (129 billion dollars of banking credits in 1985 for the twelve most indebted countries, assuming a sharp rise in the price of oil), the international banks refuse to grant them further financing. The governments of these countries then turn to the International Monetary Fund. They must wait for an answer because the governments of the North equivocate, and the economies of these countries collapse, dragging the exports of industrial countries down with them, and plunging the world into a deep recession. Such was the Great Fear of the bankers in 1982.

Finally, in the last version, the skid starts with the financial system and moves toward the oil sector: "In a political atmosphere that has become increasingly tense since the freezing of Iranian assets... there is the risk of a basic crisis of confidence in the relations between Western financial operators and OPEC countries with capital surpluses. If the banks with which the latter have deposits were to find themselves in trouble (over Brazil for example) Arab investors would discover their vulnerability to financial risk." In this hypothesis, "disappointed with their investments, [they] could adopt a strategy of withdrawal and keep their oil underground awaiting better times."[94] So the third story leads you back to the first, but through a concatenation that is made less likely in the medium term by the fall in the price of oil.

After apoplectic seizures comes cancer. A cancer that would gnaw away at the international system through the accumulation of local crises. Taken separately, each crisis could be controlled by cumbersome national administrations and by intergovernmental bureaucratic mechanisms. But the repetition of these crises would force them to live by their wits alone. Incapable of really coordinating their policies, developed countries would attend to the most urgent things first by using their own trumps, without any overall strategy. Their rates of growth would hover around zero, fluctuating with short term risks. As for a list of the crises, there are far too many to choose from: revolutions sometimes accompanied by civil war in Third World countries going through profound changes, conflicts between neighbours of the South as is presently the case with Iran and Iraq, unrest in Southern Africa, massive exoduses of refugees, slow illegal migrations, localised famines, limited military operations carried out by developed countries to protect their supplies or support friendly governments, guerillas maintained by the West or the Soviet Union, a temporary stoppage of oil or chrome supplies, a sharp fall in the output of an industrial sector affected by international competition, a storm over exchange rates, the stopping of payments by debtor countries, a loss of control over inflation, violent demonstrations engendered by the growth of unemployment, the need to rethink the whole welfare state system... The succession of shocks would give rise not to a single way of spreading the disease, but rather to a gradual deterioration of the functioning of national systems and of the international system: the stagnation of living standards in the West, the appearance in developed countries of ever larger marginalised groups, the polarisation of political life towards the extreme Right and the extreme Left (are not the vicissitudes of Labour the result of the slow decline of Great Britain?), the adoption of protectionist measures covering ever wider areas of trade, increasingly frequent government intervention in international commerce, the curbing of transfers of technology, continual conflicts within the Atlantic Alliance over the choice of suitable policies... All this could last a long time. A very long time. Until a shock that is more violent than the others carries off these organisms wasted by disease and weakened by the exhaustion of their reserves, like the peasants in the old days of wheat shortages. All the symptoms of cancer are there and 1982 was a good illustration of such a development... But social pathology cannot be reduced to a transposition of individual pathology. And there is nothing to prevent the centres of the crisis from being gradually reabsorbed. Through a reduced dependence on oil, the gradual transformation of macroeconomic policies, the setting up of a better coordination of policies between OECD countries, and by the restoration of a stable military balance between the United States and the Soviet Union.

The scene changes with the fifth story: increasingly convinced of the necessity of finding their own independent path to development, dissatisfied with progress in the direction of a new inernational economic order, and wanting to create an environment favourable to strategies that focus on basic needs, Third World countries (excluding China and OPEC countries) decide, following a historic meeting of the 77 Group, to implement a policy of collective independence *vis à vis* the OECD. They first break those links that they see as being responsible for their dependence on the North, particularly in the area of direct investments, international trade and the price of commodities. How do OECD countries react? Let us suppose for a moment that they accept this new deal. They then have no choice but to strengthen their cooperation with the United States as they did after World War II.

There is absolutely no doubt about the effects of this rupture. Compared with the continuous scenario of slow growth, both the North and the South see their situation deteriorate, but the situation will vary widely from one country to another.

Within the OECD, the least affected is North America, with a marginally smaller per capita income. The EEC is much more seriously affected: at the beginning of the next century individual income falls by about 30% compared with that which slow growth would have allowed.

Japan is even more shaken: around the year 2010 it sees half of the income that it would have had in the basic scenario disappear!

As for the Third World, although overall it loses 17% of its income (a loss that may be compensated for by better distribution within each country) the differentiation between regions becomes accentuated, because the most industrialised areas such as Latin America and Southeast Asia, and the oil producing countries (particularly North Africa and the Middle East) are the ones to benefit from the commercial opportunities offered by the breaking off of relations with the North, while the share of Southern Asia and Sub-Saharan Africa is reduced.

Which leads to two questions. Is such a rupture conceivable? Would it last?

In order for such an economic explosion to take place, a number of fundamental political conditions would have to be met. In fact the major conflicts between developing countries would have to have disappeared, and in practice, there would have to be a disarmament of the Third World that would end its dependence on the East and West for arms. A hypothesis that is all the more difficult to achieve while politico-military rivalry between the United States and the Soviet Union continues in the background.

But supposing this rupture were to come about, could it last? We must first of all note the extent of the upheavals that it would create: a general reduction of growth, a massive redeployment of activities both in the North and South, a complete alteration of financial flows, the need for an intensive policy of energy conservation in so far as all oil-importing areas have foreign balance constraints. Would Third World countries be able to maintain their political and social cohesion under such conditions? When the distributions of the advantages and disadvantages will vary widely from one to another? When the imbalances that presently exist between North and South will be recreated within the Third World between industrial countries and the others, although, admittedly, on a smaller scale? When the sirens of the North would become insistent: Japan ready to develop a policy of cooperation with Southeast Asia in order to regain a minimum of prosperity; the EEC anxious to strengthen its ties with Africa and certain Middle Eastern or Latin American countries in order to solve some of its problems.

Let us admit it. This rupture is more of a bogey for the United Nations than a probable event. This does not make analysing it a waste of time, because it highlights certain traits that will no doubt be evident in tomorrow's world.

The sixth story makes up the other half of a diptych, since the explosion of the West makes a pair with the North-South breakdown. It begins in the United States: disappointed by allies that it does not understand; exasperated from seeing their markets invaded by Japan, American industrialists and trade unionists get Congress to pass protectionist legislation. A sudden turn that is all the more easy if opponents have a limited capacity for retaliation: how could they stop the United States from paying for its oil imports in wheat, coal or dollars? Blocked on this front, the Japanese react. By concentrating their artillery on European markets. For a while, the manoeuvre seems to work, because the conflicts between the partisans and adversaries of liberalism prevent Brussels from coming to any decision. Until the day that the German Minister of Economy, the champion of *Marktwirschaft* makes a right-about turn. From that moment, everything moves very quickly. Escalating protectionism is at its zenith between the three economic poles of the West, with each one striving to attract a part of the Third World into its orbit: Southeast Asia for Japan, the whole of Africa and the Middle East for Western Europe, and Latin America for the United States. Already seriously ill, the post-war international economic system is killed by the harshness of industrial competition between developed countries...

At a time when Toyota and Honda give the directors of Ford, Fiat or Peugeot sleepless nights, the story seems familiar and could well come true. But I am not of that opinion: the more a moderate protectionism must figure on the list of probable hypotheses, the more a protectionist upset carried through to its ultimate consequences strikes me as unlikely, that is, of course, assuming that there are no other ruptures. To avoid any repetition, my arguments will be presented in a few pages when the stability of the evolutions of continuity will be discussed.

So I now have only one story left to tell you. Or rather a group of stories with a common core – conflict between the superpowers. The fact that neither of the two protagonists wishes to trigger a cataclysm that could obliterate it, is not enough to rule out the possibility of an escalation that might lead to such an end. "The processes that could link up the successive stages of a growing conflict into a chain of tragic events are errors of *perception, foresight* and *control*... Attachment to established images of its own nation or of other countries, the desire for cognitive agreement or the rejection of facts that do not conform to preconceived ideas could lead to the equivalent of sleep or blindness for governments and nations. They may not see realistically the attitudes and abilities of foreigners, or the interests, policies, abilities and constraints of other governments before embarking on a collision course with them, and on the road to escalation."[95] There are three conditions that must be fulfilled.

Firstly, one government fears a definitive swing of the international system towards imbalances that would deprive it of any reaction in the future that might have a chance of success. A situation which might arise if, for instance, the United States were convinced that the Soviet Union had eliminated the threat of a nuclear second strike (the third control deficiency).

Secondly, the structure of one of the national political systems makes it possible for it to have an inaccurate perception of the situation on the field, of the intentions and aims of the enemy, of the respective efficacy of military equipment, and of the final consequences of a confrontation. Something that could happen to a Soviet bureaucracy that is too closed to the outside world (the second control deficiency).

Thirdly, that the fear of humiliation, or hope of the 'war to end all wars,' generates anger and hatred, or quite simply the determination not to give in (on the part of one nation at least), while the other, consenting and resigned, accepts to be kneaded like soft dough in the hands of its leaders (the first control deficiency).

The spark could come from disturbances in Europe (Poland? Yugoslavia? Turkey?), conflicts in the Third World (Cairo, Ryad, Teheran,

Islamabad, Havana or Central America...), from an about-turn by China which would now align itself with the Soviet Union. And as for the possible escalations, it is useless to try to describe them. Many an author has done that before me. However, two possibilites merit reflection: a preventive coup by the Soviet Union in order to get its hands on the Middle East, neutralise China and vassalise Western Europe. Should this succeed, the third Rome would have won the first of the new Punic Wars; the progressive engagement of the whole of American military might under pressure from exasperated public opinion calling down a fire of vengeance and purification on the enemy.

These are some of the monsters that lie hidden in the bowels of the earth. They obviously have many chromosomes in common. Evidence of these chromosomes is to be found in the seeds of explosion as well as the chains of propagation.

War or revolution in the Middle East, a serious nuclear accident, a stoppage of the repayment of international debts, revolutions or conflicts in the Third World, the USA or EEC swinging towards protectionism, a Chinese about-turn, Soviet coup, American explosion... These are some of the seeds detected throughout this book.

Spiralling inflation, a cumulative recession, an epidemic of protectionism, the collapse of the house of cards of international credit, destruction of democracy by the economic crisis, trails of revolutionary gunpowder, military escalation. These, on the other hand, are the principal chains of propagation that are produced by the economic, political, military and social tangle.

However, the probability of such ruptures has notably decreased in the past few years: the ease on the price of oil, partial control of the debt crisis, the strengthening of American military might and the installation of Pershing in Western Europe; these are factors that have helped to stabilise the international system, and which make it possible to end this chapter with a transition to a major key proclaiming the victory of continuity.

# The range of continuities

If we would write the history of the next twenty years (one generation), it is not enough to chase away the spectres of the great ruptures, because there still remains a vast spectrum of possibilities. Even with a prospective approach that limits itself to combining a few simple elements. The ingredients of this alchemy for scenarios of continuity have appeared progressively throughout this book: the nature of the relative balance between the United States and the Soviet Union, the intensity of cooperation between the great Western countries, the evolution of the oil supply, the choice of their strategies of development by the groups of societies of the Third World, the form of relations between West and South, the dynamics of aspirations and values within industrial countries, the greater or lesser plasticity of the social oligopoly of these countries... Let us analyse these ingredients: by eliminating the incompatibilities and by stressing coherences. The result is four scenarios. If the first embodies the continuation of a moderate and irregular growth, the other three personify three attempts to escape this development: a return to sustained growth thanks to the vigorous and coordinated policies of Western governments; the great industrial countries turning in on themselves through the development of a moderate protectionism; the initiation of a 'new growth' through a rapid and profound transformation of social aspirations. We shall entitle them: *Prolonged Stagnation, Rediscovering Growth, An Exploded World*, and *A Different Development*.

However, one preliminary remark: never has it been more important to distinguish between medium-term evolution and short-term fluctuations. Let us not be like those travelling salesmen who base their predictions for sales over the next five years on the figure for the past fortnight! Three years might have been enough for the world to come out of the recession of the first oil crisis, but a similar period was clearly inadequate for the second, owing to the after-effects of the first crisis and American macroeconomic policy. Therefore the average growth rate of the years following the second oil crisis was lower than the probable rates of growth in the first of these scenarios.

*Prolonged Stagnation* we must take to mean the pursuit of a modest and chaotic growth, with continuing unemployment in Europe, while in the United States, the rate of growth of productivity remains below the trend of the past three decades. International trade is kept open, but the governments of the developed countries do not manage to coordinate their policies, neither in terms of macroeconomics, nor in terms of the adaptation of structures, nor on the question of energy. The fluctuations in growth rates make the profitability of manufacturing capacity investments in industrial countries so chancy that investment trails along without ever taking off again... Conflicts within and between developed countries increase the tendency of international companies to invest in certain Third World regions and to internationalise production. They prompt the governments of OECD countries to support their exports of durable goods to the developing world, whatever the technologies employed.

The result? Annual growth rates of 1.8% for the United States, 2% for Europe, and 3 to 4% for Japan. A rather slow development of the Third World. For countries in the process of industrialisation, especially those of Southeast Asia, owing to restricted markets; for the producers of commodities, due to stagnant demand; for poor countries, because of the low level of investments. Some likely figures: Latin America 3.7%, Southern Asia 4.3%, Southeast Asia 4.5%, North Africa and the Middle East 2.9%, and Africa south of the Sahara 2.5%. The social reality is grim.

In many Third World countries, rates of growth are not enough to pull the society out of underdevelopment. The absolute number of malnourished people does not shrink. For at least three reasons: more costly energy imports, lower returns from exports as a result of slack demand from developed countries, the relatively low level of aid owing to the budgetary difficulties of contributing countries.

In Europe, because of the rapid increase of the active population, growth of around 2% means higher unemployment. Under such circumstances, European society runs the risk of being ruled by increasing rigidities: the refusal of rich regions to help poor regions, the difficult situation of public finances causing the aggravation of budgetary problems in the Community, struggles over social distribution leading to continuing high inflationary pressures, and the growing difficulties of adopting a common commercial policy towards the outside world. A well and truly stagnant Europe! Unless a stronger political will emerges and initiates concerted action aimed at stimulating activity, either directed inwards (programs for communications, armaments or technological research), or outwards (financing the demand of Southern European and developing countries). Stagnation would then give birth to a cooperative Europe.

This first scenario may be plausible, but is it stable? We may well doubt this, because nothing guarantees that the social fabric of developed societies will accept unemploypment indefinitely, and that the continued liberalisation of trade will not come up against socio-political rejection of structural adjustment in industrial countries, and in Western Europe in particular. But in which direction could the trajectory of world economy then be gradually diverted?

An initial path is that of *Rediscovering Growth*. It implies Draconian conditions:

A rediscovered desire for growth in industrial societies.

The acceptance by developed countries of continual structural adjustment, resulting in the setting up of policies that make it socially aceptable.

A concerted management of total demand by the big industrial countries, aimed at stabilising the rates of exchange and reducing the constraint of foreign trade for many developed countries.

Sustained and general policies aimed at liberalising trade.

A sustained and regular revival of investment in OECD countries encouraged by a reduction of the uncertainties arising from the risks of the international situation or the future sharing of value added between wages, taxes and profits.

Reasonable oil savings policies in consumer countries.

A massive increase of financial flows to the Third World, with a significant increase in aid to the poorest countries.

A triple participation of developing countries, with OPEC countries ensuring the oil supply; the new industrial countries prefering a general liberalisation of trade to limited and uneven advantages for their exports; the poorest countries devoting financial and technical assistance to the priority of increasing their food production.

The appearance of such a scenario may be excluded, because the last decade of this century could well hold a few surprises. All the same, we shall in any case have to wait a few years for sustained growth to be established in the greater part of the economy.

Nevertheless, let us suppose that the wave of a magic wand were to establish this scenario right now. What would it mean in figures? American growth holding at around 3%, and growth in the EEC at around 3.2% beyond 1990. Much more sustained growth in all regions of the Third World: Latin America 4.5%, Southeast Asia 5.7%, North Africa and the Middle East 5.6%, Southern Asia 4.8%, and Sub-Saharan Africa 3%. Some will grumble: "That's very little for the move from moderate growth to sustained and cooperative growth." They forget however, that for the United States the difference over twenty years represents 20% of their present income! This is all you need to become aware of the enormity of the volumes involved and the length of time it would take for any distribution of incomes on a world scale.

Thus, in this scenario, the range of per capita incomes will scarcely be narrower at the beginning of the next century: by this time, the income of a North American will have increased by 50% compared with 1985. Compared with this level, the income of a Japanese person will be roughly the same, that of a Western European about three quarters, that of a South American will be one quarter, that of a black African, one twentieth, and that of an Indian, about one thirtieth.

This scenario allows the European Economic Community to recover quite substantial rates of growth and lower the risk of rising social tensions and regional rivalries; it also facilitates a cooperative Europe, but, *a contrario*, it presupposes such a Europe, because Europeans are the first to benefit from calm international relations, as well as being in the best position to take the initiative to reorganise world economic, monetary and trade regulating mechanisms.

An exploration of the second exit road from Prolonged Stagnation (a world split up into blocs) is enough to convince us. A path that is at once that of the failure of cooperation between the great poles of the North, and that of the rejection of the structural changes imposed by a slow, outward-facing growth. In the beginning, a hardening of American attitudes to the outside world or that country's increasingly marked hesitation to grapple with international economic problems and to ensure the security of the West as a whole. Faced with such behaviour, the European Economic Community strengthens its economic and industrial cooperation, develops its political independence, and gives priority to the independent reduction of its vulnerability. Japan, in turn, feels constrained to review its options. The great blocs of the North then try to make up for the (relative) weakening of their relations by developing preferential links with certain zones of the Third World: the United States intensifies its relations with the American continent as a whole, Japan with ASEAN countries, other Far Eastern countries, and so to a certain extent, with Southern Asia. As for Europe, it develops ever closer economic cooperation with black Africa, North Africa, and the Middle East. at the same time, the great developed areas adopt more restrictive attitudes to international trade, halt the pursuit of industrial specialisation, and do not leave the restructuring of their productive apparatuses up to international markets. Whence the emergence of various forms of neoprotectionism.

In terms of overall growth, the first ten years of the scenario are somewhat dull! Only North America gets well out of it and maintains the income of the scenario of moderate growth, but compared with said scenario, Japan loses 30% and the EEC 15% of its own growth. Thus, Europe, associated with relatively poor developing regions lacking strong production or absorption capacities and unable to supply it completely with raw materials, suffers from the restriction of trade, despite the agricultural opening that it finds in this scenario. There is only one beneficiary in the Third World – black Africa. Because Europe must try to compensate for losing ground in the dynamic markets of Latin America and Asia with vigorous aid to the continent with which it is associated. With the passing of time, economies adapt, the ravages of neoprotectionism become blurred, and the sky clears for the first decade of the next century.

Some readers will be thinking, "I don't understand. Your analysis goes against intuition. Moderate protectionism avoids the disappearance of all activities threatened by foreign competition, and the ossification resulting from the closing of trade only spreads in the long run." Faultless reasoning – if no country retaliates against the measures taken by another. But this reasoning collapses if protectionism spreads in a chain reaction, because, if that were to happen, we may expect changes in all the sectors in developed countries with a high export content: the car industry, electronics, aeronautic construction, mechanics, and data processing... In the same way, multinationals are forced to redeploy their activities, and by doing this they may create jobs, but they also destroy them. Nothing demonstrates better how vain is some people's hope of using customs duties to turn back the clock in a desperate attempt to preserve the present state of the economy. At the present level of interdependence within the world economy, any deviation in the general direction of protectionism is in danger of creating powerful restraints that will limit its own extent. That does not in any way rule out frequent recourse to the occasional, temporary protectionist tinkering intended to facilitate structural adaptations...

For those who find none of the above scenarios satisfactory, there remains one last path: a change in the content of growth based on a new consensus in developed countries. Where do we start? Stagnant incomes and unemployment detach a majority of citizens from long established values. But we still need to understand the nature of the swing. If it is confined to a selfish egotism, or if the desire for open spaces and natural food replaces the thirst for televisions in a sort of return to a rustic past without the least opening onto the outside world, this swing will not bring any message and the 'new growth' that it will give birth to will only be able to survive in the shelter of an inward-looking protectionism. But if the new aspirations were to feed on an awareness of globality and lead to openness towards the Third World things could be different.

But how can we describe the content of such a growth in industrial countries? Let us try to do it in a few sentences. Different arbitrages between paid work and the remaining time, with a large reduction of that part which is conventionally called 'working hours.' Many informal economic activities. Reduced unemployment. An active population that is increased by the possibility of working less, but diminished by the intensity of training. An organisation of work that is more in harmony with the aspirations of employees, and thus resulting in higher productivity which allows the pursuit of a minimum of growth. A great frugality that limits the rise in consumption and makes the development of non-market investments and services possible. Obviously, the liberation of the individual and his establishment are not enough. Economic constraints demand more. No new growth without new Puritanism.

And the Third World? It gets a bigger flow of aid from the industrial countries. And a new Western model that spurs it on to seek paths of development that emphasise basic needs. So much the better for the poorest countries, even if the countries that are in the process of rapid industrialisation, those that have banked on exports, have their expectations disappointed.

An attractive scenario? Perhaps, but an extreme form of it remains very unlikely. Why?

Because in each industrial country, the change in aspirations creates upheaval in the productive structures, provokes a crisis in some sectors, forces people to redistribute themselves in the economy. And their citizens must not only accept permanent frugality, but also temporary sacrifices.

Because the success of one region or country following a productivist scheme (a success that will be all the more easy since there will be less competition) is enough to compel the adherents of the new values to choose quickly between protection and a significant economic decline.

Because there is nothing to stop the Soviet bloc from taking advantage of such a development in the West to increase its influence in the Third World.

Because there is no guarantee of an easier energy transition if a drop in the consumption of energy is accompanied by a freeze on the development of nuclear energy and possibly of coal.

For instance, in order for Europe to be the first to adopt this style of growth, two conditions would have to be met. One has to do with relations between the EEC and the outside world, because you may ask if a Europe that is dependent in the area of energy and raw materials would be great enough to organise itself around new values of its own, sheltered, if necessary, by tariff protection, in the face of the productivist dynamism of Japan, the United States, or some of the more active Third World countries. But you may also question the probability of seeing a second condition achieved: that of a parallel development of the countries of Europe that would allow them to start off along this path at the same time. *A rift between Northern and Southern Europe would seem to be more likely. A cleavage that would reverse the stereotypes of the first half of the century, and separate the non-productive Northern societies from Southern societies passing through a rapid process of industrialisation. The adaptation of values would thus lead to an unexpected scenario of Europe proceeding at two speeds, with the role of sustained growth in the South, and with Northern Europe experiencing a marked development in the direction of the new values.*

Whence the paradox that lies at the heart of the scenario of new growth: if it were to extend over world societies as a whole, it would be more stable and less fraught with conflict than others; as it emerges it comes up against several obstacles, because the various social groups, the various advanced industrial societies, and the various groups of societies in the world all experience this changing of values at a different pace. Therefore it is highly unlikely.

This exploration of continuities obviously does not prove either the optimist or the pessimist right. If the former can point to the increase of world per capita income, the advances made by a part of the Third World, and the gradual reabsorption of the energy crisis, the latter can stress the fact that the South is only catching up very slowly, that scenarios of slow growth or of the world divided into blocs could create disturbing social consequences, and that the adoption of new values would, whatever the circumstances, begin with a difficult period of transition.

Assuming that there is no cumulative rupture, what probable development do the four scenarios of continuity therefore suggest? I shall try
to describe it as I see it, in a camaieu devoid of sensationalism whose
nuances will express the complexity of a developing world.

The slow and irregular growth of developed economies persists for
around fifteen years with continuing structural unemployment, though
with improved overall performance from 1990. The coordination of
macroeconomic policies continues to be inadequate, and structural
adjustment after a fashion is made in the shelter of indirect protectionist
measures against imports both from other industrial regions and from
the Third World. Some countries (Japan in particular) show a greater
flexibility, and their productivity rises without making the productivity
of any other country a kind of ceiling. Governments have a difficult job
arbitrating between perennial traditional demands, and the new
demands coming from active minorities. Only a few countries opt more
decisively for new growth and regulate some of their trade with the the
outside world in order to make the chosen development possible.
Altogether, the performances of developed countries in terms of growth,
inflation, employment, energy independence, and foreign balance gradually move apart. The European Community finds it more difficult to
adapt than North America, and from 1985 to 1990 growth is slower than
in the United States or Japan.

Third World countries, for their part, continue to diverge. In the
poorer continents, some countries try reformist or radical development
strategies in order to satisfy better the basic needs of the majority, but
there is no guarantee that these efforts will succeed. Third World
countries also try to organise cooperation with each other but this is only
partly successful, and all the more so because for cultural, political,
military and economic reasons, there are still close links between Latin
America, North America and Europe, between Africa and Europe, the
United States and Europe, and between Southeast Asia and Japan.

Despite the semi-protectionism that exists within the North, and
between North and South, as well as within the South, there continues to
be an intense redeployment of economic activities in the world, and the
countries that are in the process of industrialisation increase their trade
with the developed countries. Without really becoming a part of the
world market, they depend on it more and more heavily.

But such a picture is not less disturbing because it is possible:

Unfulfilled aspirations emanate from the people: the governments of
the developed countries have to face the claims of an aging population
that voices both new demands and a strong need for security; in the

Third World, revolutionary movements thrive, and absolute poverty only retreats slowly in relative percentages.

Harassed by the multiplicity of problems to be solved, and caught in the numerous conflicts created by interdependence, governments do not manage to establish cooperation on a foundation of regularity and trust. Many issues are resolved belatedly, and the solutions correspond above all to what economists call non-cooperative equilibria.

Continuities and ruptures. How do we improve the former or block the latter? The time has come to replace forecasting with questions about politics.

# REFLECTION FOR ACTION

"The most pessimistic view of man and things, of life and its value, is perfectly consistent with action and the optimism that action demands."

Paul VALERY
*Regards sur le monde actuel*

# Elusive decision-makers

Quick! A conference of heads of state! Without their mobs of aids and body guards. At Lichtenstein or in Bermuda. In a few days, the world's top scientists will explain the facts to them and provide them with the evidence. Then, having seen the light, they will return to their offices and act. And the the face of the world will be changed.

But what an awful caricature of reality! For two reasons:

1. Getting a pedestrian to cross at the lights by explaining how traffic lights work is the easiest thing in the world. But when you are dealing with a thousand pedestrians, things are different. Whether you address them all or simply inform the 'leaders,' you won't get them crossing in an orderly fashion in groups of four. And we would all say "Thank goodness for that."

2. Besides, why should the pedestrians wish to cross to the other side? Action cannot be inferred from knowledge and there is no guarantee that these pedestrians share the same values or have exactly the same conception of the best of all possible worlds.

Reflection on action must be based on these two observations.

The first one shows that changing the future presupposes a transformation of the three control deficiencies; the international system is the seat of the first one, the second is firmly embedded in the national systems, and man himself is the carrier of the third.

Let us set the last one aside for the moment, pointing only to the failure of the 'cultural revolutions' to construct a new man, the uncertain balance-sheet of psychoanalysis in so far as the modification of people is concerned, and finally the immense future power of genetics and neuro-pharmacology. The day is approaching when man will be able to change man. Who will be subject? Who will be the object? Our hopes are as great as our fears.

Let us rather consider the second control deficiency. Where are the West's decision-makers? Everywhere and nowhere. Heads of state with narrow political majorities, criticised by the media, and challenged by pressure groups. Compartmentalised governments, better suited to making decisions on copper, VAT or housing aid, than to the development of comprehensive policies. Corporatist structures incapable of subjecting their particular interests to a global vision. Business concerns bound by the indispensible consideration of profitability. Citizens torn between the limits of their egotism, the Utopia of their generosity and the feeling of their powerlessness. But that does not prevent any of them from taking decisions and influencing the evolution of systems. Besides, this book is not only aimed at the so-called leaders, but also at all the men and women who help to mould history. It intends not so much to dictate their conduct, as to suggest a conceptual framework that makes today's world and that of tomorrow intelligible. The top priority is understanding, because understanding can generate different attitudes and encourage different behaviour. And then, each decision-maker, whatever his place in society, will look at his problems from a new perspective, and will invent a solution that is suited to the society that is being created, without anyone being able to say precisely where the main initiatives that will radically change the system will come from. We should therefore not misjudge the meaning of the pages ahead: it is for the sake of convenience that they refer to the classification of problems inspired by the usual simplistic model of the state, and as a result often give the impression of having been written for governments.

The decision-makers? They are no easier to identify in the international system, and the vision of a country reduced to being a 'Father of the People' is patently naïve.

Equating Iran with the Shah may have been a convenient diplomatic fiction. We know what became of it. The state of the world is not only caused by the clash of the schemes of the politicians in power. It also depends on the behaviour of high officials, the executives of multinationals, trade unionists, polemists, scientists, religious leaders, the leaders of revolutionary movements... Despite the fact that from one country to another, from one group to another, they do not analyse the present in the same way, many of them are seeking a common language that would allow them to recognise their areas of agreement or conflict. If this book (thanks to a message that derives its acceptability from a systemic vision of the world) were to be, for some of them, the beginning of such a language, it would have achieved its aim.

However, indispensible though it may be, an awareness of the fact that decision-makers are scattered all over the world is not enough to provide the basis for a philosophy of action. No endeavour of this kind can dodge the second observation: the inevitable debate on the finalities.

Some believe that man is not only his own guardian, but also the guardian of Life, the protector of all the animal and vegetable species that live on the earth. If a single species of mosquitoes disappears somewhere in Oceania, they mourn as if it were the smile of a child that had been put out.

For others humanity is the only acceptable reference. The whole of mankind. Nothing but mankind. The rest of life, all aesthetic or historic heritage, only makes sense in relation to humanity: present or future humanity. In its name, they refuse to make distinctions between people. Nations, cultures and wealth are in themselves valueless. But these defenders of humanity do not all belong to the same school of thought, and within the socialist family, for example, the differences between brothers, cousins or allies are not negligible. The revolutionary who is ready to sacrifice any individual whose existence threatens the advent of enlightened tomorrows for the human masses, is opposed by the conscientious objector who refuses to spill blood for any reason whatsoever.

Next comes the band of those who only look at the world through the future of a national group. *Rule Britannia* and *Deutschland über alles* are now *passé*, but this does not in any way prevent nationalism from flourishing on every continent, or governments from continuing to be above all the guardians of the perpetuity of the national state.

Two clans bring up the rear: those who identify with other human groups apart from the national state – sons of Israel, defenders of the faith, adherents of negritude..., and those who are only concerned with the survival and welfare of their family or even just saving their own skins.

This is an overly simplistic typology, because most people feel they belong to all these worlds, even if the importance given to them varies widely from one individual to another. It is an inadequate typology, for in order to determine the finalities, we must go beyond the mere reference group alone. In two ways. By arbitrating between the present and the future, between short-term and long-term interests. By combining the six great dimensions of social finalities: efficiency, equality, liberty, participation, security, and adaptability.

And we should not be surprised that social projects that the Soviet *apparatchik*, the Japanese business man, the Egyptian peasant, the Parisian intellectual, the militant ecologist, and the abandoned Bogota child carry within them should be incompatible. Even for a European of the 1980's like myself, the range of objectives remains immense.

Since human history will come to an end anyway, I could resign myself to absolute catastrophe in a huge nuclear holocaust. For once humanity had disappeared, would there still be someone who would attach some meaning to such an adventure?

I could accept Western disarmament followed by the extension of the Soviet Empire over the whole world to free humanity from the third control inadequacy, in the hope that after decades of servitude, the conquered would have managed to contaminate the conqueror and give socialism a human face once more.

I could militate for a World Revolution, for a revolt of the peasant masses in each developing country and for a Third World attack on the 'haves' in the East and West.

I could dream of a world-wide Fourth of August during which the representatives of the West transfer their wealth to the rest of the world in an act of magnanimity.[96]

I could forget the world, cast into outer darkness all that is not Europe or the West, and argue for our society to turn in on itself in the hope of protecting this island of relative prosperity from the stormy sea.

I shall do none of these things. I shall accept the ethical reference to the whole of life, but within this, giving priority to humanity, and, within humanity, to the two historical entitities to which I belong – French society and European civilisation. I shall refuse to disregard the long-term consequences of our present decisions without, for all that, sacrificing the present for the future. I would argue for the adaptability of our societies, and for a balance between efficiency, security, equality, liberty and participation. Referring to history and to the examples that it gives us of societies whose inability to adapt set them on the road to irreversible decline, and of societies which, through their creativity, have survived and blossomed despite the upheaval of their environment, I shall ask about the paths that developed countries can adopt to face probable developments and face the unforeseen. Governing elites have never had a stake in revolutions; and it must be added that they have not countenanced them. But they have often thought they could guarantee their safety by maintaining the status quo, and it is their refusal to adapt themelves that has led them to the final catastrophe. Will the same be true of the leading states of the Western world? That is the fundamental question today, and one which I believe has only one answer: developed societies will only guarantee their future through a progressive reformation of the international system and their national systems. A reformation that must be executed with resolution and flexibility, and one that reduces their vulnerability while at the same time adapting their international relations to the embryonic new power games. We have within us all the elements of decline: mentalities that evolve more slowly than the environment, a social oligopoly that creates fixity, a tendency to give priority to the short term. Since societies are not changed by decree, the future will be the product of profound attitudinal changes on all levels, and of coalitions between social groups for long-term projects. Let us not forget that societies are like elephants: we may poke and pull and push them, but we never know which way they will turn. I am only a small mahout, or rather (since I am in the pachyderm), one of countless neurons. Each person is free to adopt the goal I offer and the answer that I propose or to content themselves with the conceptual framework previously constructed; the one does not necessarily follow the other.

What should be the content of these reforms? In order to analyse it, I had to make a choice. I could either put myself into the shoes of an American citizen and speak as if I lived in Los Angeles or Houston, or remain myself and adopt the perspective of a European nation and its actors. The first option would have made my message strike home more forcefully to an American reader, but it could not be truly authentic. Moreover, I thought it would be better to accept my Europeanness. This choice will in no way prevent American or Canadian readers from transposing my reflections, using their continent as a reference.

The projector will point in three directions one after another: foreign relations, domestic transformations, and the education and information of people.

# Towards a new geography

All foreign policy consists of tactics and strategy. Without tactics, there is no management of crises, no exploitation of opportunities, and no adaptation to the terrain. But without strategy, there is no interpretation of the facts, no lasting influence on the plans of others, no possible reorientation of the course of things... The whole art is a question of deducing the former from the latter by preserving flexibility in action and not forgetting that every society is a complex entity with multiple finalities whose numerous actors dream of different priorities.

The strategy that this book proposes is like two sides of a coin, one addressed to multipolarity and the other to interdependence.

The response to multipolarity should be the establishement of a new hierarchy of solidarities. A program that may be summarised in one formula: the seven circles of cooperation.

The first of these circles? Obviously, the European Common Market. Each citizen is free to give it a transcendental value or not, by transferring to it the national Imago. The essential thing is that long-term parallel interests outweigh everyday conflicts. Faced with new economic competition, faced with a haunting Soviet presence, faced with the enduring shortage of energy and raw materials, Europe is a reducer of uncertainty and acts as a bearing on world affairs. Everybody knows the priorities. A permanent secretariat for foreign affairs, greater military cooperation (particularly between France and Great Britain for nuclear arms, and between the countries of the hard core ofthe European Community for taking space defence into account) a European monetary system capable of absorbing shocks, a trade policy that breaks the force of storms without hindering adjustment, a common agricultural policy that is faithful to its principles but with its methods reformed, industrial and research operations with freedom of choice in the most advanced fields, and a common core of energy policies. And finally increased exchanges between those who will be responsible for the future: future government or business leaders, young scientists, new journalists, young militant trade unionists or politicians...

The second is not the North Atlantic but the Trilateral circle: Western Europe, Japan and North America. Beginning first of all by strengthening the weakest link in the chain, by developing a political collaboration between Japan and Europe that challenges and goes beyond economic competition. Does not Europe stand to gain from helping to make Japan aware of its world-wide responsibilities? Then defining (pragmatically) more balanced relations with the United States, relations within which Europeans will behave like adults and not like adolescent old men.[97] Rediscovering the direction of some major solidarities that the developed world must preserve despite its conflicts of interest, and despite the relative weakening of its leader: solidarity in democracy, solidarity in growth, solidarity in military protection, solidarity in oil supplies, and solidarity in the reform of the international economic system.

Then comes the circle of the three-way dialogue between Europe, the Arab world and black Africa. Separated and united by the Mediterranean, and shaped by a long history of mutual influences, the Arab and European worlds need each other. Flows of oil and sometimes of labour, from the South and East to the North. Technology, industrial investment and agricultural aid from the North to the South and East. Capital and tourists in both directions. Rarely have two groups of countries so geographically close to each other been more complementary. The fact that the superiority complex of the West, the instability of the Arab world, and mutual grievances make relations delicate and tenuous does not in any way justify giving up on gradually establishing preferential links. As for poor black Africa, according to the outlook for the end of the century, it is not at all a decisive economic stake, despite its reserves of raw materials. However, it is in the interest of Europe and the moderate Arab states that it take its fate into its own hands, ensure its political stability, be able to resist foreign influence, and rid itself of the spectre of a food disaster. Do we need to mention Chad to be convinced of the difficult life that this *ménage à trois* will have?

Fourth circle: now into the ring come the new industrial nations; and there must be cooperations with them to extend the foundation of the developed world. A new development that concerns Europe in two ways.

Through the old links that it has with certain Latin American countries, through the challenges that these new markets and new competitors give its economy. Some paths to explore: agreements over opening their frontiers to each other, setting up joint undertakings, strengthening scientific and cultural cooperation, and contributing to a widening of the OECD...

The fifth circle embraces the whole of the Third World (except China). The overall objective has recurred again and again in this book like a leitmotiv: to contribute, through relations on all levels, to a reform of the international system, while at the same time avoiding having the actions of the developed countries jeopardise the development of the poor countries. A thorny question that has not yet ceased to create jobs for journalists: what to do in the case of a Third World country when political struggles pit against each other corrupt authoritarian ruling classes and brutal revolutionary juntas? The former expect a life-buoy from the West. The latter hate what the West stands for. Violence against violence. What solution should we adopt? Take refuge in a strict neutrality? Not interfere until others do? Take the side of the masses, having faith in their future development? Back the leaders? Push for the democratisation of dictatorships? Chili, Cambodia, Angola, Iran, Nicaragua, El Salvador, the Central African Republic... The list of these past dilemmas of the West is long, and the list of future dilemmas will be longer still. The answer must perforce be pragmatic, for it must neither forget human rights as they are defined by the West, nor power games on the international level, nor the dynamics peculiar to the countries concerned.

As for the content of policies, it must spring from the reality of the differentiation of the developing world, in order to explore as much on the world level as on the bilateral level all the possibilities of mutual benefit. However, there is one Third World country which, by virtue of the size of its population defies all classification: India. Its size allows it to be both a tremendous agricultural country with a very low standard of living and a new medium-sized industrial country, while, because of its geographic position, it cannot be indifferent to Soviet advances towards the Middle East. It would be a good thing if in the future there were closer relations between India and Europe than there have been over the past quarter century.

China alone will constitute the sixth circle. A long-term investment for Europe that is of the primary importance: the training of people, of young Chinese people who will be in positions of leadership in thirty years.

And finally, there is the last circle, that of peaceful coexistence with Eastern Europe. Why mention it so late, given that it includes countries which are closely linked to Europe through their history? Obviously, because the only state in the world that constitutes a military threat to Western Europe is to be found there. Europe's strategy, contrary to what many think (or say), is practically mapped out (or should be): sticking to a global concept of détente linking various issues, not renouncing its convictions, and, if necessary, not shrinking from ideological debate with this ossified form of communism, stepping up trade with the most independent East European countries, sticking to constructive exchanges with the Soviet Union, and never compromising on national defence.

It is through these seven circles that the problems of interdependence must be tackled. And since its dimensions have already been the subject of analyses, a few supplementary quotations will suffice.

We cannot but see that defence policy must become a major priority once more. With modalities that will naturally vary according to the situation of each individual European country. Take France, for example. There are various conceivable options, many of which are illusory or unacceptable: a pacifist doctrine which, in tomorrow's dangerous world, would mean quashing our freedom of choice without having any pulling power; strict sanctuarisation that would ignore the importance to France of equilibrium in Europe, the Middle East and Africa; a system of European defence that would require conditions that are difficult to bring together, at least for the moment; a return to NATO that would go against the geographic evolution of the world. And finally there is the option of continuing along the chosen path, but with a considerable reinforcement of the volume and security of strategic nuclear forces and the development of long-distance intervention forces, and preparing together with other EEC countries to take space into account in European defence thinking. direction that demands a larger share of the domestic product for the defence budget, and savings on the bulk of defence spending that does not contribute anything to the defence of France; but fighting for peace also presupposes active diplomacy, particularly in Africa and the Middle East.

Finally, Europe can contribute to the construction of a more balanced world, in at least four ways:

1. By taking part in the stabilisation of the international monetary and financial system. The setting up of the European monetary system is a step in this direction. There must be others. The introduction of basic

controls of the growth of Euromarkets, the gradual consolidation of a part of dollar balances, the development of long-term investments by countries with balance of payments surpluses, more transfers of resources to Third World countries. All these are objectives that Europe can make a practical contribution to realising.

2. By associating itself with international action in the area of energy: consultation on the policies to adopt in case of crisis, negociations with producing countries, helping Third World countries to develop their own resources, transfers of energy technologies.

3. By adopting constructive policies for international trade. Whether it is a question of developing the international trade of manufactured products, promoting adapted technologies, regulating commodity markets, strengthening the agricultural potential of the Third World, setting up an organisation of trade that cuts down the risk of permanent or unforeseeable protectionist barriers while at the same time time making possible temporary measures for adjustment announced in advance.

4. By supporting operations aimed at protecting the common heritage of humanity, and by facilitating the making of a rich fabric of non-governmental international organisations.

Nonetheless, the most important thing remains to be said, because the great innovation of the next twenty years will be that foreign policy will no longer be the business of specialists. It will be the work of all the decision-makers. The novelist whose novel will be translated, the teacher who will educate the people of Mali or Guatemala, the technician who will perfect a method of saving energy, the young man who will replace his military service with voluntary service overseas, the trade unionist who will include international constraints in the formulation of his demands and the navy officer who will patrol the Persian Gulf, will be both its inventors and artisans.

Encouraging, supporting and channeling this host of actions will be a new task for governments. The learning process promises to be a tough one.

# Adapting by creating

Two words by way of introduction, aimed at destroying certain myths.

The first ties the future of European society to international constraints. What was a useful swing of the pendulum after several years of denial, is now likely to occult our domestic problems and obscure our options. The new frontiers are not only to be found in foreign markets. They also pass through our employment pools and urban suburbs. Denying our margins of freedom is another form of resignation and ossification.

But we should not fall into the opposite myth, believing that all things are possible, dealing with the wrong planet and blinding ourselves to the harsh reality of tomorrow's world. The backlash would then sweep like a hurricane over the barely opened roses of socialism.

As for the other myth, it consists of substituting the Japanese challenge for the American challenge in the *Manager's Vademecum*. Japanese society provides food for thought? Fine. It leads us to ask questions about ourselves? Excellent. But any illusions on our part of imitating it are quite absurd. In the Sixties, European leaders believed they were adopting American style management. In fact they invented something new. Our motto should be clear: we should take inspiration from outside ideas without shame, but that should be done in order to draw solutions from the heart of our own culture.

And since this is the time for peremptory simplifications, I shall regroup under six topics the areas in which European societies must both adapt and create.

1. The first priority: demographic renewal. Far from contributing to the equilibrium of the world by refraining from adding a few more mouths to feed and bodies to warm, industrial societies, if inhabited by old people, will hold back desirable developments, meet the great challenges of the hour with inertia, and accelerate the decline of their own culture. Without moderate population growth in the West, the gradual reformation of the international system is in serious danger of turning into a long period of blockage followed by a series of explosions. This needs to be repeated again and again.

2. The second topic will surprise no one, but action has nothing to do with looking for originality and paradox: despite the drop in the price of oil, the slip-knot of energy dependence must be undone as quickly as possible, by stressing energy savings, by continuing nuclear program- mes, changing over to breeder reactors, by buying foreign coal mines and converting our oil-fueled factories to coal, and by preparing the advent of solar energy.

What is true of energy is also, on a smaller scale, true of raw materials. The objective? To reduce our vulnerability at every stage, from ore to metal, depending on the distribution of reserves, worked mines and processing factories. But not at any price.

3. The third topic is vast. Because of its scope: productive activities as a whole. Because of the finality that it involves: competitiveness on intra-and extra-Community markets. Because of the policy that it calls for: 'liberal interventionism.'

Why this neologism? And how can it be justified?

The major characteristic of the productive structure of a developed economy has a name – complexity. Countless goods and services. A host of professional specialities. A wide variety of units of production, from the huge factory to the laboratory or the artisan's workshop. A perpetual renewal of productions and methods. Anyone who thinks that such a structure may be managed by means of a barrage of regulations or direct state interventions is deceiving themselves. Competitiveness would disappear like a mirage if it were not founded on the creative capacity of the whole of society.

The state, on the other hand, has its own responsibilities: strengthen- ing the key points that economic agents are not capable of assuring, defining the rules of the game, informing, encouraging, foreseeing, and absorbing shocks.

Two examples of key points: energy with the electronuclear program, and research responsible for the upstream stages that are the bases of the technical innovations of companies. But in the latter case, let us remember that finding demands more than spending. Let us beware of accumulating snowball mediocre researchers; they never warm the furnace of invention. Let us concentrate our attention on the weakest link in the chain – the transfer from the laboratory to productive activities.

As for the rules of the game, they should be less norms or constraints than signals of correct prices. Signals that reflect accurately the *social* scarcity of the various factors of production for the European economy. An insufficiently dissuasive energy price is a crime. Labour costs that discourage recruitment are an absurdity. Negative real interest rates that do not guarantee savers a return on their capital are wrong. Giving free services that users would be prepared to pay for is a mistake. But do not let this plea for an efficient price system deceive you: it demands a counterpart – the protection of the weakest groups. A subject that will be dealt with a few lines hence.

Acquiring information is more than a minor task: interdependence is in the process of increasing rapidly the volume of information necessary to run a business. The general manager may need to know the growth potential of the Brazilian economy, the details of the Japanese market, the characteristics of its Korean competitor, the level of wages in Mexico or Singapore, subsidies granted to the Ivory Coast, the Indonesian tax system... If the firm is the only one that can generate part of this information, the rest of it can be gathered and disseminated by the state. Directly and indirectly.

Moreover, the Ministry of Industry should (like Japan's MITI[98]) periodically make known the sectors that it deems to be heralds of the future, and the strategic sectors in which it would wish to see a strengthening of the productive fabric of the country. Less to take the place of the market in the selection of winners, than to awaken initiatives and encourage them through c stimulation. From this point of view, liberal interventionism answers strictly the needs of a medium-sized open economy that is neither an ITT-like supergroup headed by the Industry Minister, nor a simple arena of competition within which the activities carried on do not matter.

Stimulation also presupposes foreseeing, or in other words, guarding against the creation of new capacities in sectors approaching maturity, or those where the comparative advantages of foreign competitors could prove decisive. Beware of tomorrow's iron and steel industries! It would be better to avoid them by anticipatory adjustments.

Finally, the last role of the state – that of absorbing shocks. When the shock hitting the productive structures is socially too severe, or is only the result of an accidental phenomenon without long-term effects, it might find it necessary to curb developments, but it must avoid getting caught in the machinery. It is so easy to move from the temporary to the permanent, and to end up being forced to amputate an arm where it would have been enough to cut off a finger.

If the state does this, what is there left for companies to do? Everything. Or nearly everything. Because the above recital of facts is not a call for concubinage between civil servants and employers. The staff of public or private companies are not to waste their best hours in flattery aimed at getting aid from the young marquises of governments. Such staff have better things to do: invent products, create markets, get financing, build production capacities, and manage at the lowest possible cost. In times of prosperity business concerns have experienced the era of creators, an era whose growth often turned its mistakes into anticipations. For some years now, they have experienced the era of managers who tighten bolts, slash investments, and eliminate risks. To the detriment of the future. They are going to have to combine these two types of men and find their way to a form of management that is firm but creative, because good management without strategy covering the future will lead them to ruin just as surely as would a chaotic innovation that would no longer be sanctioned *a posteriori* by growth. They are going to have to think about the new aspirations of men and women in order for their firm to respond to them and base its efficiency on their (relative) satisfaction. Otherwise, their blissful wait-and-see policy (to which short-term problems act as a screen) is in danger of opening onto some nasty surprises.

4. On the other hand, liberal interventionism calls for a complement and counterweight: a new macroeconomic policy, a *NEP* of the Eighties. Its aim is extremely simple – reduce inflation and limit unemployment so that it is not allowed to create groups of rejects from the social and economic system. But as long as the *two big groups of instruments* (without which a developed economy is no longer controllable) are not combined, the problem will remain unsolved.

On one hand, there are the traditional instruments of the regulation of demand, the total amount of money in circulation, and budget deficit, which attack Keynesian unemployment and inflation. Their possible applications are however greatly limited by the tendancy to import, and, in the present state of the monetary system, by the extreme sensitivity of exchange rates.

On the other hand, there are new instruments designed to combat classic unemployment and inflation through costs.

If unemployment is to be reduced, the relative marginal costs of labour and equipment must first be changed. By cutting down the shocking level of social insurance contributions based on salaries only. By relaxing the regulations governing dismissal which encourage employers not to take on staff in the face of an uncertain future. By avoiding any excessive rise of the guaranteed minimum wage, and perhaps even by eliminating this constraint. As for a reduction of working hours, it is unthinkable except under draconian conditions: as long as it does not degenerate into extra paid holidays; as long as it does not reduce the length of time during which capital equipment is used; as long as it does not lead to a rise in hourly wages that is higher than the rise in productivity; as long as it does not hit (at least temporarily) the rare categories of personnel, those whose activity conditions production capacities. Two indispensible flanking measures: a close watch on non-salary income, and a more extensive recourse to a minimum guaranteed family income to compensate for the weakening or disappearance of the role played by the statutory minimum wage.

As for inflation, it can only be combatted by attacking its structural roots: insufficient competition, tacit agreements, the use of prices by the government to guarantee incomes, the coexistence of an indexation of prices for some resources with a lack of indexation for others (such as the rate of interest). Should harsh, instant action be taken? It may be preferable to a long interest war, but the very nature of the causes makes success ever precarious.

5. Thus, and more than in the past, macroeconomic policy cannot be separated from action on structures by its two sides: the struggle against inequalities and the struggle against unearned incomes.

If its aim is to dissolve everything in the grisaille of mediocrity and create a society of people on welfare, the struggle against inequalities will only increase rigidities at the expense of a new victim – the user or consumer. On the other hand if it frees the live forces in society and attacks unequal opportunities and the privileges of status, if it recognises ability more than diplomas or birth, and if it opens up educational possibilities right throughout life, it will liberate the vital forces of society.

However this will not be enough. Behind the total unemployment figures rises a menacing spectre for the future of European societies – the emergence of large minorities of déclassés incapable of defending themselves in the struggle for survival. They are characterised less by their low incomes than by their inability to fit into economic and social life. People with several inequalities. Rather than handling enormous sums that generally go back to the people they were taken from, like the present National Health Service, rather than regulating working conditions (that are a unit) by cutting them up into abstract strips (duration, accidents, sickness, laboriousness), the Welfare State would do better to turn itself first of all towards the defence of these minorities, focusing (in the case of the majority) on protection only in the case of exceptional circumstances. The strain that the low growth rate will impose on the state budget will force governments to undertake this reform of the Welfare State.

As for the fight against unearned incomes, (whether these incomes are the result of tax exemption, barriers against entry into certain professions, regulations that suppress competition and divide the market into segments), it will be needed to vitalise the economy by slimming it down and making it fitter. and the government must definitely not be excepted from this process.

One objection, and it is a major one: won't the social oligopoly ruin this lovely programme? Maybe. But we should not rule out the possibility that certain groups that are part of it may revise their strategy, realising that in the world ahead, the effective pursuit of their aims requires other methods.

6. The four topics preceding this one belong to traditional economics. The final one will have a totally different source of inspiration. If, in the future, the principal activity does not occupy more than four days of the week on average, if aspirations, as they are modified, blossom into a variety of behaviour patterns, the framework of life, environment and culture will become a source of major concern coming immediately after employment and health. Concern that will give rise to conflicts surrounding the arbitrages between the environment and economic profitability, between the environment and freedom, between the environment and participation, between conservation and creation. These new social struggles will have their actors: landlords and tenants, central governments, local communities, neighbourhood-based groups... The role of governments? It will be less doing than allowing the expression of the right to be different, without challenging the proper management of the common national heritage. A marvellous terrain to explore.

The search for adapted and creative development. In the full awareness of international commotion and the effervescence peculiar to European societies, could there be a better subject for reflection on the part of political parties that would throw off dogmas in order to pursue their truth?

# Education and information

Once more, my son, before I finish this book, I think of you. Not to speak to you, but to ask myself if the adults of my age will know how to educate your generation and those that precede it so that they may invent a creative answer to the problems of the future.

There is no task more important than this one.

Furthermore, we need to inform ourselves, to broaden our parochial outlook, to know where Korea is and what is a micro-computer... The fact that there are several possible interpretations of the world (and this book only offers one of many) does not excuse any of us from trying to know, analyse and understand, and then, if we can, to pass on facts and propagate interpretations.

But let us return to you, my son. Without tackling the whole of your education, I should simply like to ask myself some questions on three aspects that throw light on reflection focusing on the possible future developments of the world: professionalism, opening oneself to the outside world, and the meaning of life.

Being a professional means knowing practically and theoretically all the subtleties of your occupation, being aware of all foreseeable techniques, being ever ready to learn about new improvements, being capable of innovation, able to conceive, undertake and fulfill all the tasks that this occupation involves. Contrary to the twaddle that those who specialise in generalisations would have us believe, a professional is never a robot that repeats preprogrammed movements mechanically. Furthermore, a person who has known how to be a professional from the beginning of his life will be a professional all his life, even if he changes jobs. And there is no contradiction between this call for professionalism and the statement that in tomorrow's world education will continue through life, and that most men and women will have a series of different occupations.

Why this hymn to professionalism? Because in the long term, Europe's only incontestable asset in international competition lies in the ability of its men and women to work together as professionals. My son, the Europeans of your generation will be competing with the Chinese of Singapore, American biologists, workers from the suburbs of Santiago and Rio, Japanese university graduates, the multitude of men and women consumed with the hunger for knowing and doing, burning with the desire to improve their condition, strained with the will to prove something to themselves.

In countries like France, Italy or Spain, professionalism is a recent and fragile conquest. Ask the old English and German leaders the image they had of these countries on the eve of the Second World War. They Their industrialists? They were conservative and shallow. Their generals? They stopped thinking twenty years ago. Their politicians? They knew nothing about economics. Their economists? Apart from a few exceptions, they would not have been able to keep up a discussion with Cambridge economists... If you want to be convinced, reread the political speeches of the time, glance through pre-war economics textbooks, run through the menus of the French *Grand Quartier Général* in 1940 (you are what you eat). You would be more embarrassed than amused. One of the major victories of the post-war generations has been their attainment of professionalism. And we need only look at Britain to observe the opposite development: British industrialists and officials in the first half of the Nineteenth Century were professionals. In the Twentieth Century they have gradually ceased to be such. This hard-won victory is, because of the deficiencies of our secondary education, the weakening of our universities, the idleness created by unemployment, the dulling of the need to excel in danger of being lost at the very time when it is becoming more necessary than ever.

Long live competence! But it must be complemented by an openess to the world. If our adolescents are psychologically premature, that has its advantages and disadvantages. On the other hand, turning them into social dwarves may well hand them over defenceless to the agressions of the world ahead. A decided return to history, geography, economics and an introduction to politics in school curricula is essential. They must be able to construct an interpretative framework of the world, by appropriating their past once more, by knowing the beginnings and development of the other great civilisations, finding their place in time and space, in order to understand other cultures, to perceive the work of time in the leavening of society, to become aware of the rise and fall of human groups. That implies the assimilation of dates, figures and precise concatenations, for there are no great constructions without scaffolding, and you need to know that Louis XIV of France lived before Napoléon in order to be able to put relations between Europe and China into their proper framework. Another necessity: the knowledge of languages. Firstly their own, for if they cannot handle it, thought atrophies. And then foreign languages, which are vital to communication and trade.

Professionalism and openness to the world means breaking free from the old anachronistic debate over the difference between 'well-made heads' and 'well-filled heads,' a debate inspired by one of Montaigne's most outdated texts, because it was written before the emergence of scientific thought. As if heads that were inadequately filled could be well made, incapable as they would be of organising and combining material and, consequently, knowledge! We must also throw out this old European idea that education, attested by a diploma, confers professional competence. An idea that forces so many young people today to accumulate diplomas of general knowledge in order to gain access to the rare but cushy nests of administrative posts whose content has not changed. That is the snare that the conjunction of the social oligopoly, the spread of unemployment and the perversion of our education system is gradually trapping us in. Far be it for me to think of eliminating access to education, that means which allows each person to discover and fulfil himself. Every country with a high standard of living has a duty to make the extension of education to all one of its main objectives. But it is a mistake to believe that education creates professionalism and automatically ensures openness to the outside world. It would be better for the future of European societies if they would realise this as quickly as possible.

The third aspect that I should like to bring up is only an indirect result of prospective analysis, and there is no reason why each reader should be obliged to follow me; but I am convinced that it will only give developed societies the strength to overcome the problems of the future if those who comprise them are able to give meaning to their existence by reinventing an ethic of discovery, creation and excellence. Morality has been swept out of our education. The young people of the Eighties who are searching within themselves in vain for the Super-ego on which they could anchor their personality no longer know what to rebel against. They see no new frontiers. For them there are no new worlds to conquer. The future is less

what you make of it than a source of anguish and fear. And the time has
no doubt come to make ethics the backbone of our education once more.
It is not a question of resurrecting the sexual taboos and boggeymen of
an outdated Nineteenth Century, but of having the courage to formulate
one or more morals of action that take into account both new foreign
horizons and aspirations that are springing up in our societies.

# EPILOGUE

"One day we shall speak of: when there were
nations."

Alfred de VIGNY
*Le Journal d'un poête*

# A lesson in prospective analysis: the year 2000

Paris. 6th October 2000. In a *Conservatoire National des Arts et Métiers* that is even more decrepit than today, the professor who has just been appointed to the newly created chair of Economic and Social Futurology is giving his first lecture. He begins with a solemn homage to the pioneers of this discipline, in other words, for those who know how to read between the lines, a catalogue of their mistakes and an indictment of the insufficiency of their methods. He underlines the poverty of the statistics they used, the inadequacy of the concept of national income that they employed, the mechanical rigidity of the models of the world that they constructed, the theoretical weakness of all the analytical instruments they used, from Delphi to Micmac, from structural analysis to the dynamics of industry. That is past and gone. Prospective analysis has made inestimable progress in twenty years.

In the interpretation of facts. Thanks to the development of sociology, economy, and political science.

In the gathering and transmission of data thanks to *télématics* (if you want a series of statistics all you need to do is ask for it aloud and it will appear on the large screen in the lecture room. To get the results of an estimated model in real time all you need to do is key in the raw data on the professor's terminal. To get a film on rice cultivation in Thailand or maps and photographs of the cities of India, all you need do is call an audio-visual bank).

Similar progress has been made in the versatility and complexity of the models constructed. Thanks to systems analysis, the unwieldly models of yesteryear having been laid to rest; and in their place we now have hosts of linked models, models that tolerate different degrees of precision, that absorb both quantitative and qualitative data, and may be used in parallel or in series.

"Nonetheless," adds the professor who is honest and clear-headed, "the fundamental difficulties remain. The self-organisation of human systems continues to be a source of creation and unpredictability. Their complexity continues to defy attempts to synthesise them. The criteria of the scientific base of prospective analysis are barely getting off the ground..."

Among the old people present listening with the somewhat intermittent attention characteristic of this age, there is one man who is surprised. Less by the development of the discipline, less by the fact that it has kept the same name all these years (vocabulory has seen so many ups and downs in a quarter century), less by the deepening of epistemological thought on the subject, than by the fact that a frank and open lecture should be given in this place. With no hymn to the glory of any political 'ism,' without any reference to the protective friendship of any 'brothers,' without eulogies of a national or foreign 'Papa Doc,' without any funeral oration for a recent or imminent holocaust. Twenty years earlier, this simple fact was far from guaranteed.

The professor continues, upbraiding his audience: "If some of you think that our futures up to the year 2025 depend on the development of science, then you are mistaken. The prospective analysts of 1986 already knew this."

True, says the old gentleman to himself, but look at the number of things that have been discovered in the last quarter century! We had an idea of the areas (immunology, neurophysiology...), but the capsule containing them remained sealed. We would never have imagined this new point of departure, and those of us who, twenty years ago, got to the heart of the Twenty-first century to a considerable extent knew that the upheavals that would be caused by science would prevent us from straying from the straight and narrow. Relationships between Science and Prospective Analysis are curious indeed: within twenty years, everything is fixed; within fifty, everything is possible.

The analogy with demography is obvious. For today's lecturer, the two major questions of 1985 have been answered: the drop in the fertility rate of the Third World is now irreversible, and it is now becoming easy to estimate reasonably accurately the ceiling of world population; as for birth rates in Western countries going up again, it confirms that in these countries, lengthy swings in fertility are much more likely than a steady downward trend.

And the old gentleman realises that he has just discovered an obvious fact, an important obvious fact: humanity is within a few years of the summit of the Great Transition, and the mountains that blocked the horizon in 1985 now allow us to see further ahead. He thinks about energy: the cost constraints of solar energy have been eliminated, the fears about the dangers of nuclear power have been dispelled, the unknown element of the technical possibility of fusion has just been eliminated. The move to renewable or quasi-renewable fuels will require a few more decades, but it has become a certainty. He thinks about agriculture: famine has not yet diminished, but in developed countries, it is unarguable that the trend of per capita consumption of food is down, and the vast majority of Third World countries have retained the eating habits of their middle classes. Some even predict that malnutrition will have disappeared by about 2050. He thinks about mineral resources: no one speaks of their physical scarcity any more, and doctoral theses in history are devoted to the analysis of the intellectual influence of the first report to the Club of Rome. The title of one such thesis is "Of the emergence and propagation of the ideology of zero growth as a contributing factor to the Great Fear of the year 2000." He then thinks of the physical environment: knowledge of the climate has made decisive progress and the intricacies of the interactions between climate and human activities have been unravelled. Ecology is no longer the subject of conflict and has become an integral part of everyday culture; it has become part of our way of life. Seriously, but not to an extreme. Nonetheless, we are still faced with a tremendous task. Checking erosion. Providing drinking water for all. Preserving the genetic diversity of life.

And now the professor broaches the subject of geo-economy. He speaks with confidence on two points on which the prospective analyst of 1986 had only ventured a few timid words. There is no longer any argument as to whether China (which has halted the growth of its population and strengthened its self-sufficiency in food) contains regions where industry has got off the ground, and is on the way to becoming one of the great powers of the second half of the century. As for differentiation in the Third World, it has reached its peak because of the considerable dispersal of the group of nations moving up to development. But what is new is that some people now dare to speak of convergence, a convergence that they place at around 2050, when the concept of economic growth will have lost all meaning for a Westerner, when Latin America, Eastern and Southeast Asia, will have become developed zones, when the huge sore of poverty on the world map will have begun to be reabsorbed.

The old gentleman remembers. In 1986, the final question of a journalist would always be: "Are you optimistic or pessimistic?" And had he written such a thing then he would have been immediately classed with the optimists.

How ironic! For international conflicts have never been as frequent as they are at the beginning of this century. The spectre of war has never been more in evidence. The contradiction between economic, political and cultural interdependance, and the organisation of national societies into states, has never been sharper. The problem of the third control deficiency has become a glaring one, and the lecturer brings it up, announcing that his course of lectures will discuss at length some possible results of the crisis of the international system. Speaking of anihilation, he predicts that our fate will be played double or quits up to the last minute.

He pauses for a few seconds, and then continues. Turning to the old industrial countries, the ones that created the great adventure that was the Nineteenth Century. Why does God no longer live in Rome, Paris, London or New York? Why is He now Chinese or Brazilian? Why has Western civilisation, like so many others, entered the era of ossification, resistence to change and exhaustion of creativity? To the point that it feels beleaguered by these young nations that are inventing short-cuts to the future, throwing the shafts of their architecture up towards the sky and experimenting with new political forms... Never has the debate over the second control deficiency been more relevant than at this time of crisis for the great democracies.

The speaker is coming to the last pages of his notes. And focusing his attention on Man, he announces a forecast on Morality, and sketches the trends as they may be perceived in the work of writers, poets, men of religion, scientists, and the founders of sects. A sign of the times, he speaks of universality, the unity of ecosphere, communion with living things, and the care and moderation that such concepts imply. But he also speaks of the diversity of options and practices, the freedom of small groups, the right to creation and innovation. And finally he asks himself what can be the content of an ethic of the transformation of man by man, and how human society will manage the first control deficiency, the one that lies at the heart of each one of us. The day when individuals will only see each other as *Meccano* constructions whose parts may be changed and nuts and bolts more or less tightened.

Polite applause waken the old gentleman. 1986? He had never left it, and he has only been dreaming of one of the countless prospective analysis lessons of the early Twenty-first Century. If he had had a heavier lunch, he might have had some real nightmares! But what does it matter? Didn't William of Orange say that action is not born of either optimism or pessimism? And as for the future, we should only seek to anticipate it, in order better to create it.

# BIBLIOGRAPHY

Given the variety of subjects discussed in this book, even a partial bibliography should list hundreds of titles. But I have deliberately limited it to about thirty titles without repeating the sources quoted specifically in the text. And, having supervised the publishing of *Facing the future: Mastering the probable and managing the unpredictable*, (final report of the *Interfutures* project, OECD, 1979) and *Demain la France dans le monde* (France in Tomorrow's World), (Rapport du Commissariat Général du Plan, La Documentation Française, 1980), I have chosen not to mention borrowings from these sources.

M.R. BISWAS, A.K. BISWAS: *Food, climate and man*, New York, John Wiley, 1979.

A. BRESSAND: *Ramses 1981, Coopération ou guerre économique*, annual report of the Institut Français des Relations Internationales, Paris, Economica, 1981.

J.W. BOTKIN, M. ELMANDJRA, M. MALITZA: *On ne finit pas d'apprendre*, report to the Club of Rome, Paris, Pergamon, 1980.

H. CARRERE D'ENCAUSSE: *L'empire éclaté*, Paris, Flammarion, 1979.

H. CARRERE D'ENCAUSSE: *Le pouvoir confisqué*, Paris, Flammarion, 1981.

A.P. CARTER, W. LEONTIEV, E. PETRI: *The future of the world economy*, New York, United Nations, 1976.

B. CATHELAT: *Les styles de vie des Français 1978–1998*, Paris, Stanké, 1977.

B. CAZES: "La crise de l'Etat protecteur dans les économies occidentales," *Commentaires*, vol. 3, No. 12, hiver 1980–1981.

M. CROZIER: *Le mal américain*, Paris, Fayard, 1980.

A. DANZIN, A. BOUBLIL, J. LAGARDE: *La société française et la technologie*, Rapport du Commissariat général du Plan, Paris, La Documentation française, 1980.

J. DELAUNAY, D.H. MEADOWS, D.L. MEADOWS, J. RANDERS, W.W. BEHRENS III: *Limits to growth*, London, Earth Island Ltd., 1972.

F. GIROUD, P. d'ARVISENET, J. SALLOIS: *Réflexions sur l'avenir du travail*, Rapport du Commissariat général du Plan, Paris, La Documentation française, 1980.

M. GODET, O. RUYSSENS: *L'Europe en mutation*, Bruxelles, "Perspectives européennes," 1980.

M. GODET: *Demain les crises*, Paris, Hachette, 1980.

J. GRAPIN, *Radioscopie des Etats-Unis*, Paris, Calmann-Lévy, 1980.

W. HAFELE: *Energy in a finite world*, Laxenburg, International Institute for Applied Systems Analysis, 1980.

P. LAGADEC: *Le risque technologique majeur*, Paris, Pergamon, 1981 ("Futuribles").

B. LUSSATO: *Le défi informatique*, Paris, Fayard, 1981.

M. MESAROVIC, E. PESTEL: *Stratégies pour demain*, Paris, Seuil, 1974.

A. SAUVY: *La machine et le chômage: le progrès technique et l'emploi*, Paris, Dunod, 1981.

J.-J. SERVAN-SCHREIBER: *Le défi mondial*, Paris, Fayard, 1980.

J.-P. SUDREAU: *La stratégie de l'absurde, l'enjeu des années 80*, Paris, Plon, 1980.

J. TINBERGEN: *Reshaping the international order, report to the Club of Rome*, New York, E.P. Dutton, 1976.

A. TOFFLER: *The Third Wave*, New York, Morrow, 1980.

*Catastrophe or New Society: A Latin American model*, Ottawa, International Development Research Center, 1976.

*Global Future: Time to act*, a Report to the President on global resources, environment and population, Wahington, U.S. Department of State, Council on Environmental Quality, 1981.

*La nouvelle frontière technologique*, Paris, Ecole Nationale des Ponts et Chaussées, Journées prospectives "IPC 2000," 24–26 avril 1979.

*The global 2000 report*, Washington, U.S. Department of State, Council on Environmental Quality, 1980.

Readers may also find it useful to consult the journal *Futuribles*, in particular the following issues: February-March 1980 ("L'Europe face aux défis du futur"), July-August 1980 ("France: les perspectives à long terme du VIIIème Plan"), September 1980 ("L'Informatisation"), January 1981 ("Crise de l'Etat protecteur? L'économie souterraine: une réponse ambigüe), March 1981 ("Perspectives énergétiques mondiales"), April 1981 ("Systèmes de valeur et styles de vie"); the *Revue du Centre d'Etudes Prospectives et d'Informations Internationales* (CEPII), in particular the following issues: January 1981 ("Redéploiements géographiques et rapports de force industriels"), April 1981 ("Aspects de la politiques économique soviétique"); *Politique Etrangère*, journal of the Institut Français des Relations Internationales, the *Revue Politique Internationale*, the annual reports of the World Bank and the International Monetary Fund, as well as the publications of the OECD.

# NOTES

1) J. LESOURNE, *Les Systèmes du destin*, Paris, Dalloz, 1976
2) As Director of the OECD 'Interfutures' project. The final report was published under the title: *Facing the Future: Mastering the Probable and Managing the Unpredictable*, Paris, OECD, 1979.
3) D.H. MEADOWS, D.L. MEADOWS, J. RANDERS, W.W. BEHRENS, *The Limits to Growth*, London, Earth Island Ltd., 1972.
4) Reserves are that part of identified resources from which usable ore may be extracted economically and legally, at the date of evaluation. The figures for potential resources are usually much higher than those for reserves.
5) A. de TOCQUEVILLE, *Democracy in America*.
6) South Korea, Hong Kong, Taiwan, Singapore, Malaysia, Thailand, Philippines, Indonesia, North Korea, Vietnam, Laos, Cambodia.
7) Will China definitely opt for a decentralised economic system in which individual intiative would play a significant part?
8) This last figure is less significant because the international rice market is smaller.
9) C. LAMBROSCHINI, "Première puissance agricole du monde," *Le Figaro*, 12th May, 1979.
10) Except Eastern bloc countries and China.
11) Except Eastern bloc countries and China.
12) J. SURREY and W. WALKER, "Energy R and D: A UK perspective," *Energy Policy*, June 1975, pp. 90–115.
13) Special Drawing Rights (on the International Monetary Fund).
14) A. BIENAYME, "Un symptôme trompeur de déclin," *Le Figaro*, 12 May 1978.
15) C. FREEMAN and A. YOUNG, *The research and development effort in Western Europe, North America and the Soviet Union*, Paris, OECD, 1965; M. BORETSKY, *U.S. technology trends and policy issues*, Monograph 17, Program of policy studies on science and technology, George Washington University, Washington D.C.; for a more general view, see the works of K. Pavitt at the Science Policy Research Unit, University of Sussex.

16) K. PAVITT, *The Future of technology in advanced industrial societies*, working paper for Interfutures.

17) C. STOFFAES, "Y a-t-il un déclin industriel?," *Le Figaro*, 19 May 1979.

18) A social oligopoly is a situation in which social groups are organised to negociate between themselves or with the government.

19) See M. OLSON, *The political economy of comparative growth rates*, paper presented at a seminar of the University of Baltimore (December 1977).

20) C. CASTORIADIS, "Vers la Stratocratie," *Le Débat*, Mai 1981.

21) Ministry for International Trade and Industry.

22) Association of South East Asian Nations.

23) According to the most optimistic hypothesis, that is to say, supposing that the situation deteriorates no further, West Germany will have 50 to 56 million inhabitants by the end of the century. It will then have a smaller population than that of France, Italy, or Great Britain.

24) H. KISSINGER, *White House Years*, Vol. 1, 1979, p. 421.

25) M. GODET, O. RUYSSEN, *L'Europe en mutation*, Bruxelles, Commission of European Communities, 1980, pp.54–56.

26) These calculations have been based on 1970 exchange rates. Note that results may tend to vary according to the rates chosen for converting the national incomes of the different countries into dollars.

27) S. NORA, A. MINC, *L'informatisation de la société*, La Documentation française, Paris, 1978, p.114.

28) I. PRIGOGINE I. STENGERS, *Order out of chaos: Man's new dialogue with nature*, New York, Bantham, 1984; quoted from the French edition, p. 296.

29) Ibid.,p.27.

30) A. TOFFLER, *The third wave*, New York, Morrow, 1980.

31) Heavy bombers.

32) Because of MIRVS.

33) The low altitude American Cruise Missile, the Soviet Backfire bomber, Soviet medium-range SS 20 missiles which could reach the United States in their third stage.

34) *L'Europe, les vingt prochaines années*, La Documentation française, 1980, p. 49–50.

35) Quoted by J. GRAPIN, *Radioscopie des Etats Unis*, Calmann-Lévy, 1980, p. 313–315.

36) J. GRAPIN, *op.cit.*, p. 337.

37) E.M. BROOK, E.R. GRILLI, J. WAELBROECK, "Commodity price stabilisation and developing countries: the problem of choice," *World Bank staff working paper*, 262, Washington D.C., 1977.

38) With the exception of rice, and in some years, pork.

39) The year 1976 has been chosen because estimates of the consumption of non-commercial energy are available for that year.

40) P. DESPRAIRIES, *L'Avenir du pétrole classique dans la perspective énergétique mondiale*, Seminar on energy – Académie Pontificale des Sciences, 1980. The following quotations are from the same source.

41) G. HANSELMAN, *Le Défi du recyclage des pétrodollars*, Publication 72, Union de Banques Suisses, Zurich, 1980.

42) Cf. WOCOL study. Figures are in tonnes of coal. One TOE is roughly equivalent to 1.5 tonnes of coal. The WOCOL figures apply to the year 2000, but

following a slowing down of world growth, there is no chance of their being achieved until 10 years later.

43) Excluding non-ferrous metals and refined oil products.

44) United Nations Industrial Development Organisation.

45) While the GGT (*Confédération Générale du Travail*) is the French union connected with the Communist Party, the CDFT (*Confédération Française Démocratique du Travail*)is an independent union, though it leans towards the Socialist Party.

46) J.J. SERVAN SCHREIBER, *Le Défi mondial*, Fayard, Paris, 1981.

47) Where Nixon and Pompidou met in 1971.

48) Where the heads of state of the great Western nations met in 1977.

49) R. TRIFFIN, *L'Avenir du système monétaire international*, from the *Commissariat du Plan* (1980).

50) M. LAURE, "Le Rééquilibrage économique et financier mondial à la suite des chocs pétroliers, ou: Pour une coopération mondiale organisée," a lecture given at the Institut Français des Relations Internationales, 11th May, 1981.

51) General Agreement on Tariffs and Trade: international organisation responsible for preparing and following up general agreements on international trade.

52) United Nations Commission for Trade And Development.

53) L. ARMAND, M. DRANCOURT, *Le Pari européen*, Paris, 1968.

54) See the fifth Part of this book: DEVELOPED SOCIETIES: CONTESTATIONS AND OSSIFICATIONS.

55) For France, data is from COFREMCA and from the *Centre de Communications Avancées*; for Europe, the Eurobarometer for the Commission of the European Community ; for the United States, research by David Yankelovich.

56) L. ROUSSEL, "La crise de la famille," *La Recherche*, No. 111, May 1980, p. 548.

57) F. GIROUD, P. ARVISENEL, J. SALLOIS, *L'avenir du travail*, La Documentation Française, 1980, p. 93.

58) A. DANZIN, *Science et Renaissance de l'Europe*, Chotard, 1980.

59) I.e. guaranteeing their members collective advantages.

60) M. OLSON, *The political economy of comparative growth rates*, paper presented at a seminar of the University of Baltimore (December 1977).

61) This definition is wider than that of the Welfare State, because it includes the services of national defence.

62) N. PARKINSON, *The law and the profits*, John Murray, London, 1960.

63) B. CAZES, "La crise de l'Etat protecteur dans les économies occidentales," *Commentaire*, No. 12, Winter 1980–1981, p. 581. This chapter is also often inspired by Cazes' analyses, both in *Interfuturs* and in personal works.

64) R. BACON and W. ELTIS, *Britain's economic problem*, London, Macmillan, (Second edition), 1978.

65) BACON and ELTIS, *op. cit.*, p. 162.

66) B. CAZES, *op. cit.*, p. 584.

67) BACON and ELTIS, *op. cit.*, p. 163.

68) J. FONTANET *Le Social et le Vivant*, Plon, Paris, 1977.

69) B. CAZES, *op. cit.*, p. 585.

70) A. de VULPIAN, *Les Pouvoirs publics face au changement socioculturel en France. Contribution à la conférence internationale sur l'avenir de l'administration publique*, Ecole

nationale d'administration publique, Québec, 1979. Both this and the following text (see note 2) are quoted by B. CAZES, op. cit., p. 587.

71) M. CROZIER, *On ne change pas la société par décret*, Paris, Grasset, 1979.

72) Cf. Paul McCRACKEN et al., *Vers le plein emploi et la stabilité des prix*, OECD, Paris, 1977. 73. A. SAUVY, *La Machine et le Chômage*, Dunod, Paris, 1980.

74) M. ALLAIS, *Rapport d'activité scientifique du Centre Clément-Juglar*, Paris.

75) J. P. BENASSY, R. BOYER and R. M. GELPI, *Régulation des économies capitalistes et inflation*, CEPREMAP, 1978.

76) J.-P. BENASSY, R. BOYER, R.-M. GELPI, *op. cit.*, p. 7–8. I have changed the termilogy on one point, by speaking of 'oligopolistic deregulation' instead of 'monopolistic deregulation' as the authors do. For two reasons: this terminology seems more appropriate, and besides, it fits in with the terms used in the preceding chapters.

77) A combination of 'telecommunications' and 'informatics' – data processing. See S. Nora and A. Minc, *op. cit.*

78) A. DANZIN, A. BOUBLIL and J. LAGARDE, "La société française et la technologie," *Rapport du commissariat general du Plan*, 1980, p.29.

79) P. JEANJEAN, *La Nouvelle Frontière technologique, synthèse des travaux.*

80) P. JEANJEAN, *op. cit.*

81) *Ibid.*

82) J. POLY, *op. cit.*

83) P. JEANJEAN, *op.cit*

84) A. TOFFLER, *op. cit.*, p. 134.

85) A. TOFFLER, *op. cit.*, p. 367.

86) F. GIROUD, P. ARVISENET, J. SALLOIS, *Réflexions sur l'avenir du travail*, La Documentation Française, p. 143–144.

87) Has not the shortage of wood cropped up in our history several times?

88) A. BABEAU and L. LEVY, "Les effets économiques et financiers de l'évolution démographique," *Consommation*, No. 2, 1979.

89) Possible levels of female activity between 1975 and 1990, in order of magnitude: from 53.1 to 60.8% in the US; from 48.5 to 52% in West Germany; from 55.3 to 60.2% in the United Kingdom (*Interfutures*, op.cit. p. 148).

90) The protection of nature, barricading oneself into one's home, and the backward-looking fashion in architecture are expressions of a rejection of change by some people.

91) *Réflexions sur l'avenir du travail*, La Documentation Française, 1980. The text quoted itself contains quotations from Amado and Stoffaes: "Vers une socio-économie duale," annex to the report on *La société française et la technologie*, La Documentation Française, 1980.

92) Or of a 'plural society,' – the term used by M. GODET in *Demain les crises*, Hachette, Paris, 1980, p. 134.

93) Op. cit. p. 152–153.

94) Institut français des relations internationales, *Ramses 1981, Coopération ou Guerre économique*, p. 85–87.

95) K. DEUTSCH, *The analysis of international relations*, Englewood Cliffs (New Jersey), Prentice Hall, 1968.

96) It was on August 4th, 1789 that the French *Constituante* assembly voted the abolition of privileges.

97) As insufferable as adolescents and as faint-hearted as old men.

98) Ministry of International Trade and Industry.

# Index